JX/6

A SPIRIT OF ADVENTURE

A SPIRIT
OF ADVENTURE

The memoirs
of Ted Quigley

The Book Guild Ltd
Sussex, England

The Book Guild Ltd
High Street,
Lewes, Sussex

First published 1994
© Ted Quigley 1994
Set in Baskerville
Typesetting by Southern Reproductions (Sussex)
East Grinstead, Sussex
Printed in Great Britain by
Antony Rowe Ltd.
Chippenham, Wiltshire.

A catalogue record for this book is
available from the British Library

ISBN 9 86332 911 X

CONTENTS

1

EARLY DAYS

Chesterfield in the county of Derbyshire was my birthplace. Unlike the leaning tower of Pisa a crooked spire on Chesterfield's 14th century parish church has not earned it fame much beyond regional mileage. Yet, to give the town its due, Chesterfield deserves far greater recognition nationally and internationally than it has earned.

The Romans started it. It grew to be a market town and it received charters from King John in 1204, from Henry III in 1233 and from Queen Elizabeth I in 1598. George Stephenson, builder of the first successful railway locomotive, spent his last three years in the town and is buried in Trinity Church there. There's a memorial hall in his honour. Its diversity of industries, mostly based on coal mining and heavy engineering production, reflects well on the enterprise of its citizens now in the region of nearly 100,000. Manufactures in Chesterfield include cast iron pipes, chemicals, mining equipment, machinery, surgical dressings, pottery and electric lamps.

It was not long after the armistice of 1918 had ended the Great War that I started my schooldays in Chesterfield – a daily walk of four miles to St Mary's Spencer Street elementary school. Dreamy and far from bright, my first two years in the infants section passed in a trance-like regret that for some unknown reason I was less clever than most of the others. Segregated in our seventh year the boys moved upstairs while the girls remained at ground level. As the change drew near, boys up above, who had already passed through standards one and two, filled us with foreboding for the future. Frightening stories came of the canings and chair-leggings inflicted by Miss Martin in her efforts to instil learning and maintain discipline. We saw the famous chair leg only infrequently. From this we assumed, I think rightly, that the advancing years had softened Miss Martin and the self-imposed ration of ten or so strokes per session she shared out amongst us as aides to learning and good behaviour. During those first two years she taught us the three Rs and transformed us from infants to boys.

Moving from Miss Martin's small classroom to standards three and four under the tutelage of Miss Hobbs who, in common with all teachers taught all subjects, presented new hazards. We now came under the eye of the headmaster, John Greenan, who sat behind a tall desk on a raised dais which gave him a clear view of standards three to six – and of course seven and 7a which with an iron hand he taught himself.

We were kept painfully aware that behind that desk hung a selection of six canes ranging from the light 'cutter' to the thick heavy 'bruiser'. Even now I recall that oft-experienced stab of fear as, prompted by some sixth sense during a whispered word to a classmate I would look up to find one of them levelled wordlessly at me before the peremptory downwards sweep summoned me to the desk. Canings were never given immediately. The rhythmic reaching down for another exercise book from the shelf behind the desk might continue for an hour or more, each with the hope that it was the last, until finally the appearance of the cane would be the signal for us to move into line for the canings which never came light.

A boy up for caning was accorded full sympathy from the other boys but critically watched when under punishment. Heaven help he who so much as flinched or worse still cried. The taunts levelled at him after school would be a measure of the very real contempt felt by the rest of the school. I always remember the shocked incredulity when called to the desk for the second time one day to be given only comparatively light strokes one on each already bruised hand, a hitherto unknown concession by stern disciplinarian headmaster Greenan. An ostentatious blowing on bruised hands was a sign of weakness but the application of the juice of a raw onion when a heavy caning, known to be imminent after a bad showing in an examination, was accepted practice. Oddly enough, perhaps due to the inborn toughness and mental maturity of those days and an awareness that it would follow on any slackness or wrongdoing, punishment was accepted without rancour and an appreciation of its necessity. 'Telling' was an unforgivable sin and a caning taken for a boy not man enough to own up resulted in taking it out of his hide later.

Schoolmate Frank Navin introduced me to the world of Tom Merry of St Jim's and Harry Wharton & Co at Greyfriars School by lending me tattered copies of the *Gem* and *Magnet*. I doggedly ploughed through these and later copies acquired from his elder brothers until the skipping of difficult words was almost eliminated by constant practice. Soon, with twopence earned weekly from the collection of horse manure for the family allotment I was buying *The Rover* to enjoy the exploits of those more mature characters who adventured to the exotic Orient or the sandy wastes of Africa and Arabia.

Short time working in the 1920s forced my father to leave the Bryan Donking engineering firm (now one of the world's industrial giants) and obliged us to move into town to be nearer the new job he had taken as a labourer on the coke ovens at nearby Stavely. Our new house in Joel's Row off Hipper Street had two bedrooms. There was a living room equipped with a gas ring, a plain table and four chairs. A cold water tap dripped into a stone sink. From the tap we filled the boiler at the side of the old black-leaded fireplace to give us the hot water for the Monday wash.

Twice weekly in the side oven mother baked bread that had risen from dough placed under a towel in front of the coal fire. The front room faced the blank wall of the town's Rowton House a few feet distant and in consequence was always cold and damp in winter. (These Rowton Houses which spread through every town in the Midlands had been bequeathed in perpetuity by an old family of that name to provide local indigents with twopence (1p) to spare, a bed for the night and a bread and jam breakfast the next day.)

For family evacuations, almost a public spectacle in working-class areas in those days, there were six 'privvies' three in a row and placed back to back. These served all the families in the over-a-century-old terrace of twelve houses on which the first landlord had bestowed the name Joel's Row. Four in our family and seven next door shared the luxury of one of these and each in turn threaded together the squares of newspaper which we hung behind the door.

Simple pleasures then: pushing iron hoops at the run, whips and tops, marbles (played in gutters on the way to and from school), sliding on winter ice, street football. Sneaking into Markham Road slaughterhouses to watch butchers poleaxing bullocks, slitting the throats of the

10

more docile sheep and the loudly protesting pigs. Often to emerge in haste when, aiming to rid themselves of their ghoulish young admirers, the slaughtermen slung dripping intestines at our much-darned stocking-legged knees and heavy-boot-shod feet.

Behind this was the cattle market, also used as a fairground when the gypsy show people paid their twice-yearly visits to Chesterfield. Then we paid a penny to climb to the top of the helter-skelter to slide down and round its circular tower on coconut mats. To admire the gleaming brass decorated steam engines belching smoke as they powered and brilliantly illuminated the garishly coloured roundabouts, penny-a-go rifle ranges and coconut shies. There was always the old gypsy woman in a small darkly lit tent who, after consulting her magic crystal ball would, provided her palm was crossed with silver, foretell the future.

On the other side of Hipper Street at its junction with Markham Road there was still the ruins of one of the town's old silk mills. In its shadow there still stood what remained of the ancient town's ducking stool and the mill pond into which by popular request the town's shrews and witches were repeatedly immersed until they promised to forgo their evil ways.

The old outcroppings outside town gave us good muscular exercise as we dug out coal leavings to supplement the coal priced at twelve shillings and sixpence a ton (in new currency 62½ pence) that all employees at Stavely were granted as an allowance.

From the outcrops we viewed with envy the nimble railway shunters riding cross-legged on poles thrust between the wheels of fast moving trucks. With these poles they uncoupled selected trucks to travel of their their own volution to join goods trains being made up to take them to their separate destinations.

Great fun was to be had on dark evenings. With a long piece of thread agitated from a distance to cause a button previously inserted into the frame of a window to tap against the glass. Despite a lightning emergence the occupant saw nothing more than an apparently empty street. Another diversion was to tie the knobs of two adjoining front doors loosely together by a stout piece of string before knocking on both. The first to respond could open his door only to the extent of the slack in the rope by which time his neighbour, meeting resistance would exert his full strength and slam shut the first door and start a brief tug o' war. All went well until one of our victims who must have got his wife to pull at the door while he sped round from the back, enjoyed a field day punching ears and kicking backsides.

We rarely had twopence to attend the Saturday afternoon cinema shows. However I still remember those long flexible poles used by the male attendants to crack down on the heads of those who climbed onto the backs of the long wooden forms the better to warn their cowboy heróes of fast approaching dangers. Pandemonium broke loose when repeated pole assaults on the high-perchers toppled them more often than not on the heads and knees of those on the form behind.

Our favourite films in those days were starring cowboys Tom Mix, Jack Holt or William Farnum. The weekly serial misadventures of Pearl White, usually tied to a railway track with an express steaming at speed towards her, always ended with a flash. 'End of part five – part six next week.' We roared with laughter at the antics of Charlie Chaplin, Buster Keaton, Harold Lloyd, Fatty Arbuckle and all the other great stars of the Mack Sennett era. As I rarely could raise twopence I failed to become an afficionado of the silver screen but I still remember stars like Rudolf Valentino; Pola Negri, a sultry siren if ever there was one; Alice White, Emil Jannings, Lilian and Dorothy Gish, Douglas Fairbanks senior and all the other great names of the time when we read, or tried to read, the dialogue as it was flashed on the black-and-white screen. Simple days compared with the Technicolour masterpieces of today, but we thanked our lucky stars that, unlike our parents, we had avoided the boredom of their magic lantern shows.

Coke oven workers in common with all coal miners worked eight hours seven days a week including all holidays. Starting on alternate weeks at 6am, 2 and 10pm. With sixteen hours straight on the Sunday they changed from the early to the late shift. Only twice in eighteen years, due to his relief's failure to report for work, did my father enjoy a Christmas dinner at home. His festive fare – work's canteen bread and cheese washed down with beer. Furthermore, he was obliged to start work again on Boxing Day at 6am as usual, just eight hours after completing his sixteen hours' long Christmas Day stint. That was bad enough but worse was to come: the memorable occasion when his relief failed to report for work on not only Christmas Day, but Boxing Day too. The result was that father worked sixteen hour shifts on both days which, after deducting travelling time, left him on both days with less than seven hours at home.

Work on the coke ovens was physically hard as I saw on school holidays when I accompanied my father on the bus to Stavely. I watched the men he was about to relieve discharging from the ovens tons and tons of compressed wet slack in an eye-searing white hot heat, and in clouds of sulphureous smoke to drop as coke into waiting railway wagons below. This explained why my father always had the appearance of a man who had spent a lifetime in the tropics.

I will always remember the occasional visits with

13

brother, father and mother to the cinema and the return home in darkness to wait for father to strike a match and light the gas mantle. Then there'd be a mad rush to the four walls of the room to cut off the retreat of hordes of cockroaches, to stamp on them and kill them clear of rugs or the fireplace tiles. If the bag was ever less than forty father always wanted to know who had been slacking. We and all our neighbours scrubbed, scoured and laid insect powder between shrunken skirtings and rotting floorboards but the ageing houses negated all our efforts.

Walton Wood, a short walk over the fields then, gave us in season the blackberries that mother joined with apples to make the jam for the sandwiches we carried to school as our lunch. She baked the bread and, for a Sunday treat, made the hard toffee we broke into small pieces to suck with relish. We always managed to have the Sunday joint of beef and this lasted us, cold and sliced, until Wednesday when the remnants became a stew laced with a meat cube. Like all the women of that era mother could call on an amazing variety of cheap ingredients to give us what we called savoury ducks: squares of flavoured mincemeat, black puddings, roly-poly puddings steamed in cloth coverings, pies with meat or fruit from our own garden allotments, potted meat – a seemingly never-ending source of recipes handed down from mothers to daughters and kept intact year after year, generation after generation, in mind.

With most fathers on seven-day working in the local industries the family allotments were tended by the children and for the table we provided potatoes, cabbages, beans and peas enough to keep us going throughout the year. Any of us could have told the writer of a letter to the London paper that his spuds were green because he had not hoed them and consequently they had grown exposed to light. I'm still a keen gardener more than sixty years and worldwide travels later.

Chesterfield, an ancient town, held its market days on Mondays, Thursdays and Saturdays and no better entertainment could be found today on TV screens or in any of the multifarious segments of show business.

There was the chap from Staffordshire who, after selling only one of his good quality tea sets would quickly dispose of several cheaper ones, 'More suitable for you unrefined lot'.

That led him to what he called the toilet set which in those days when bathrooms were non-existent in working-class homes, had to contain a chamber pot. Holding a specimen sample in the light of the hissing naptha flare in wintertime he would flick it with a fingernail to prove its musical soundness.

Searching through the crowd he would ask the fattest woman present to step up and be measured.

'I'm sure it's just your size. It'll fit you like a glove.'

Still addressing her he'd offer the advice that a pot that size would certainly carry enough beer from the pub on Sunday to provide a dinner gargle for her old man, herself and 'a regiment of relatives'. Strange that today these relics of long-forgotten bedroom appurtenances are being sold as household ornaments, plant-holders, antiques. No doubt many of the old Chesterfield varieties could well be adorning some collector's palace of a home in Beverley Hills or Boston – secured on a European trip at some fancy price that would have the Staffordshire market salesman turning madly in his grave.

As this diversion drew temporarily to a close the crowd would drift to the adjoining stalls of Bill and Alf who sold respectively domestic goods and sweets. It all started when Bill decided to inspect Alf's array of sweets by holding at arm's length a yellow and black peppermint whirl which could easily have been mistaken if placed on the ground or on park grass for an animal deposit – in shape at least. Assuming an expression of disgust and still holding the sweet at arm's length he would ask if anyone wanted 'a bit o' wot t' dog left in t' entry'.

The show proceeded to the amusement of the large crowd when Alf, who had pretended not to notice Bill's seizure of the first sweet, caught him stealing another and in instant dudgeon knocked it from Bill's hand to land back on the stall. As Alf turned away the hurt expression on Bill's face would give way to energetic chewing as he popped another sweet he had previously palmed into his mouth and then stop a split second before Alf turned to discover the cause of the crowd's sudden laughter.

Bill affecting not to know that Alf had tied a long rag to his back before both decided to visit Oliver Kirk's pork butcher's shop then on Low Pavement at the bottom of the market. The crowd followed them as the two took over serving in the shop after fastening butcher Kirk inside his cold room. There followed typical Mack Sennett chaos as customers received the wrong orders and the butcher appeared, cleaver in hand, to chase the couple out – but not before they had legitimately sold off what remained of his pies, sausages and the like.

And so the comic couple left the shop amid screams of laughter as the crowd saw the long trail of dummy sausages that Bill had fastened to Alf's back with a handily placed pin. Back at the stall angry Alf, finding the sausage tail, knocked a bucket from Bill's stall. As he picked it up in obedience to Bill's angry command he got a hefty kick to his backside and, in a retaliatory move, he then sold to a grinning bystander for one shilling the bucket clearly priced at two shillings. This was the cue for the duo to start selling the large quantities of soap and toiletries that the crowd had been put in the mood to buy. Immediately the demand from this stall abated the crowd's attention was quickly switched to the purchase of sweets from the other.

As the 10pm market closing time drew near, the several butcher stall holders commenced to auction what prime beef joints still remained unsold. These were eagerly snapped up by late market shoppers at the unbelievably low price these days of around sixpence (3p present day money) per pound.

At school, where possession even of an old tennis ball placed a boy two or three rungs above the rest, our games were simple, boisterous and strenuous. There was the kind of tag that was started by one lad extending his arms shoulder high with fingers extended to be grabbed by about twenty others. Once he had yelled 'Pigs – fries – snerks' then there was a general stampede by the crowd as he attempted to tag a victim. The first tagged boy joined hands and soon others were touched to form a long chain that swung furiously around until the last player was collared.

There was another game, 'Husky-fusky' played by about thirty boys divided into two teams. Which one should have first jump was decided by the captain of one team guessing correctly in which of the two extended clenched fists of the other a marble or similar object was concealed.

The weakest boy from the losing side then took up a stance with back against a wall. The next less strong boy, bending to press his head into the stomach of the boy against the wall, clasped both arms round his back. The next boy pushed his head through the straddled legs of the first and hooked both arms round his thighs. This was repeated until the strongest took up the last positions in what looked like a straddle-legged crocodile. Starting

17

with the most agile, the other side then jumped in turn over the back of the last boy in the crocodile using both hands in a down and forward thrust to land up the crocodile as far as possible. Once landed, no further movement was permitted nor any part of them to touch the ground. Soon the whole team was astride the by now grunting boys beneath. The last to jump then raised either finger or thumb and called 'Husky-fusky-finger-or-thumb.' The outcome of this decided which team should be the next to jump.

We had what we called camel races and, less rowdy but certainly more skilful, games with marbles obtained gratis from the necks of broken bottles at the neighbouring bottling plant. Those bottles in which the glass marbles at the top were pushed down to let the lemonade or other drink flow are now collector's items.

We collected 'fag cards' issued by the big cigarette companies, Players, Wills, Carreras, Gallahers and others who were to disappear after World War II within the giant cartels – and the cigarette cards with them! Wonderful series they were: railway locomotives, army uniforms through the ages, birds, animals and the most informative 'Do you know' sets.

Collections then – as they are today as pricey relics of an era well on to antique rarity – were jealously hoarded and the swops saw each set with its particular value. A rare one, for instance, might be gained for two hundred cards of lesser collector's value. I wonder how many are left today who skimmed the cards in a game in which a card was leant against a wall to be knocked down by the accurate aim of a skimmer. The winner usually counted his winnings in hundreds as he picked up the cards of the unsuccessful contestants. Along with my pals I kept close watch on cigaretts smokers. If we saw one opening a new packet then we'd waylay him with the request, 'Can I have your fag card Mister? Please!'

Ingenuity we had in great quantity. Money was scarce. Thus with old pram wheels and a few boards we made trolleys capable of seating four for a high-speed descent of a steep hill of which Chesterfield had plenty. From the rubbish tips we salvaged the remains of bicycles minus saddles and brakes to carry three. The only way to set this contraption in motion was for the proud owner to stand precariously on the pedals. The way to stop was for the second lad seated on the crossbar to press one foot hard down on the front wheel and the third lad on the back step together with the pedaller to drag one foot along the ground to achieve a wobbly halt. This usually happened when we saw a policeman whose wont it was, as we well knew, to clip ears first and then deliver a lecture on the inadvisability of idiots like us riding bicycles without brakes.

In winter the snowball fights were exhilarating, especially if the opponents were grammar school boys who never resorted to the practice of other elementary school boys of throwing balls made of rock-hard slush. Once during a temporary lull some of their girls appeared on the scene so, to fill in time until more boys appeared, we filled their wellington boots with snow. Contrary to expectations they accepted this with such good grace that we all agreed that these grammar lasses, despite their being only girls, were first class sports.

When the Christmas spirit was abroad in Chesterfield we felt as if we were in wonderland. Those were the pre-supermarket times when the brightly decorated shops around the market place square bore such names as Maypole, Melias, Lipton, Home & Colonial and there were in less affluent support the home-owned shops ranging from chemists to the ubiquitous bakeries and fruiterers.

In the lighted windows we saw the streamers, multi-coloured, bearing the seasonal reminders of holly and mistletoe and the great spread of decorative cotton wool that heralded the snowfalls we seemed to get in greater quantity in those days. Old Santa Claus, red faced, merry and brimming over with good cheer, either in the flesh in the big stores or in model form, smiling at us through plate glass or outside the shop doors. Everywhere the warmth and the friendliness of the season of peace and goodwill made us forget in the glow of thousands of lights of many hues, reflected almost as brightly from the rain-wet pavements on which we stood, that our home-fire Christmas was not likely to be as scintillating in effusive spending as those gilttering window displays had been.

Softly, the radiant beams coming through the stained glass windows of the Royal Oak, 900 years old and renowned as the place where the Knights Templar planned The Crusades, reminded us of the antiquity of Chesterfield. Nearby, the cheery glow from The Vaults still bore the Dickensian memory of the stagecoach. The old buildings stood in a narrow lane off the Shambles between Low Pavement and Burlington Street where multiple tailor Montague Burton opened his first ever shop, Packers Row, still offering sight of the much-worn packhorse loading stage standing outside the Penny Bazaar, and the market place. One could well imagine the toot-toot-toot of the guard on his high perch and the clippety-clop of the horses' hooves as down the narrow lane it passed an outgoing coach, both almost touching the buildings on each side. The stagecoach draws to a halt, the steaming horses are uncoupled and the passengers alight to warm themselves in front of a roaring fire in the inn with glasses of brandy to warm the cockles of England's hearts of oak.

And then back to the mechanical era of automobiles, steam locomotives and early aeroplanes as each footstep left behind the aura of old Chesterfield and took us to the market place, the largest open-air mart in the country. From there to Low Pavement to view the fairy lights casting their brilliant beams on mouth-watering displays of chocolates and sweets behind the old, rounded bow windows of a shop that, even more than half a century on, evokes a nostalgic glow in the taste buds of an old man.

Our Christmas at home despite the work-ridden absence of father was usually a heartwarming family gathering that brought father's sister from Burton-on-Trent carrying roast duck and homemade mince-pies – a visit always heralded to mother's intense annoyance loudly outside the back door by the elderly postman before producing from behind his back the postcard from which he had gleaned his knowledge.

Mother baked and iced the Christmas cake and made the plum puddings – enough for Easter and to celebrate all our birthdays. We had various meats and sauces and all the trimmings that celebrated the greatest Christian festival. Money was scarce, indeed, but there was not one working-class family near us then who would deny their children the joy, limited though it might be, of the best Christmas they could afford. Apart from then and times like Easter, we were never given such things as chocolate, sweets or ice cream. The probable reason why we still had our natural teeth right until our late sixties.

Eventually there came a move to Sanforth Street, north of the town. A house offered for rent, father took it as it was much nearer his workplace. It was practically a copy of our old home but it did lack the lodging cockroaches and that was a blessing indeed. We had our own privy –

outside to be sure, but ours and ours alone. Gone was the blank-wall view from our old home and in its place was a vista of fields covered in season with wild flowers, buttercups, dandelions, daisies and hedgerows adorned with wild roses, blackberry bushes and a profusion of flora the like of which has long since vanished from the hedgeless expanse of modern farms.

Among our new neighbours was an old woodcarver and his cabinet maker son. On the other side there was a locomotive driver and his son, a woodworking machinist. It was the engine driver who brought me the nearest I was ever likely to get to fulfilling an ambition towards engine driving when, on a school holiday, he took me on the footplate of his engine working in the yards of the Sheepbridge iron works. The highlight of that experience came after darkness descended. I watched spellbound as he pushed to the top of a huge slag heap wagons filled with molten waste from the furnaces and then tipped them to send streams of white-hot slag down the side of the tip in spectacular, great, bounding leaps to strike older deposits. There they forked into myriads of shimmering rivulets which, in the darkness, looked like liquid silver.

The time came when at the age of fourteen I had reached standard 7a at my elementary school. There had been particular emphasis on arithmetic and copybook writing. The reason was that accomplishment in these two subjects led to apprenticeships in craftmanship rather than descent into the coal mines. Quick and accurate calculations were, so we were told, the hallmarks of good apprentice material. From seven to fourteen I had not avoided the pitfalls of delinquency in one form or the other and the canings that followed. Discipline then was stern. Often punishment at school, reported to parents, would result in further thumpings from father.

Britain might have slipped down the wealthy-nation league but we still ruled an empire over which the sun, we were told, would never set. At school we were given to understand that this would go on forever. Our navy was still the biggest and most powerful, though this claim was challenged by the United States and we had to admit that, though comparisons then as now were odious, the American fleet was equal to ours in numbers and fire power. Japan, our ally in World War I, had built up a third-place navy. So, as we now know in post-adolescent sapience, Britain's world leadership could well have been taken over at that time by its biggest creditor, the United States. Isolationism across the Atlantic still gave us Britons, poor as church mice though we might be, dominion over palm and pine and regal authority over the old Empire countries.

The time had arrived to think of school leaving and entry into the workplace. I was pretty good with my hands and a report from the woodwork teacher at the large Central School to which we trooped each week suggested that this might be my vocation. The headmaster felt that as I had shown an aptitude to produce recognisable drawings and a sufficiency in working out fairly accurately arithmetic posers, I might be welcomed at Grey & Lewis, Chesterfield's well-known cabinet makers.

Yet I had what seemed then to be an unattainable ambition to become a colonial police officer. That came about after the Chief Constable of Derbyshire, Mr Sillitoe, the man who broke the razor gangs in Glasgow and nearby Sheffield and who was later to join the intelligence service, told us about his experiences in the Rhodesian police. Stange things do happen in this topsy-turvy world of ours and, unbelievable as a colonial police career seemed then, uniformed days thousands of miles away were not too far distant.

2

CRAFTSMAN

Mr Grey of Grey & Lewis was a Scot and a craftsman in the style of those long-departed prodigies, whose works in these days of mass production mediocrity are eagerly sought as collector's pieces. In Chesterfield he was a man of renown. He arrived in town to join the largest furniture-making firm in the district and he resigned his job as manager there to start a business that soon earned distinction for its superb craftsmanship.

I offered myself as apprentice material to Mr Grey, who eyed me with such a piercing gaze that I felt he was probing the inner recesses of my mind. First came the personal interview followed by another one with my father. My father was required to undertake an obligation to ensure that once I started I should remain with the firm for the full duration of the seven years' apprenticeship. Also an assurance that he understood I should receive only six shillings for a fifty hour week and that from this sum the firm would deduct two shillings for the personal tool kit they would buy for me. Mr Grey stressed that this was rather less than an errand boy's pay but while his pay would remain static, mine would increase each year until the end of my apprenticeship when I'd be earning eighteen shillings. Subject to my father's agreement to these conditions and my suitability for the trade, assessed during a short probationary period, I could start work on Monday at seven am sharp, with emphasis on the sharp.

As my mother was obliged to rouse my father, a heavy sleeper on account of his hard physical work, at four-thirty am one week, await his return home at ten-thirty pm the next and, unlike many of our neighbours who sent their kids out of a morning with a 'doorstep' spread with lard in each hand, get my brother fed before he went to school each day, I soon learned to wake myself, cook my own breakfast and start out for work by 6.15 am.

Grey & Lewis, a partnership between the craft of Grey and the financial acumen of Lewis, had established itself in premises known as Spital Mills. Earlier, it had been Chesterfield's largest silk mill at a time when the county of Derbyshire was Britain's main producer of silk.

The machine shop, with its screaming saws and spindles, roaring jackers and planers, driven by a complexity of long whirling belts from the chugging gas engine, occupied the ground floor with its twelve-man workforce. Above was another large shop in which eight cabinet makers made all the large fitments such as wardrobes, the polishing and spray shops, the shop where mirrors, handles etc were fitted to the finished product. Beyond this was the packing shop which overlooked the loading bay. Above this again was the large cabinet shop where apprentices did their seven year training, and it was to an unoccupied bench, next to a heavily moustached, authoritative-looking man whom I rightly guessed was the foreman, that I was directed. His name was Bernard Stone and his job it was to train the firm's apprentices.

There was a short introduction to fellow apprentice Les Wilson from whom I would take on the daily duties of teaboy and, in between the brewing times, I would be engaged in the soul-destroying monotony of sand-papering the seemingly endless lengths of beads and mouldings that were extensively used in those days.

After an hour of this, Les Wilson's arrival with the tea trays, and our tour round the shops to collect the men's mugs was a welcome diversion. First I had to learn to recognise each man's particular mug. Some were made of china in various sizes and patterns and were easy, but the two dozen or so enamel type, identifiable only by the differently shaped scars acquired over the years, required some concentration at first. The tea and sugar collected with the mugs also presented a problem for a time. Old George's was not so bad as it required only two measures from the spoon kept in the tin under his bench. Others placed the tea and sugar in the mugs they habitually kept clean themselves. Old Rory's and Stan Barker's were also easy as they always premixed sweetened condensed milk, tea and sugar into a screwed up newspaper before leaving home. Sam Holmes who did likewise, screwed his up into a sheet torn from Saturday night's sporting *Green-'Un,* identified at a glance. When it came to the cleaning of the mugs, we used wet sandpaper to remove the worst of the stains. As we redistributed the filled mugs Les gave me an assessment of each man's character and his likely attitude towards shop boys. 'Not a bad sort of bloke, help you any time', or 'Watch him, kick your arse as soon as look at you', and so on.

After the tea break it was back to work at nine am to the realisation that this time last week at school the day was only just starting.

The next tea exercise, with nearly half the men going home for lunch, was even easier. My own lunch, seated on my bench with a mug of tea made from the gas-heated boiler on the floor below when compared with the school tap water, was luxury indeed.

The energetic activity of the tea-brewing marathon was

forever followed by the humdrum monotony of sandpapering beads and mouldings. Worse still came the day when a load of chairs arrived – for more sandpapering! They had been bought from a firm specialising in the making of chairs, a company obviously bereft of the presence of sandpapering boys. And so I sandpapered and sandpapered and . . . such were the crosses borne by we apprentices.

As time went on there were more enjoyable tasks to be performed such as the call for a lad to be sent to the shop below to assist in knocking together what were known as heavy robe carcases. This involved a certain amount of harmless horseplay in which I was ever ready to join. Better still was to stand behind the planer and scraping machines which were going noisily at full tilt to lift and return over roller boards that had to be fed back until the required finish had been reached.

Quite enjoyable, too, was the weekly clearing of shavings, ankle-deep, that had accrued from the extensive handwork on the solid furniture of those days. Recently I saw a photograph of present-day furniture assemblers in a workplace in which not one bench could be seen. The floor had obviously never seen shavings. Cabinet makers? I wonder.

Jokers were the bane of apprentices' lives. Returning to my bench one day after a stint in the mill I was horrified to see a block of wood had been secured to my new jack plane by a four inch nail. With the plane firmly held in the bench vice I grabbed the protruding head of the nail in my pincers and pulled with all my might. I landed backwards on the floor with a thud. Amid roars of laughter I looked at what the pincers held. It was certainly the head of a four inch nail but the four inches to which it should have been attached had been sawn through level with the bottom of the block. Adhesion of the block to the plane had been maintained by a blob of soft glue.

Tools provided much laughter for the elders. I had been made alert to the fact that I might be asked to fetch a wide variety of tools that existed only in some joker's brain. What let me down so far as real and false nomenclature was concerned were real tools with the most unlikely names. For instance, I was sent to get the plough and was handed a complicated grooving tool used to joint two boards together.

Many times I saw discipline enforced with mighty kicks on boys' backsides. Thus I had my back to the wall when I was told to procure 'heavy kickers'. They also existed in the shape of short lengths of oak to hold top drawers level when opened. Then there was the veneer hammer, an axe-like tool with blade at a right angle for glueing veneer to a surface.

Next came the good old 'glass hammer'. After all, I asked myself, since all those tools with such improbable sounding names previously called for had proved to exist, why not this? I was passed from one shop to another until finally I stood before the machine shop foreman. Bland faced he told me the glass hammer was undergoing major repairs at Markhams, the nearby engineering firm – a company which, incidentally, was destined to produce mini submarines in World War II, and many years later, build the two huge boring machines used in the drilling of the Channel tunnel.

In winter in the unheated workshops hands quickly became frozen. Warming relief there was if the order came from the foreman to get supplies from the storeroom on the same floor. Heat there was supplied by a stove over which hands blue with cold could be warmed – painfully as the warmth crept in and the cold departed. This, of course, was considered by Bernard who was never cold (he suffered from high blood pressure), to be a 'cissy, time-waster'. The penalty: a swift kick in the pants.

A blind eye was always turned to the practice of having a quick 'drag' at a cigarette in the 'castle' as the wc was called. Length of stay was controlled by those waiting outside to have their spit and drag. If impatience won the day, as it often did, then a quick glance through a small hole in the door to confirm that the occupant on the ancient, cracked porcelain was not the boss, his son or the works foreman, led to a hasty evacuation. There were two methods: thunderous kicks on the door or, failing adequate response, a shower of sawdust and shavings hurled over the door. This usually did the trick.

Mr Grey was energetic, a two-step springer when mounting stairs. An action aptly described by Frank the storeman as 'Like a man with his arse on fire', to transfix with his piercing gaze the luckless lad caught lobbing a glue block at another apprentice. Then if in the mood he would reduce each one of us in turn to a fruitless search on a shaving-strewn bench for a tool reposing in full view at his elbow leaving us mopping up hot glue from an overturned pot or sucking the first cut finger in months. Yet Mr Grey was fair in all his dealings. He set no time limit for work provided a high standard was maintained. Sometimes if speed was required to finish an order we employed every time-saving device we knew (and they were numerous). These included a drastic reduction of smoking time in the 'castle'. Always the high reputation of the firm was paramount in our minds. His thanks for a job done in time were passed down through the foreman. It was tacitly understood that future production would be at the normal pace and that visits to the castle would be as usual.

Mr Grey was held in awe. This was made plain when

fellow-worker Harry Gibbons contrived a collision with me between some wardrobes and, while poking me in the chest with his rule, told me to 'get out of the bloody way'. Later, with a mock apology he said he had mistaken me for the boss.

Without risking wear and tear of the springs of our two-and-sixpenny Ingersol pocket watches (for Sunday use only) we measured time by watching from our third floor workshop windows the passing of the scarlet-liveried London, Midland and Scottish Railway (LMS) expresses from London to Scotland as they passed by bridge over the lower-level London and North Eastern Railway (LNER) main line from the north to London and under the Hornes viaduct which carried a second LNER line to eastern England. Unique we felt it was when we saw three passenger trains, one above the other and at the same time. They were in the days before the 1960 axe of Dr Beeching removed thousands of miles of track from what had become the nationalised British Rail system. Chesterfield lost its former LNER lines but the LMS survived in British Rail livery.

The natural beauty of Derbyshire compensated me for the few pennies each week I was able to keep in my pocket from my wages. Within walking distance of Chesterfield there were some of the most scenic areas of countryside in the country. I and fellow workmate Ernie Johnson, similarly as short of cash in hand as I was, took walks through farmland fields just as lovely in pastoral beauty as they had been centuries before. We trod through bracken and gorse to the Linacre reservoirs distinguishable as such only by the presence of the stone-built pumping station standing in the shade of lichen-covered trees. In the nearby woods still densely filled with trees, we found only rabbits and red squirrels where once Robin Hood and his merry men had lived secure from the evil assaults of the Sheriff of Nottingham. The woods were the poachers' paradise, their sacks filled as they dispersed at the first sign of dawn.

A familiar sight was the highly varnished milk float of Farmer Lamb, whose high-stepping pony could have done the daily round blindfold with every stop accurately made. In the float there was the usual five-gallon can into which the farmer dipped his measures to fill the jugs of his customers.

With competence in workmanship acquired I took on private jobs. The object was to buy a touring cycle and to help with my keep at home. So I made sideboards of solid oak, automatic bureaux and extending dining tables. This kept me busy during lunch breaks and back home in the evenings. Just as industrious and far more skilful were our carvers from Belgium, real craftsmen who produced replicas of the Dutch Masters on oak panels for less than £2 each. The work was elaborately intricate in minute detail. Today they'd cost a small fortune.

Times were hard. The Great Depression had not run its dismal course. There was half-time working and, often, alone or in the company of Ernie Johnson I left home early on my new cycle to ride by way of Barlow, famed for its well dressings, and the verdant Cordwell Valley overlooked by the wild rhododendrons massed in radiant regiments as they grew on the hillsides leading down to the vale below. At Hope we left our cycles under the heather (unbelievably idiocy, perhaps, in these times of chained cycle wheels) confident that, no matter how far we wandered away, they would be still under the heather on our return.

Distance was no object so far as walking was concerned. From Hope we stepped forward to cover the twenty-odd miles that took us around Kinder Scout and the Snake Pass, always the first place in the country to become snowbound in winter. Reaching our cycles again we then pedalled home in the dark of the evening, alone in the wildness of hill and dale except, perhaps, for some lone gamekeeper spotted as a moving speck miles away. Such a vastness of moorland beauty stretching to touch the cloud-swept horizon on whichever side we looked made it difficult to realise that this was a beauteous part of a land so small as Britain rather than one of sweeping landscapes of America or Australia or some gigantic mass in Africa.

The fact that we could safely leave our cycles lying unlocked and unguarded on the moors, and even in urban streets, at that time was indicative of the trust we reposed, usually well rewarded, in human honesty. On one of our moorland jaunts, for instance, we met a labouring man on a remote farmstead. He had never seen us before and yet, knowing that we came from the town, he handed over cash equal to our combined short-time pay. His request was that we should buy hedging gloves with the money and deliver them to him by post once they had been purchased. We did that next day and hoped they arrived safely.

Down the long, winding avenues of Memory Lane now I can still see in nostalgic affection those wanderings in all four seasons over what was, indeed, William Blake's green and pleasant England. In summer the hum of the insects, the trilling of the birds and the glorious scent of wild flowers as we walked or cycled over age-old paths trodden by countless feet over the centuries. Above us the blue sky of an August day and the sun giving life to flora and fauna still adorning Derbyshire's rugged peaks and the heather-clad moorland expanses. In winter, often white with snow, the great sense of loneliness at night as, in the distance we spot the dim glow of an oil lamp on some isolated farm. Those moors of my homeland have given me greater pleasure and the most intense nostalgia than any of the sights worldwide travel has provided for me over so many years.

How the memories of those youthful jaunts flood back. I can still see clearly the notice posted on a track leading to a moorland farm that offered an Austin van for £6 – or in exchange for six piglets. There was the easy walk to the tailor's shop in the village of Eyam, where the inhabitants voluntarily isolated themselves within the village until the deadly scourge of the Plague had run its course. It was at the tailor's shop in Eyam that the cloth that brought the Black Death to England was bought and stored. A plaque outside the village recalls the courageous fortitude of its inhabitants as they cut themselves off from any outside human contact. Supplies for them were left by the good villagers of Stoney Middleton at a nearby stream. Money for their purchase was left immersed in vinegar.

On Saturdays my friend and I took walks by the River Derwent teeming then with trout. As a result it was the haunt of preying kingfishers and waterfowl. We walked through the picturesque village of Heanor where all the houses are turreted and from there to the splendid avenue of oaks in Chatsworth Park, so old that their enormous branches were supported by chains and props to prevent them from snapping off because of the enormous weight they placed on the magnificent trunk. I smile now as I recall the kindly motorist, who stopped and offered us a lift under the impression that we were walking across the Pennines to Manchester in Lancashire in search of work. He was incredulous when we told him that we were trudging through the snow for the pleasure it gave us.

'Rather you than me,' was his rejoinder as he drove off

on his moorland crossing.

In furtherance of my long-cherished ambition to join a colonial police force I wrote to the *Police Review* for information and was told that without a college education it was extremely unlikely that I would ever be considered. Applications to the Palestine and several African forces confirmed this. However, the London agents for the Shanghai Municipal Police, Messrs John Pook & Co, 168 Fenchurch Street in the City of London, sounded more hopeful. In their reply to my letter they told me they were not recruiting at the moment but they would, subject to another application from me, place my name on the waiting list. They also warned that extremely high standards, especially physical, were required before acceptance. I immediately requested that my name be placed on the list.

That was enough to raise my hopes. I enrolled for a correspondence course on police work and studied assiduously. In the meantime, of course, life continued as usual at home and at Grey & Lewis.

I was bound by the practice then that an apprentice could not receive full pay until he had worked for some time in another firm. So a fellow apprentice and I answered a newspaper advertisement asking for men with first class experience in the trade. The advertisement had been placed by a firm in the city of Leeds, located then in the West Riding of Yorkshire, Britain's largest county. We were taken on and found lodgings in Leeds.

First class the firm was certainly not. The two of us soon agreed that making furniture of ply stuck together with glue was not our particular forte. That the management were at one with us on this point was made clear on the second Friday when, given the customary two hours' notice, we got the sack.

It was in Leeds that we had our first taste of real Yorkshire pudding. Our landlady, as did all Yorkshire folk, served the famous oven-baked batter pudding in large portions covered in rich gravy as a starter. The small squares we had formerly been eating as an accompaniment to the meat and vegetables on one plate were not the 'Yorkshire pudding of Yorkshire' as our landlady told us. The pudding always came first in large portions entirely separate from the rest of the meal. That was the Yorkshire fashion and it was not, as many people thought, a ploy by the thrifty Yorkshire people to curb appetites before the main course was laid on the table. Mind you, it was filling and certainly must have left less space to be filled by the 'meat and veg' to follow.

I shall never forget our landlady's parrot. Its imitation of the sound of the bells on passing trams was perfect. The trams long ago disappeared from the streets of Leeds as they did in practically every other urban area in Britain. Now, so many large metropolitan regions, including Leeds, are easing car-choked streets by reintroducing tram services under the modern application of light railways. Pity that the old parrot, no doubt now 'ringing tram bells' in some feathered heaven, will not be able to show its versatility in giving a perfect imitation of the warning hoots of the light-rail coaches as they run over old rail tracks and through some of the city's major roads.

From Leeds the next move was to Derby's Gee's joinery works to join some former workmates from Grey & Lewis. At Gee's men worked in pairs at the same large bench and the initiation into the strange work was made easy for newcomers by being paired with one of the firm's old hands. With one notable exception. I was given a bench with an apprentice in his fourth year whose stock answers to all my queries were either, 'Dunno, mate' or 'You tell me, you're the boss'. Invariably followed by the production of a tin and the invitation to 'Have some snuff'. Nevertheless, with overtime pay no less than £5 a week, lodgings at only a pound and one shilling a week Derby was certainly closer to my heart than Leeds. The work was more skilful and done without glue.

My benchmate was eventually changed for another, more affable apprentice, whose main characteristic was an addiction to chocolate which he consumed by the slab.

His name was Tom and he had well-to-do parents. They lived with him in a village outside Derby and provided him with a car – a real luxury in those hard times. Several fellow workers also lived in the village and, to Tom's annoyance it must be said, saved bus fares by getting him to drive them to work free of charge. While Tom did not seek payment in money, he made it plain that appreciation of his free lifts could well have been shown by gifts of chocolate – just the occasional bar.

Now, one of Tom's passengers, 'Big Bill', had a sense of humour. He had collected a bag filled with samples of chocolate laxative handed out by a salesman standing outside the works gates. This he left in full view on his bench as though forgotten to be duly annexed by a sharp-eyed Tom.

Back at work four days later, and following Bill's poker-faced 'Glad to see thi back Tom. We've missed thi, lad, wha' wi' t' buses allus bein' full an' all.' Tom was not impressed by the warmth of the welcome. From the other side of our shared bench he told me, 'I'll fix those bastards soon, you see.'

I didn't see but I heard what had happened. 'Big Bill' and his mates filled the car as usual to go home from work. There were several 'misfires' and stops as the vehicle was driven towards the home of Tom's uncle where, he said, he had to pick up a parcel. He then imparted the information that he needed petrol so would they all set off in search of some place selling petrol? They did – in several directions. Once they were out of sight he re-entered the car and set off at a rate that denoted sufficient petrol-push and tooted cheerily as he passed each walking mate. For 'Big Bill' there was a special Klaxon concerto.

'You should have seen the looks on their faces as I passed them,' he told me.

Tom, naturally, was apprehensive the next day but 'Big Bill' took it all in good humour. Indeed his account of the walk home, via lanes and fields and the bulls they feared and the hedges they ran into in the darkness of a wintry day, provided laughs that were as effective as any laxative. Some found buses. Others did not. Homecomings were around 11.30pm. The free lifts started again but still without benefit of the chocolate he was too proud to ask for. This could only have left Tom with memories best forgotten.

The northern belief about people Derbyshire-born and bred was that they were strong in the arm and weak in the head. This seemed to be true enough when men, who had lost their jobs after Mr Grey had died and Grey & Lewis had closed, had found jobs in the city of Sheffield in southern Yorkshire for a wage as small as thirty shillings a week. What proved their daftness was the fact they refused to fill vacancies for much more money in Derby, only twenty-four miles by train from Chesterfield on the grounds that it was too far from home. Exactly half that mileage got them to Sheffield for their seven day week.

To some of them I quoted the case of a man on the next bench to mine, who walked nine miles to and from work six days a week, even in winter and to work long hours on overtime. They were not impressed.

Changes at Gee's in time decreed that newcomers were no longer needed. I got the sack again. I was lucky enough to get a job with a lorry body building firm ten miles or so from home. I needed to be close to Chesterfield in case there was a summons from the agents of the Shanghai police to proceed to London for interview. Body building was then a specialised trade and I was put to work on ten ton trucks being built for a major oil company. I also carried out repairs on private cars. Cabs were handmade as were doors that were fitted by men who had served a full nine year's apprenticeship. Such precision as they imparted to their work is rarely seen these days.

Back home one evening I found a letter from London. It was from John Pook & Co in Fenchurch Street. Would I proceed to London on a date given for interview as a candidate for entry into the Shanghai Municipal Police? Would I? So great was my excitement I would have jumped on my bicycle straightaway and pedalled down south there and then.

Dressed in my best Sunday suit I set forth for London on the LMS line to St Pancras. Notwithstanding the chaotic state of my mind, on emerging from St Pancras station I paused to admire the Gothic splendour of its long frontage. The most beautiful railway entrance anywhere in the country and a grade I listed building. From there to the equally beautiful curving terraced offices that was Fenchurch Street and in which Pook & Co, agents for Shanghai and Colombo occupied number 168. Sadly, all those early Victorian terraced offices were demolished in the 1970s and replaced by much less impressive concrete and cement four storied buildings. I was nervous, but still confident I could make a good impression. I felt I had little to fear even though my education was not college-given.

My confidence almost dropped to zero when I looked at my fellow applicants for selection: scarlet-coated guardsmen, immaculate in walking-out uniforms, boots polished to diamond-bright perfection; large men in uniform trousers and sports jackets, obviously policemen off duty. All exuding confidence. What chance, I asked myself, had I the rustic from Derbyshire got against this lot? I was given the examination papers and told not to rush things as the others still had to be interviewed. Eventually, Mr Pook, briefly scanning the completed papers, ushered me back to the by-now empty waiting room. Soon it was my turn to stand before the selection board. This was composed mainly, I learned later, of those senior police officers who chanced to be home on leave from Shanghai. A questionnaire sent to me previously, asking for a detailed account of my activities from the age of five to the present, was on the table in front of the chairman.

There followed fifteen minutes of questions, most of which appeared to be aimed at sorting out those with a bent for a Sax Rohmer-type role, or an inclination for the Arabian Nights pleasures that Shanghai, known then as the Paris of the Orient, offered in plenteous and sensual profusion. Outside again, I was informed that my application was still under consideration and because my four-hour journey to London had placed me last on the day's list, I should make all speed to the agents' doctor in Middle Court, a Dr Lee.

At the end of his very thorough examination Dr Lee told me I had still one more medical to take in Harley Street, but having been passed by him I could be quite sure of acceptance. With what appeared to add authenticity to this assertion he solemnly warned me to be careful of the drink and women when I got out there in a manner which excluded any likelihood that these desirable temptations might not soon be forthcoming. After the Harley Street examination, a picture of all those self-confident fellows with whom I had shared the waiting room came to mind. I heard the specialist's phoned report to the effect that if I was the last man, then only he and Reece had passed today. Would I be sailing soon? I prayed with all my heart that good news was on the way.

It was. I received a letter to confirm that I had been accepted. There was a form to fill in that called for my agreement to sail in three weeks to China. There was also a list of injections I would have to have. I handed in my notice at the body building firm and prepared myself for the voyage to come. A second letter telling me that sailing would be delayed by two weeks found me working locally in a firm constructing Chesterfield's new town hall. Again I was paired with another man. I suggested if he liked to lead then I'd be happy to follow, whereupon it transpired that he also was a cabinet maker and had been hoping to follow where I led. However, we managed all the unaccustomed jobs with credit. We really came into our own when the council decided to restore and transfer to the new building all the valuable oak furnishings from their old offices. We were offered permanent jobs at pay levels which with overtime bank managers would have envied. I wasn't even tempted. Shanghai called me. It was a strong call that could not be denied.

Finally, a sailing date was fixed – aboard the Peninsula & Oriental liner, *Corfu*. I had wanted to have a farewell run around the peaks of Derbyshire. It was not to be. My foreman begged me to work to the last possible day which I did.

41

3

P&O SHIP TO CHINA

My departure from home on the first leg of my journey to China was brief and to the point. As a family we had never demonstrated discomposure when troubles in one form or another had befallen us. Emotions we certainly had but we kept them in check as, indeed, did most of the northern stock amongst whom we lived in that era when life was encumbered with many sad afflictions.

I kissed my mother goodbye. Luckily, father was on late turn for work. As I prepared to leave the house he shook my hand. He looked over at Mother and told me to write to her regularly.

'Let her know how you're getting on,' he said.

Later that day in Messrs John Pook's office at 168 Fenchurch Street I met the other nine recruits with whom I was to sail that day for Shanghai on the P&O China ship SS *Corfu*. The other half of the squad which like us had been selected from the first thousand applicants from a total of double that number, were to follow on another P&O ship, *The Chitral,*two weeks later.

Two groups carrying on animated discussions about the Irish and Scots Guards and the RAF on the one hand, and A and B divisions on the other left little doubt as to their previous callings. After a long interval of this a tall redhead who had been listening with obvious impatience took a chair next to mine and after checking that I'd been in neither the Guards nor the Metropolitan Police said that was a big relief because as a Glasgow-born ex-prentice seaman he had begun to think that he was all on his own with this bluidy lot. To our mutual relief Sandy (Cockburn) and I were in the same cabin which we shared with Jock Kinloch late Scots Guards and Gammie ex-RAF. As we left the river below Tilbury, which we cleared much to my surprise dead on time at 4pm we toasted each other with strong Worthington bitter which I still remember cost less than three of our new pence per pint.

Dinner was announced by a melodious tune played on a xylophone by a steward walking around the corridors below decks and the public rooms above. A custom discontinued with the war but so common then, that when berthed in line with other British ships in three major ports en route we were entertained by the music from this tuneful instrument rising and falling in the darkness as each in turn sounded its own distinctive call to dinner.

Shipboard routine started with tea in the cabin followed by a real English breakfast with the P&O curry as an option. Lunch with curry as a third choice was followed by 4pm tea, a full meal in itself for those without the will to resist. Cakes and sweetmeats were made fresh every day in superabundance. A few hours engaged in deck sports worked up the thirst which put an edge on the appetite for dinner. This was always preceded by the solemnly-observed ritual of the nightly bath. Escorted individually by a Goanese bath steward to the appointed bathroom, we had the choice of using salt water soap to bathe in the hot salt water-filled bath and sluice down afterwards with a large basin of fresh water. Alternatively, we could wash down with the fresh and immerse after in the salt to remove the lather. Compared with my existence in Chesterfield life aboard the *Corfu* verged on the luxurious. Happy ages away from the tin bath in front of the fire at home, heated as always with hot water from the kettle on the fire.

The dark oak-panelled dining saloon, contrasting with the gleaming cutlery laid out on snowy tablecloths, softly lighted by the red-shaded lights on the panelling gave an intimate and truly authentic Oriental atmosphere which I have never seen equalled in any of the many Asian eating establishments I have visited in London since. The Indian table stewards in white and green livery stood at intervals round the walls. They were from Goa, then a Portuguese colony in India which was, in 1961, taken over by the Indian military.

That aura of romance redolent of the East, which permeated those old China ships of the P&O so saturated those that travelled on them with their own indefinable mystique that any subsequent ship travel undertaken paled into emasculated mediocrity by comparison. Always there was that indefinable something missing.

The ship itself in drab tan and black, with the P&O house flag, might not appear as anything remarkable. Perhaps it was the crew, from its commander, Captain Chaplin, down to the lowest Goanese steward, exuding efficiency, pride and confidence born of the knowledge that they were part of the most powerful marine force in the world. A legend in the Far East. Possibly it was the passengers themselves: an officer of the Bengal Lancers, an accomplished pianist returning from home leave.

The ship was steaming outward bound for over five weeks along that most romantic route of all, the old 'Red Route' from London to Yokohama. A voyage redolent of the romance of the East on the ships of the P&O that had sailed into oriental dependencies since the days of the British East India Company and Lord Clive. In the bar the talk was of the good old days, nostalgic flashbacks of the old hands that took scant notice of the fact that the Union Jack flew proudly over the sterns of most ships we saw at sea.

The Empire was still a major force in the world and this was certainly evident so far as the *Corfu's* passenger list was concerned. There were the military advisers bound for the princely states in India – Jaipur, Hyderabad and the rest. In the bar army officers exchanged greetings with planters returning to India, Ceylon, Malaya, Borneo and elsewhere after home leave. Some would be back on third or fourth 'stints' in the tea gardens or the rubber plantations tanned, leather-skinned, tough and hard drinking. A few were on their final 'tour' before retirement back home in Britain, a fate that, according to the barman, who had served successive generations of 'colonials', would see the lure of the East bringing them back as his customers after only a few months of pining for the old times beneath the grey skies of every English season.

After Gibraltar and Malta, Marseilles with the dominating Basilica of Notre Dame la Garde and its Fort St Jean of 'Beau Geste' fame which as a boy I had read so avidly about was the first call of any real interest. A fellow passenger who, with the benefit of a solitary overnight stay in Paris, warned us to be wary of the women who would approach us ashore. That was before he left us in the hope that one of these highly desirable women would accost him ashore that night. In the meantime several of us joined Sandy on a nostalgic tour of his old drinking haunts round the docks. My deep concentration on a late-night rendering of Santa-Lucia in a late-night bistro was abruptly broken by a poke in the back and a request in a familiar voice for the loan of a quid till we got back to the ship. The profit of doom was back in our midst. After generous doses of cognac had loosened his tongue we

45

heard the reason for his sudden descent into insolvency. He had accompanied a lady to a cheap hotel where, before switching off the light, she had carefully placed his suit on a hanger and hung it in what he had assumed was a closet. On waking later to find the lady gone he opened and stepped through the 'closet' door to find himself in a passage as bare as the pockets of the familiar suit lying in a crumpled heap at his feet. We lust and learn!

From Marseilles to Port Said and the entrance to the Suez Canal built by Frenchman Ferdinand de Lesseps, whose statue looked over the waterway that had become an overseas goldmine for Britain thanks to the financial genius of British Prime Minister Benjamin Disraeli. In 1875 he brought off a celebrated coup, the purchase of the Suez Canal shares from the financially embarrassed Khedive of Egypt. The canal remained in joint British and French hands until, in 1956, Colonel Gamel Abdel Nasser, the revolutionary leader of a new Egypt, expropriated the entire waterway after a brief military confrontation with Britain, France and Israel. The statue of de Lesseps, most unfairly considering the wealth the canal would bring to an independent Egypt, was toppled and destroyed by raging crowds.

The *Corfu* berthed in the harbour to await a place in the next convoy of ships to navigate the canal. I got my first whiff of the aromatic odour of the East: the scent of many spices, the perfumed bouquet of Biblical frankincense and myrrh, the pungent tang of Arabic coffee and the appetising smell of the seemingly countless cafes that Port Said then offered the traveller on his forays into the teeming streets of the port. It was a fascinating event in my life I can never forget.

British troops lived in barracks in Port Said and learned bad Arabic in various encampments down the length of the canal to Port Suez. The decks teemed with traders with passes to sell an amazing variety of goods: brightly coloured clothing, handicrafts, postcards of the pyramids, of the Sphinx and others of a less salubrious nature, produced discreetly from an inside pocket only at the approach of unaccompanied men.

In these days of hourly flights by aircraft I wonder if the operators of the large flotilla of bumboats that clustered around passenger ships in the old days of six-week voyages to the Far East are still operative. They were fascinating times. From the *Corfu* deck I watched the bumboat men bargain with railside passengers over the price of goods contained in baskets and hauled up by ropes for inspection by potential buyers. When sales were made the goods were removed and the cash lowered down in the basket. The bargaining between bumboat man below and railside potential buyer enacted in increasing decibel strength as more than fifty became involved brought forth a cacophony of yells that must have shaken the foundations of the headquarters of the Suez Canal Company visible in the harbour entrance. Fascinating was the unerring skill of boy money-changers, who had never seen the inside of a school, to quote not only the exchange rate for pounds and dollars but for all the world's major currencies at that time. Their amazing speed in working out mentally the exact exchange totals for currencies offered would have delighted my old headmaster back in Chesterfield, a mathematics fanatic if there ever was one.

The dhobi-wallahs, laundrymen, who had taken away our dirty shirts plus other items in huge bundles loosely tied together returned them four hours later laundered and ironed in spotless condition. Not a single item had been lost from the individual neatly tied parcels brought to our cabins just before sailing time, at a greatly reduced cost against shipboard laundry prices.

Soon we were in a convoy consisting mostly of British ships for passage down the canal. We sailed slowly on the waterway to watch from our high, deckside vantage points the road, railway and sweetwater canal on one bank of the enormous cutting. On the other side, the Sinaii region, there was nothing it seemed but a vast expanse of mud. We passed Ismailia and El Kantara and waved back as British servicemen in the pith helmets and khaki shorts of the era greeted us on one side or the other. It was hard to imagine what the scene must have been as thousands of men toiled in incredibly harsh conditions to dig away the millions of tons of sand and earth to leave a wide channel deep enough to accommodate some of the largest steamships in the world. Deaths ran into thousands of Egyptians employed as labourers. Finally, in 1869, the Suez Canal was opened to international shipping. It is more than 104 miles in length and today it can accommodate ships of 37-feet draft.

Passing through the Bitter Lakes we entered the heat of the Red Sea. As we viewed first the distant sand and rocky scene to starboard, Abyssinia, now re-named Ethiopia by Mussolini's conquering legions, and the same unreliev-ed terrain to port I mentally commiserated with those unknown members of the British and Italian colonial services who were living out their widely separated lives in those arid wastes. I little knew that I would one day be considered an authority on both.

Aden, as it remained until recent years when it became part of Marxist-led South Yemen, was a shopper's paradise or so the cheapness of its offerings seemed to suggest. The old naval and merchantmen coaling port, built on solid rock, gave us avenues and narrow streets of shops, either Arab-owned or operated by Indians. Alas, all the incredibly cheap cotton shirts we bought in

Steamer Point to save on ship's laundry bills before reaching Bombay, tailored with an economy to match their price, split at the seams within minutes of dressing.

'How's your shirts?' I asked Sandy.

'Sew, sew,' he replied.

Bombay was spicy, indeed. Here we were in the gateway to India, a major port and commercial and industrial city second only in size to Calcutta.

Ballards Pier, still there in independent India but a pale shadow of its shipping importance at the time of the British Raj, drew the colourful crowds of pukka sahibs, of memsahibs, Anglo-Indians and the 'natives' to welcome the liners on the Far East run. Nearby – and still there today – was the real Gateway to India, erected to welcome the King-Emperor George V, a magnificent monument as famous in the Orient as the Arc de Triomphe in Paris. We hastened to set foot on Indian soil or, rather, Indian city pavements there to be nudged, pushed and shoved into the road by the 'untouchable' cattle that roamed the streets freely – and certainly dangerously.

We toured the bazaars, passed by the red double-decker trams omnipresent then in most large urban centres in Britain. British-made, they reminded us of the public transport back home but the crowds grimly hanging onto precarious footholds back, sides and top left us in grave doubt about their safety.

The oriental aroma, rich, pungent and often overpowering in the markets, stayed with us as we gazed in wonder at Bombay's many handsome buildings: the Victoria railway terminal, the Taj Mahal Hotel, still one of the best in the world, Elphinstone College, Grant Medical College, the Sassoon (a man to be more than familiar in Shanghai) Institute and the big department store of Whiteway & Laidlaw.

We reached the beautiful hanging gardens on Malabar
Hill and there, in somewhat awesome amazement, we
stood outside the high wall of the Parsee Temple of
Silence below which dead bodies are placed on the
ground for the ugly vultures perched hungrily on walls
and trees to tear apart down to the bare bones. This still
today is the Parsee form of 'interent'. There is a large and
mostly prosperous community in Bombay. Ethnically
the Parsees are the original inhabitants of Persia driven in
large numbers into exile by Arab invaders.

We were importuned by beggars, still as numerous
and pestilential today as they ever were. We watched
snake charmers. Groups of sari-clad women, muscular
arms bared high, flailing with heavy thuds on stones or
on concrete slabs, shirts and other garments heavy and
wet. We wondered if the shirts we had handed to the
dhobi-wallah who had boarded the *Corfu* were
undergoing this heavy form of punishment and, if so,
would they survive the experience. Evidently they did.
They came back clean, well pressed and intact.

Bombay had delighted us. It is still an interesting city
today, much bigger now with a population of about eight
million souls, Hindu, Muslim, Parsee, Christian,
Buddist and of such other faiths as Judaism.

The next leg was to Colombo in Ceylon, where we
passed with salutes a Royal Navy flotilla berthed
offshore.

Ceylon, Sri Lanka now, British-controlled since 1818
when the kingdom of Kandy was overthrown, offered us
the varied attractions of Colombo, the capital city, that
had been in succession administered by the Portuguese,
the Dutch and, finally, the British. While the port had
prospered on exports of tea, rubber, spices and
agricultural products, the main attraction of the capital
for the *Corfu's* female passengers were the long lines of

shops selling the country's gem-stones. For us, alas, only window shopping as the gems in multi-coloured shapes and sizes, beyond our financial standing, spread their lure in sparkling flashes.

After leaving Colombo the ship travelled at low speed for a whole day in a humid fog. Once the fog had cleared we put on speed, a significant engine-room asset that enabled the *Corfu* to survive as an armed merchantman during World War II. She arrived in Penang dead on time.

At Penang, or George Town as it was generally known then, we had our first glimpse of Chinese life. To all intents and purposes Penang could have been part of the old Chinese empire. It lived and breathed and prospered on the enterprising genius of its majority Chinese population brought initially as labourers by the British, who took over control of the island as part of the Federated Malay States.

Chinese dialects were in evidence everywhere. True enough, we saw indigenous Malays and Tamils from India but, apart from the large British 'hongs' as the Far Eastern companies were called, business, industry, shopkeeping, almost every endeavour, was a Chinese monopoly.

Under British rule there was little indication then of the ethnic violence that would ensue many years later between the politically ascendant Malays and the Chinese, dominant in the economic life of the region. For us, ashore in wide-eyed wonderment at our first contact with the Chinese people among whom we were to live and work in Shanghai, the impact on our rapidly weakening 'homeside' insularity was strong.

From Penang and then Swettenham, the port of Kuala Lumpur, we sailed to Singapore where we were joined as fellow passengers by Chinese from the city and other parts of the Straits Settlements. They were heading back to the land of their ancestors. Most of our British passengers had left for their various colonial pursuits at the ports of call on what was for us a wondeful voyage of discovery. Each port had given us an insight into the kaleidoscopic lifestyles of a large section of the world's inhabitants, isolated then by great distances and what would be described today as the rudimentary travel facilities of that era. We felt we were a privileged few. Indeed we were the beneficiaries of Britain's imperial power, the selected servants of the Crown leaving behind in homeside insularity the mass of the population. The international tourist market of today's more affluent societies was more than half a century away.

Singapore, like Penang, could have been China itself. The majority of its population was Chinese, mostly Fukien in origin. Then, as now, it was a major port and prosperous trading centre.

It had been since 1922 the principal base for the defence of British interests in the Far East but, despite its strong fortifications, it fell to the Japanese on February 15, 1942, a defeat that was to have its effect on us in Shanghai.

Hong Kong, then still architecturally colonial with its balconied waterfront buildings, was our last call before the *Corfu* set course for Shanghai. We went ashore in Kowloon which was essentially residential and dominated by the Peninsula Hotel, still renowned the world over for its luxurious hospitality. Yet to come was the post-war transformation to metropolitan splendour with its skyline completely dominated by skyscrapers spread in glittering arcs along its shores. Its fame as one of the century's greatest success stories and eventual return to Chinese control were more than sixty years away.

We crossed the busy harbour by the Star Ferry to

Victoria island, the business centre, and there we met and entertained an American couple who returned our hospitality with strong beer in the beautiful, oak-panelled bar of the German liner, *Potsdam*. Many years later I was destined to travel on that splendid ship.

As we steamed the fourteen miles up the Yangtse to Shanghai, I saw for the first time that local phemomenon caused by the heavy silt carried downstream in seemingly solid blocks of differently coloured water, each of which, failing to merge with the next, appeared to be separated by invisible barriers. As we neared the impressive skyline of Shanghai's famous Bund, more resembling Liverpool than a city in China, we anchored in midstream in a line of mainly British ships off Holt's Wharf in Hongkew. A P&O pilot tug, with that ex-Navy Shanghai character Harry Webber in charge, took us ashore from where we were taken in two police vans to Ping-Liang Road Training Depot in Yangtsepoo.

4

RECRUIT IN THE SHANGHAI MUNICIPAL POLICE TRAINING DEPOT

After disembarkation from the *Corfu* we were taken through the teeming streets of the largest city in China to the training depot of the Shanghai Municipal Police in Ping-Liang Road. I shared a room there with Bill Carr, a Yorkshire man who had completed service in the British Army in Shanghai and stayed on in the police.

Shanghai was not a colony. It was a treaty port on the soil of China. In the 1830's the Manchu government suppressed the importation of British-Indian opium into the port of Canton. This led to the Opium War of 1839-42 with Britain. By the terms of a series of treaties signed with Britain and several Western powers betweem 1842 and 1860 the defeated Manchus grudgingly became party to the 'unequal treaty system', the principal features of which were the opening of specially designated ports, including Shanghai, Canton, Foochow, Ningpo and others, to Western 'residence'. Hong Kong was totally ceded to Britain and became a Crown colony.

Shanghai, an inconspicuous fishing town, was opened to foreign trade under the terms of the 'unequal treaties' and a British settlement established there. From then on the growth of Shanghai was phenomenal. The French followed the British and established a concession adjoining the British area. The Dutch, Portuguese, Americans, Japanese and several lesser Western powers followed the British and in 1863 the International Settlement of Shanghai was established. The French remained aloof and retained their own concession under strict French control. Adjoining the borders of the two concessionary areas was Chinese-controlled Greater Shanghai with headquarters located at Kiangwan.

The Settlement, or 'English Town' as it was known by the Chinese, was governed by the Shanghai Municipal Council. This administrative body comprised five British, five Chinese, two Dutch, American, Japanese and Portuguese members with one from each of seven other countries. Law and order was maintained by the Shanghai Municipal Police. There were also foreign military forces stationed in the Settlement. These consisted of two British infantry battalions, a regiment of the United States Marine Corps and Japanese and Italian troops as well as naval units from these countries. The French, of course, maintained a garrison and naval units for the protection of their concession.

The imperial Manchus had long since gone when I arrived in China, but Pu Yi, the boy emperor and the last of his line to rule China, had been installed by the Japanese as the ruler of Manchukuo which was the name they gave to Manchuria, Chinese territory they invaded and captured in 1931. The revolution that had seen the rise to power of Chiang Kai-shek and the Kuomintang (Nationalist Party) had posed problems of defence in the foreign-controlled areas of Shanghai. So, to augment the strength of the international regular forces in the city, the territorial, citizens 'army', the Shanghai Volunteer Corps, was formed. It was commanded by a British officer and consisted of British, American, Eurasian and Chinese units. There was one regular battalion formed of young White (anti-Soviet) Russians, a well disciplined and most efficient unit that came to the aid of the police when the Japanese bombed Shanghai in 1937.

British influence was then supreme in Shanghai and, indeed, throughout China. In overall command of the internationally composed Shanghai Defence Force was British Major General A P D Telfer-Smollet. The Shanghai Municipal Police commissioner was former British Army officer, Major Kenneth Bourne. His deputy, Captain H M Smyth, had served in the Indian Army in Gurkha battalions.

The police force in the Settlement was, indeed, a 'League of Nations' in the cosmopolitan composition of its members: predominantly British and Chinese with some White Russians, eight hundred Sikhs, six hundred Japanese plus sprinklings of other nationalities. Its duty was to preserve law and order over a foreign enclave nine miles in length and a mile inland from the long Whangpoo River boundary. Additionally there were some fourteen miles of extra-territorial roads extending westward into Chinese territory.

There were fourteen police stations in the Settlement of which Louza held the record of being the busiest in the world so far as handling crime was concerned. Yangtsepoo was the largest. Headquarters were in the British defence sector in central Shanghai. A count of flags flying in the city conducted from the eighth storey of the Foochow Road central headquarters revealed that more than eighty per cent were British. Apart from the stateless White Russians and the Germans, Austrians and other nationals of defeated countries in the 1914-18 war, most foreigners living in Shanghai had extraterritorial rights, Empire nationals were subject to control by the

British Consulate-General in the city. Located on the central Bund in extensive grounds its facilities included the British Supreme Court in China, magistrates' courts and ancillary departments. Close to the police head-quarters were the American Consulate-General and the US Supreme Court in China. Other treaty-power nationals had their own courts. The White Russians, the Germans and their former allies in the 1914-18 war, together with the Chinese residents in the Settlement, were tried in what were known as the Mixed Courts.

The dividing boundary between the six square miles of the French Concession and the Settlement was the wide boulevard, Avenue Edward VII which was built over a small creek running into the Whangpoo River. There were no restrictions on movements between the two foreign areas. Indeed, many of the Settlement people, foreigners and Chinese, chose to live in the architect-urally more attractive French area.

Newcomers to Shanghai we might have been but it did not take us long to realise that there was a full scale war on the city's doorstep. Death, doom and disaster were omnipresent and almost everywhere outside the confines of the two foreign areas there was human suffering on a vast scale. In July 1937, the Japanese, on the pretext of being the victims of a Chinese attack at Loukouchiao, near Peking, unleased their formidable military forces in a full scale war against the government of Chiang Kai-shek. Despite heroic resistance by the Chinese the Japanese advanced quickly to occupy practically all the coastal region of China. There had been heavy fighting around the Settlement and the French Concession and the victorious Japanese had advanced to conquer the capital, Nanking, and to advance further inland. Chiang had retreated well into the vast interior of China to set up a wartime capital at

Chunking in Szechwan province.

The two foreign areas became massive refugee camps as thousands of Chinese from the hinterland fled from the scene of hostilities and sought sanctuary under the protection of the French and Settlement councils. A French Roman Catholic priest, Father Jacquinot, established a camp at Siccawei in the French area while in the Settlement a large dilapidated movie theatre, later to be renovated and reopened as the Roxy, was used to accommodate about 500 refugees, mostly women and children.

Despite the inevitable drift to war in Europe following the rise to power of Adolf Hitler in Germany and Benito Mussolini in Italy and, much nearer home, the threatening worsening in relations between Britain and America and the militarists in Japan, the foreign areas in Shanghai remained neutral. Japanese forces were still part of the Shanghai Defence Force and their sector was the Hongkew district which, containing a large Japanese population, had become known as Little Tokyo. Law and order was still maintained by the Shanghai Municipal Police although the deterioration in the international situation had provided many difficulties in so far as increasing Japanese interference was concerned. Garden Bridge over the Soochow creek at its junction with the Whangpoo River was the boundary line between the British sector and the Japanese defence area. Kilted Seaforth Highlander sentries stood midway on the bridge a few yards away from Japanese soldiers.

Other defence sectors in the Settlement were manned by the Fourth Regiment of the United States Marine Corps and the Italian Savoia Grenadiers.

At the Gordon Road depot we were issued with handmade and made-to-measure footwear and summer and winter uniforms. After that we watched one of the three units of the Settlement's world-famous riot squads deal with a noisy mob. Each unit carried a mix of forty-six Sikhs, Chinese and Russians and British officers. They were carried in two red vans on Leyland fire-engine chassis armed with swivel-mounted Tommy guns. The first and larger vehicle carried a shotgun and a large indicator panel from which the commander of the squad would duplicate in characters his shouted orders. This removed the problem of crowd noise blotting out the sound of his voice. This was shown when the British officer in charge of the squad was able to form his men into four ranks which then each in turn charged and withdrew until order was obtained. All this was performed without a single vocal command from the officer in charge standing tall and helmeted in a deep recess behind the driving cab. In the second vehicle officers were similarly placed, usually three abreast, in the recess behind the cab taking their orders from him.

Fitness, we maintained through early morning runs commencing daily at 6am which, considering it was high summer with day temperatures around 120 degrees with very high humidity, went some way to offset any ill effects of the beer consumed the night before. These early morning runs were our introduction to those highly varnished, beautifully made miniature barrel-like receptacles for a family's twenty-four hours accumulation of night soil, and known as 'Mo-dungs'. Minus their tight-fitting lids, they were placed outside each house at 4.30am and their malodorous contents collected by coolies with hand carts before 7am. Known as 'honey-carts' their gaseous contents, swirling in liquidity, were borne to creekside barges for journeys up-country there to be laid on the crops that would soon appear in Shanghai's markets. Liberal splashings of potassium permanganate, we were told, would protect us from any unwelcome ill effects.

Square-bashing, the descriptive army appellation for drill, followed the runs. The instructor, Police Sergeant Knifton, late of the Brigade of Guards, was hardly enamoured of the performance of Sandy and me. The ex-army and the former British police recruits found little difficulty in reacting immediately to his shouted commands. For civilian types such as Sandy and me, confusion replaced what should have been split-second obedience. The remedy we found, was to fall in on each side of old soldier, Bill Carr, who could be relied on to give us *sotto-voce* guidance when some difficult movement had been ordered.

Sometimes, alas, he could also be relied on to say 'right' when the advice should have been 'left'. Or vice versa, with the result that following the stamp of feet preparatory to the smart wheel to the right of the rest of the squad Sandy and I took one to the left and marched off by ourselves leaving two conspicuous gaps in the ranks. After each of the advanced squad, those in the depot when we arrived, had put us through our paces under Sergeant Knifton's watchful eye he would call for volunteers from the new men. Something of a joker, Carr, absolutely deadpan of face and in a voice remarkably like mine, would make me the first volunteer, then, with a perfect mimicry of Sandy's Glaswegian accent, make him the next.

One thing was certain: any drill displays to which Sandy and I might be party would never attract the crowds of multi-national viewers to the racecourse whenever the pipes and drums of the Seaforth Highlanders performed the ceremony of Beating Retreat. Nor, indeed, inspire the very real praise from the many American Marines always present for the precision of the Scots in carrying out, without spoken command, intricate quick-march and slow march manouevres.

Every Thursday, Sub Inspector Dan Cormie, a heavily built Scot with a bitingly sarcastic wit capable of reducing his victim to pulp and all those within earshot into paroxyms of laughter, lectured on all known small arms. Emphasis was placed on the American Colt · 45 with which we would be armed on leaving the depot for transfer to station duty. Three times a week we attended the range and took what was probably the most comprehensive police arms training anywhere in the world outside America. It was definitely necessary. Armed crime in Shanghai in one month was greater than that in America in one year and that despite the presence there of Al Capone and his machine-gun murderers. It was said that the Capone mob and ourselves in the SMP were the first organised units to be armed with Tommy guns. We used them in the maintenance of law and order unlike Capone in Chicago. From early 1940 police casualties from shoot-ups were, on average, one or two a day. Mainly Chinese.

Precision in drill and firearm accuracy had to be watched by a similar proficiency in colloquial Chinese. Three bonuses totalling more than £150 in English money were paid to those who passed the final examination in three years. Contracts with those who failed to pass the examination within five years were not renewed. Each of us in training had to undertake duty in the depot office from 4pm to 10pm in turn. There was a teleprinter to record all police messages and, if a button was not pressed at the end of each message, there would soon be a query from headquarters wanting to know why. There was also a nine-bank telephone switchboard on which two calls on each bank could be taken provided the first two keys were raised and the next two down, or vice versa. In those days when telephones were still a rarity both Sandy and I became utterly confused when buzzers and lights terminating one or more calls coincided with incoming calls. Frantically we tried to push in keys in an effort to make connections. Often, by miraculous flukes, we succeeded but we also cut off callers in full conversational flow. Reconnections were not always acknowledged politely.

Once, in a panic caused by the clatter of the teleprinter and phoned queries from headquarters demanding to know why the last message had not been acknowledged, I cut off a call by a senior officer to the Commissioner and then re-connected him with his deputy in the office next to his and the Commissioner with a startled recruit, who had answered the phone ringing in the dining room on the floor above the offices.

Almost as ridiculous was the time when I answered the phone and a voice speaking Chinese came on. Despite my insistence that I didn't speak Chinese the voice went on and on and I really started to worry. Thinking the call might be important I ran to the floor above in search of a local born Chinese-speaking recruit who might help out. There I found senior recruit John Blackley still talking into the phone which in my panic I had forgotten I had linked to the outside exchange. What I had believed to be the voice of a Shanghai Chinese was that of Blackley reading romanised questions and answers from the Chinese-study book he was using to prepare him for his next exam. Such were the trials and tribulations of virgin telephone operators.

My roommate Bill Carr, who had served as a steward on British merchant ships, had an inexhaustible fund of stories from voyages that had taken him seemingly to every port in the world. Indeed, he had sailed round the world four times before he joined the army for a seven-year

year enrolment that ended in Shanghai. Carr had been a member of the crew of the *Doric Star,* which established the world's longest tow when the captain of a disabled British vessel just out of New Zealand insisted on being towed to Liverpool where he had been bound when the breakdown occurred.

My Scottish pal Sandy's assertion that stewards got fat keeping seamen thin recalled for Carr the time when he made good a five per cent deficiency in jam by cutting the ration by ten per cent and then, on receiving the inevitable complaints from the crew restored five per cent to the mutual satisfaction of all.

Shanghai provided for us sartorial splendour that could never have been obtained back home in Britain. Tom the Chinese tailor was our *haute couture* cutter and stitcher. Working with Bradford or Huddersfield cloth lengths this western-style tailor, always clad in well cut suits of his own, gave us suits expertly cut and sewn at less than two pounds sterling – on credit. Whenever settlement of larger-than-usual mess and canteen bills left us short at the end of the month he would waive repayments seemingly with little concern. He knew full well that people in our vocational situation would fulfil our commitments and order new suits and overcoats. This we did, without fail. Tom the tailor was certainly a first class specialist in sartorial expertise. A police officer on leave in the United Kingdom wearing a Tom-the-Tailor creation completely astonished a London tailor, who had noted hem-stitched buttonholes back and front and lapels similarly hem-stitched.

Told the price paid the English tailor was open-mouthed in surprise and asked where in the world could a suit, good enough for Savile Row, be made so cheaply and with the best Yorkshire cloth, too.

That was Shanghai. For us foreigners, as we were called

by the Chinese, the two foreign areas of the city gave us privilege and sybaritic living at a price that would have been unbelievably cheap in such world capitals as Paris, London or New York. The temptations, alas, were far too numerous and our expenditure soared so that, usually, only small change reposed in our pockets before the next payday. It was the local chit system that led us into insolvency. Meals, drinks in most bars, cabaret dance tickets, even taxis could be obtained merely by signing a chit. Collections at the end of the month left most of us bemoaning our collective flare for cashless high living.

Our social life was somewhat hampered by the fact that the training depot was situated in the Japanese eastern defence sector. Only a few miles away there had been heavy fighting in such Chinese areas as Chapei and Kiangwan. The ravages of war in some areas had spilled over into the Settlement and Japanese military patrols were apt to make outings rather dangerous by their habit of shooting at every shadow that moved. Luckily we were able to cross Garden Bridge three times a week into the glaring neon-light welcome of the western half of the Settlement. A million lights might flicker on New York's Broadway but, as even the Americans had to admit, that great highway could not hold a candle to Shanghai's brilliant nights. Shops, restaurants, night clubs, cabarets, bars were illuminated in electric multi-hued effulgence that converted daytime drabness into a fairyland of brilliant colours reflected in fiery glow in the over-hanging sky. Compared with the monotony of the eastern district over the Soochow Creek the western region provided us with streets teeming with cosmo-politan humanity. Trams and double-decker buses ran side by side with automobiles, rickshaws, carts, itinerant hawkers, food stall owners and a multi-racial law and order force seen nowhere else in the world: turbanned

Sikhs, Shantung Chinese in flat-capped blue, White Russian cycle patrols in the French Concession, British SMP officers armed and vigilant and, outside the banks and the money-changers, Sikh, Muslim and Hindu guards cradling rifles or with holstered revolvers.

Carr was an obsessive cinemagoer. In Bubbling Well Road running by the racecourse and its inner sports complex was the British-owned Grand Theatre, a large and imposing construction showing first-run movies. After a matinee or evening performance we walked the few yards to the Foreign YMCA there to enjoy the then unfamiliar American hamburgers served by white-coated Chinese waiters. From there self-consciously seated in rickshaws for the first time in our lives we crossed into the French Concession, or Frenchtown as it was commonly known, to be welcomed at DDs, a popular restaurant-cum-night club on the tree-lined wide Avenue Joffre, the main Concession thorough-fare.

DDs provided an attractive decor, music and the lure of cover-girl beauty provided by its White Russian hostesses. Its long black glass bar with chrome foot and hand rails was overlooked by full length mirrors and bottle-laden shelves. Black velvet draped the walls to make an attractive mating with red pile carpets. It was within this warm, sophisticated setting that the silky allure of its hostesses lured daily a large racial mix of males all alight with lustful desire, easy prey for the siren calls of 'Buy me a drink, darling,' that left many in month-end insolvency.

We had joined a group of American Marines at the bar, all of whom obviously had succumbed to the temptations of the flesh and were in hope of sensual reward for large outlays of cash. One of our party, Jimmy, similarly afflicted with fleshy desire roused by the beauty of the hostesses suddenly poured forth with words that were hardly likely to gain a place in the book of sweet expressions of love but which, nevertheless, were more than fully expressive of his fertile ebullience:

'I'd walk the length of Nanking Road barefoot over broken glass just to smell one of their farts'. A sentiment shared by all of us.

The girls were members of anti-Soviet White Russian families who had formerly lived and worked in Manchuria, especially on the Chinese Eastern Railway at a time when Russian influence in that northern region was extremely strong. The conquest of Manchuria by the Japanese and its emergence as Manchukuo had led to a mass exodus of the White Russians to the open-city freedom of Shanghai. There they lived in stateless exile, mostly in the French Concession, and there the daughters of parents, who had once been in happier times affluent in the north but who faced a poverty-stricken existence in Shanghai, offered their 'Russian Princess' attractiveness as night club hostesses, cabaret partners, bar girls and even prostitutes. For all of them the goal was an American, British or other passport that would replace the insecurity of stateless existence. The marriage rate was high for most of the White Russian women. Many of them with ex-Tsarist-officer fathers, offered beauty with graces far above the level of their spouses' backgrounds.

Once out of Shanghai and ensconced safely in husbands' territories divorces often followed arrivals. Yet there were many unions that proved happy and lasting for a lifetime.

In DDs and Shanghai's other social venues the girls worked solely on commission given on the drinks they enticed from male customers. The 'brandies' or 'whiskies' that the bar boys handed to them were cold tea. In the cabarets they existed on dance ticket commission and the charge to a customer for a girl sitting at his table for a stipulated period of time. If they were willing, of course, they could be 'bought out' at a price that promised greater reward.

The dice box played a significant part in bar-room life in Shanghai. When the drinks flowed only in sluggish infrequency a girl would produce the circular leather dice box and suggest a throw or two or three – or maybe more – to see who would buy the next round, and the one after that and so on. There were many variations among which liar dice seemed to be the most popular – a kind of poker-style bluff in which the possession of completely expressionless visage could mean easy pickings. The girls were experts. Of that there could be no doubt. The usual ploy when a customer was slow to challenge was to space the dice across the bar and then, seemingly miraculously, place the inverted box over each one and with a few deft twists of the wrist lift all the dice in turn back in the box. Another variation was to place the dice one on top of the other to be picked off individually in the inverted box without disturbing the ones beneath. These tricks were to be seen nowhere else in the world. Constant practice made any kind of dicing appear child's play. If, however, by some stroke of misfortune, mistiming or just accidental misadventure a game was lost then losses were always honoured – unless, of course, as usually happened the challenge came, 'Double or quits'. Lady luck seemed always to be on their side.

French pride in its long and far-famed history was reflected in street titles in the Concession. Avenue Joffre paid tribute to the 1914-18 war leader. Others in that great conflict such as Foch, the British Field Marshal Haig, Petain and Pershing were similarly remembered. French courtesy to foreign monarchies was evident in the

naming of Avenue du Edouard VII and Avenue du Roi
Albert (of the Belgians). There was Route Victor Emanuel
(of Italy) and Rue Lafayette recorded the fame of one of
France's greatest heroes. The French names afforded
much pronunciative difficulties for Chinese rickshaw
men or taxi drivers. Rue Lafayette became 'Lah-fee-tah
Loo' and Rue Tenant de la Tour 'La-too Loo', 'Yaffay
Loo' was, by far, the busiest thoroughfare in Frenchtown. 'Loo' of course, was Chinese for road or street.

The pre-eminence of Yaffay (Joffre) Loo came about
not only because its wide, tree-lined straightness and its
buildings were reminders of the architectural heritage of
Paris, but because it offered countless variations for those
in search of the seamy side of life. Seek a quick drink and
you'd find a welcome by the girls in hostelries that
seemed to exist cheek by jowl along practically the whole
length of the avenue. And there were countless more on
the side streets.

French delight in *haute cuisine* found *gourmets* from
practically every nation in the world seated in the Cafe
Renaissance, where the 'Bing Crosby of Russia',
Vertinsky, sang every night, or the Hungarian,
Tkatchenko's, the Cafe de Paris, Leonardo's and many
others, not forgetting the popular and inexpensive
Chinese restaurants serving the dishes of Canton and
many other provincial regions.

Culture the French provided with the assistance of the
Russians and other ethnic groups. The British-owned
Lyceum Theatre in Rue Cardinal Mercier, off Avenue
Joffre was the home of the British Amateur Dramatic
Society. It was much better known as the venue for
productions by the Russian Light Opera Company, the
Russian Ballet and Russian theatre group – all
professionals who had chosen stateless exile rather than
accept the artistic controls imposed in the Soviet

Union.

Nearby was the Russian Cathedral in Route Doumer, the scene of beautiful Orthodox Easter services and the spiritual home of most of the Russian community in Shanghai. There was, of course, a small Soviet group but they played only a small part in the everyday life of Shanghai. Indeed, they were kept under constant surveillance and many of them suffered severely later during World War II.

For me the experience of living and working in Shanghai was fascinating after the mundane existence I had known in Chesterfield. Never will there be in this world a city that offered so many diversions, such varied scenarios, such metropolitan sophistication, such privileged living for the foreigner, such contrasts as Shanghai – a wicked city certainly but yet a home for the devoted missionary, for the political exile, for the money-seeker, the banker, the baker, the candlestick maker; a huge assortment of the world's disparate human beings all congregated in two foreign concessions on the soil of China.

From DDs we followed Carr, our Pied Piper, to Pop's, a bar at the other end of the scale owned by an old Russian Jew. There a gaggle of multilingual hostesses, who had certainly seen the passage of more years than their sisters in DDs, made British, French, American and Italian military and naval servicemen happy to be able to converse in their native languages. In fluent Shanghai dialect they passed on orders for drinks to the bar boys as their commission earnings rapidly increased.

Carr, who was our guide and mentor because of his army service in Shanghai, was warmly welcomed by two Russian brothers in the bar. Their gesture to a bar boy produced beers lifted over the heads of the animated throng closely crowded with their female partners all along the bar. Their role in the place soon became evident when one of the brothers seized the arm of a noisy drunk demanding a dance of no one in particular in one hand, and his waist in a bear grip in the other. Then, after waltzing the drunk smoothly through the door held open by his brother, he rejoined us at the bar to resume the conversation at the point it had been broken. Later that night a belligerent drunk looking for a fight got a well timed punch to the jaw from one brother, was grasped under the arms from behind by the other before his recumbent form hit the floor, and then tossed outside by both.

Some time later I visited the bar with Mike Harman, a former hunter in Manchuria who had joined the police in Shanghai. I was a little nonplussed by the curt nod without handshake with which the brothers acknowledged my introduction to them of Mike, and this proud Georgian's acceptance with near obsequious servility of this apparent snub. Later he explained that because of their birth and high status in the Russian community his standing was much inferior to theirs.

I had reason to remember DDs some time later when one of the most flamboyant characters in Shanghai, an American named Jack Riley, fell foul of the law. Riley had made a fortune as the slot machine king in Shanghai. His imported one-armed bandits, as the fruit machines were known, were piling in the money in cabarets, night clubs and bars and he bought DDs, which like his other ventures flourished in the free-spending social whirl of Shanghai.

High-living Riley, who was an extremely popular figure, became one of the first victims of an edict issued by the American consulate in the Settlement that any American nationals arrested by the SMP or the French police should be fingerprinted and their prints sent to the security section of the consulate. It was after an accident that the Settlement police laid a charge against Riley and took his fingerprints which were sent on to the American authorities.

Two days later came the bombshell that earned headlines in the press. Riley was a fugitive with a criminal record. He had escaped from Alcatraz and, like many other men fleeing arrest in several countries, had landed in Shanghai to make a fortune and to earn press prominence as both businessman and florid show-man.

It was the end of the reign of 'King Jack' in the city. Pictures of his arrest appeared in the leading English-language daily *The North China Daily News,* and several other newspapers. The Settlement police took a calculated risk when they allowed Riley freedom to settle his affairs.

He faithfully kept his word to honour that privilege and he reported back to the police. He was taken aboard one of the American President liners that regularly visited Shanghai. It happened that SMP Sergeant Jack Day, who was proceeding on leave to Canada, via New York, was appointed Riley's 'guardian'. On his return to duty Day told us how Riley, in appreciation of the freedom granted by police after his arrest and his own non-curtailment of his shipboard life, had insisted on paying for all the drinks they had together during the voyage.

I met Riley once in a Frenchtown bar presided over by Angella, and after noting my acceptance of her usual practice when serving those she called her friends of adding a brandy to the price of my beer, this genial stranger ordered another round and suggested we play liar dice to see who would pay for it. With the combination of luck and the obvious wealth of my opponent who doubled the stake every time he lost the throw ended up with the result it inevitably must, with me as the loser. He suggested I wager my jacket and if still unlucky, my shirt after that.

Many international criminals found refuge in Shanghai. One of the most notorious was the Buddhist monk, Abbot Chao Kung. In reality he was the Hungarian-born Jew, Trebitsch Lincoln, who was living in the Foreign YMCA. He went to England before World War I and became a Church of England curate and then Member of Parliament for Darlington. Despite the fact that he lost heavily as an inveterate gambler in Monte Carlo, that he had failed in business and was an ex-convict, he was appointed British postal censor in 1914. He offered his services as a spy to Britain on the outbreak of war with the Kaiser's Germany but was turned down. He then crossed to Holland where he forged some documents and engaged in negotiations with the Germans. He sailed to America and in New York confessed to being a German spy. Extradited to Britain he served imprisonment for forgery and was deprived of UK citizenship and expelled from the country. He went to China and entered a lamasery. In the 1920s his favourite son, Natzl, was hanged for murder in Britain. Lincoln rushed to Europe to try and see his son but was refused permission to land. He bore an intense hatred of Britain. He died in Shanghai in 1943.

We were still in the depot when a headquarters detective, Lok-Ah-Wei, was murdered. A long-serving Chinese officer he was almost totally illiterate but he had become one of the most powerful men in Shanghai. Such was his influence in the underworld that a person wanted by the police but known to be hiding in some remote village far away from the city would be returned to face justice on the strength alone of a letter bearing his chop.

All influential Chinese had their individual chops, an embossed, often intricate set of characters on a signet ring or special stamp to be used as a seal in business transactions or as a sign of good faith and identification. The chop was an invaluable asset when a fugitive simply by crossing the Whangpoo river from the Settlement side to Chinese-controlled Pootung could place himself beyond the reach of the SMP.

As it was felt that the funeral of Lok-Ah-Wei would be one of the biggest Shanghai had ever seen our instructors at the depot were assigned to street duties and we had a whole day off.

As it was close to the end of the month Jimmy and I found that our pooled resources would just about cover a cinema show and the tram ride to Louza station where we could sign for a few beers and lunch. That was, provided we walked the five miles to the tram stop by the dining room windows of the Palace Hotel on Nanking Road by the Bund in a humidity of such intensity that the local recruits dressed within minutes of showering without patting themselves into a semblance of dryness as we newcomers did. Either way, our shirts were invariably soaked by the time the first button was fastened.

Leaving the depot in the regulatory jackets and ties we refused an offer from recruits Dan and Henry, similarly attired in jackets and ties, to share a taxi. We made it clear that such luxuries might have been possible at the beginning of the month but our name so late in the month was not Rockefeller. Off they went and left us to walk.

Eventually, sweat-soaked and weary we arrived at the tram stop outside the Palace Hotel. There, our mutual congratulations at having got over the worst were interrupted by discreet tappings on the window behind us. A glance over the shoulder revealed the still immaculately clad Dan and Henry urgently beckoning us inside, the normally astute Jimmy was too quick to assume, to meet the attractive English girls seated at their table. With a foreboding of what I guessed was about to come I reluctantly followed Jimmy as he eagerly responded to the request. Entering the foyer I was just in time to see Henry, with a dexterity born of desperation, pull him behind a palm to ask for the loan of two dollars that Dan, in his new-found knowledge that signing chits in the Palace was taboo, was urgently requesting from me behind another.

After a rueful comment from Jimmy, 'And not even a knock-down to the girls', a quick check of what remained in our pockets ruled out the tram ride to Louza and with the exception of the funeral, everything else.

Lok's funeral procession was almost as long as a Lord Mayor's Show in London and almost as colourful. Large open-backed lorries carried huge pictures of the dead detective and banners bearing euolgies were borne in other vehicles. Behind the lorries clad in sackcloth with heads covered and bowed in sorrow walked the male members of Lok's family. Professional mourners in long white gowns, hired for the occasion, wept, wailed and beat their chests as they extolled the virtues of Lok. We watched the procession from the roof of the Foreign YMCA building opposite the racecourse.

Chinese detectives mingled with the dense crowds lining Bubbling Well Road. European detectives, guns in hand and eyes searching both sides of the road for possible bomb-throwers or assassins, slowly followed the hearse in open automobiles. The coffin, red in traditional Chinese style with black-lacquered adornment, was covered not in flowers but boat-shaped replicas of the old silver dollars which would smooth the detective's journey to join his ancestors. Behind in long procession walked Lok's colleagues in the police, mourners from the French police, relatives, friends and household servants.

Afterwards we walked down Nanking Road to halt outside the windows of the large Whiteway Laidlaw department store. Jimmy took a stand in front of one of the display windows and, for exactly a minute, itemised in his mind what he had seen. He then turned round, back to the window, and recited quickly every one of the sixty-odd items in the window: a range of coats, suits, shirts, a wide micellany of haberdashery and accessories, without a single error or omission. There was no doubt he had not had a preview earlier of the window's contents. They were as new to him as they were to me. On many subsequent occasions Jimmy performed similar remarkable feats of memory. In the depot a quick run-through of the instruction book was enough for him to repeat almost the whole *verbatim*.

When he passed the final 500-dollar bonus examination in Chinese two years later he went on the following week to pass the German examination, which earned his retention in the German-affairs office to which he had been posted on leaving the depot. He also threw a mean punch in the ring and played rugby union. Quite a man was our Jim.

Despite innumerable disapproving comments by the former London policeman that 'We never did it that way in the Met.' the depot courses came to an end, and coming out sixth in the passing-out exams I was posted to Chengtu Road, the third and smallest station in A Division.

5

CHENGTU ROAD POLICE STATION

Chengtu Road station was well placed as far as amusements were concerned. By far the biggest attraction was the racecourse inside which was a large sports arena where football and basketball, rugby union and cricket were played. In the basement of the stands overlooking the wide track the Seaforth Highlanders were accommodated. Nearby was the Union Jack Club, the social centre for the British members of the Shanghai Defence Force. The main thoroughfare in the district, Bubbling Well Road, led to large shopping centres such as Yates Road, Seymour Road and Taku Road where markets daily attracted large crowds.

Bars and multinational restaurants, which included the popular American-owned Chocolate Shops, remained open until late at night. The New World amusement centre, or as the Chinese knew it, the 'Sing-S-Ka', on the corner of Bubbling Well Road and Yu-Ya-Ching Road was well patronised by Chinese. Just as popular with the Chinese was the Old World (Lau-S-Ka) situated at the extreme northern end of Yu-Ya-Ching Road at its junction with Avenue Edward VII. A popular rendezvous for the cosmopolitan residents in the district was the second-run Uptown cinema reached through a long arcade in Seymour Road.

All persons not belonging to the Han (Chinese) race in Shanghai were known as foreigners. I came under that heading. So did the Americans, the French, the Italians and anyone not fortunate enough to have been born in the Celestial Kingdom but of outside barbarian stock. In the early days we, together with all members of the British Empire, were known as Englishmen (Yinka Nyings), but early in the 1930s we lost this distinction. From then on we joined the ranks of lesser mortals and became merely foreigners.

It was generally accepted that our police-trained boys, who butler-like tended to our domestic needs, were the best in town. Boys they were certainly not. The number one boy in the palatial home of some millionaire foreigner could be in his late fifties or even older. Houseboy was in no way a derogatory term. In a restaurant a shout of 'Boy' would bring a waiter to the table. Boys they were, born in the China of that era and boys they remained to the end of their days.

My boy in particular was fastidious in providing a service second to none. On leave nights my civvies were carefully laid out on the bed in the order of dressing. I still remember the time when, like an errant schoolboy, I tried to explain to my boy why, the previous night, I had worn a suit of my own choice rather than the outfit he had laid out for me. That same feeling of guilt enveloped me when he told me that the vests I had bought would have cost half as much had I left the purchase to him. And that, as I well knew, would have included his cumshaw, the omnipresent 'squeeze' that was accepted everywhere in China as the illegal legality. Strangely enough, though our boys were servants none of them would take on houseboy duties if one 'master' married and left station quarters to live in a flat. Invariably they would go back to the depot to look for another unmarried master. In my case, on my arrival at Chengtu Road I took over the boy of Sergeant Wilson due to proceed on seven months home leave. That enabled him to remain in quarters and add my contribution to the half pay left by the departing officer.

Chengtu Road station was a new, four-storey building laid out in the form of a square with bullet-proof gates. The offices were on the ground floor with single and married quarters above. Although adequately furnished the single rooms were rather small. Sandy's reaction on viewing the accommodation was to ask which cell was mine. For leisure moments there was a canteen with billiard table, easy chairs and a fine mahogany bar where a bottle of Johnny Walker Black Label cost four shillings (twenty pence).

All prisoners considered to be dangerous were held at Chengtu Road as it was virtually escape-proof and could well accommodate more than a hundred. To the east the district was bordered by Louza station and the the west Bubbling Well. On other sides there were Sinza and, beyond our jurisdiction, the French Concession.

I spent the first month on night patrol with Sergeant MacCachy, an exceptionally hefty ex-Ulster policeman. This enabled me to learn routine duties and to familiarise myself with the district. We were extremely careful not to overstep the boundary and encroach on Concession land, which could easily be done as roads ran into roads and there were no border-crossing signs. On one occasion I was told, a Settlement probationer straight out from the depot had been returned to Chengtu Road station by the French police with the advice that they could well look after law and order in the Concession without his help.

MacCachy at 11pm called the parade and as each man answered to his number he read out his duties in English. As the men on parade were Chinese this seemed to be a strange performance. Yet, as I soon learned, the only

English the Chinese officers were required to know were their own numbers, beat numbers and drill commands. At the end of the parade MacCachy asked in Chinese if everyone had understood his orders. Those in doubt took one pace forward and the Ulsterman repeated the whole again in Chinese.

On one occasion within minutes of leaving the station we came across a half-drunk British able seaman in uniform holding a coolie on a rickshaw seat with one hand while he tried to lift the shafts with the other. His response to MacCachy's query as to what the hell he was trying to do was slurred forth to reveal a commendable impulse which was that since the coolie had pulled the rickshaw for the first half of the journey it was only right that he should give the puller a rest while he became the puller for the remainder of the journey. His amiable agreement to MacCachy's suggestion that a doubling of the fare would be more appropriate saved him from landing in the ungentle hands of the international military police patrol which appeared on the scene as the rickshaw coolie, not anxious to lose a double fare, sped off in more than double-quick time.

War clouds were hanging threateningly over Europe as Adolf Hitler in Nazi Germany built up his military forces to underprop his strident tirades against such neighbours as Austria, Czechoslovakia and Poland and, in particular Britain and France. The decision of El Duce Benito Mussolini in Italy to throw in his lot with Hitler had resulted in a unique situation in the International Settlement which persisted even after the war had broken out in Europe.

This was the international military police patrol, much photographed and publicised in the British and international press. Usually the then neutral American Marines took the middle part of a three-nation patrol which comprised men of the Seaforth Highlanders or other British battalion to one extreme and Savoia Grenadiers at the other. This international patrol varied in composition. The British element might be men of the Durham Light Infantry or the East Surreys, depending on which battalion was on Settlement duty. The Italians, after war had broken out in Europe in September 1939, were stranded in Shanghai as the Royal Navy had command of the seas and any Italian forces in China would be unable to return to their homeland.

While in the Western Desert British troops and Italians were engaged in full hostilities, in the Settlement, the international neutrality of which had to be observed, two Italian gunboats remained unmolested and secure in the Whangpoo River lying almost cheek by jowl with such British cruisers as HMS *Belfast* or gunboats such as the *Ladybird,* the *Petrel,* the *Cockchafer* or the *Sandpiper.* It was after war had broken out in Europe that the Lloyd Triestino liner, *Conte Verdi,* was stranded in the Whangpoo River where it had to remain completely useless to the Italian war effort as were Mussolini's gunboats or Savoia Grenadiers.

So far as Shanghai was concerned the war was conducted verbally either in the press or over the radio waves. The Franco-British effort was espoused by the *North China Daily News,* the British-owned *Shanghai Times,* the French *Journal de Shanghai* and the friendly American-owned *Shanghai Evening Post and Mercury.* German and Italian propaganda came in English from the Nazi Transocean news agency and its Italina counterpart, Stefani.

Even before hostilities in Europe began the radio-waves war waged fiercely in Shanghai. By far the most popular broadcaster in Shanghai was Carroll Alcott, the newsreader and commentator on the American-run station XMHA.

The Chinese were involved in multifarious crimes that involved loss of life. Not only were we in the police confronted with hundreds of armed thugs, kidnappers, minor petty thieves and the like but Japanese aggression against the government of Chiang Kai-shek had led to a spate of political murders and, in Shanghai and elsewhere under Japanese military domination, a permanent state of war between Chiang's 'Chunking underground' and the Japanese and their Chinese puppets.

Chiang's retreat to the mountain fastness of Szechwan province had seen his right-hand man, Wang Ching-wei, lured away by the Japanese to become president of the Chinese puppet government installed by the Tokyo militarists in Nanking. Thus, the two foreign areas in Shanghai were surrounded by hostile puppet local authorities which had pledged alleigance to Wang Ching-wei. The Japanese and their puppets were the targets of Chiang's underground resistance groups and their murderous assaults by gun and bomb often involved Settlement and French territory in the violent incidents in which many people were killed. Often the dead included members of both the SMP and the French police, mainly Chinese.

I was on patrol one night just as the food and hot water shops were closing when, for the first time, I saw what one of my school books had described as 'the legendary Chinaman with a fire on his back'. He was a food hawker with a long bamboo pole resting midway on his shoulders. Behind him at the end of the pole there was a charcoal fire, red and glowing, in a metal container. At the other end in front of him was a glass cabinet filled with Soya beans and meat patties. As he moved forward with a sinuous motion that equally balanced the

81

suspended weights on the pole ends his swinging shoulders activated a loud clapper, tock-tocking the message to all and sundry that he was ready to cook and sell what for many would be their only meal of the day.

Shanghai winters were cold and icy in contrast to the steamy heat of the summers. I was thankful for the warmth provided by my cotton-padded tunic and greatcoat and chamois leather gloves inside my woollen issues. The Chinese eschewed all forms of house heating, preferring to rely on body heat provided by soft, cotton-padded jackets and long gowns with sleeves drawn over their hands. They cooked on charcoal stoves and bought their water from hot water shops.

Thousands of refugees from country regions who had lost their homes and livelihood during the fighting in 1937 and 1938 between the advancing Japanese forces and the retreating Chinese, had fled into the security of the Settlement and French Concession. They could be seen huddled close together for warmth in every doorway or alley that offered some shelter from the freezing wind and rain. Some gathered round cooking stoves still warm outside closed food shops to take advantage of what heat was left in the clay linings of the stoves.

Each night hundreds died from hunger and exposure to the bitter cold. Bodies were collected in daylight by the Shanghai Public Benevolent Society and stacked high in the institution's compounds. In one of the repositories near the racecourse I watched children of staff members playing hide and seek between the high-piled bodies with no more concern than that shown by their fathers when they threw the bodies over the high sides of motor trucks to the chants of 'One, two, three' as they swung the bodies to gain momentum for the final heave. The corpses were taken to Yangtzepoo where I had seen huge pyres burning day and night from the police training depot.

On my first solo street patrol I saw a beggar, obviously dead, lying on Avenue Edward VII. Wishing to be certain that life was extinct before I phoned the station to get the body removed, I applied the back of my hand to his frozen cheek. This brought derisive screams of laughter from a line of prostitutes watching me from the Concession side of the road. Death was omnipresent and in all classes of society there was a callous indifference to it and, for that matter, to life itself. Later I came across the frozen forms of a father, mother and two children who had died that same night on the open road before they could reach the illusory warmth of a nearby alley.

Detailed one night to pick up and remove to the mortuary any refugees who had died on the streets, we had difficulty in locating one, whose body had been seen and reported to the station. We were directed to a heap of rags under some old straw matting from which emerged the skeletal-like figure of the wife of a man whose corpse we had been looking for. For two days she had remained in his embrace as a shield against the biting, razor-sharp wind since he had died.

The myth that the Chinese lack humour was exploded on the night I called the duties as MacCachy had taken the first of his twice-monthly leaves. At the end of the parade I called out in Chinese the routine inquiry, 'Does every man understand his duty?' Almost to a man, to my embarrassed discomfiture, the entire parade, by taking one pace forward, gave me my answer – a resounding NO. Eventually, in my halting Chinese, I got them back into line and marched out of the station by their section sergeants. Confidence was restored in part later when an amused Harry told me: 'The buggers always do that with new recruits taking their first parade.'

I awoke one night with the feeling that someone was raking my chest with a frayed bamboo pole from a position on the verandah, but could not reconcile this activity with the nauseating stench assailing my nose. As I heaved into a sitting position, a long-haired sewer rat the size of a tomcat jumped from my chest to the floor. I can still hear the sharp claws that had been digging in my chest scrabbling for traction on the polished wood floor between my bed and the open French window through which it escaped.

A large wild cat came to the compound every day for the sport of killing the rats caught overnight in our multiple traps. As the rats were tipped from the cages to the ground, the cat killed with lightning speed, often two at a time. Yet even this ferocious feline cowered away when faced by brown rats, preferring to leave them for us to despatch.

The Chinese method of dealing with the rats that ate their food, bit their sleeping children and multiplied much faster than the Public Health Department could destroy them was the time-honoured ploy of releasing a few caught with lighted kerosene-soaked rags tied to their tails. As they ran down their holes the belief was that in their passage below ground they would flush out the rest and cause a general stampede for safety well away from the homes thay had invaded. Often this practice caused fires beyond the ability of the excellent Shanghai Fire Brigade to quell and we in the police were left with the near-impossible task of evacuating the tenants of houses more intent on saving their goods and chattels than themselves. The situation was invariably made worse because the thrifty Chinese had reduced by half the size of their rooms by installing false ceilings. They sublet the upper half to others who, in turn, subdivided what they occupied to take in more people. On average about forty persons would live in one house, built for two families at most.

Fires with heavy loss of life were constant hazards in Shanghai. I attended a fire in a three-storey house that had raged into an inferno beyond control within a few minutes. No sooner had I started evicting the residents than they were running back inside to make last attempts to save their possessions. Quickly the blaze spread to other houses in the row and the same desperate attempts were made by residents running back into the burning buildings in the hope of salvaging practically all possessions. When only three charred bodies were found in the ruins next day I was surprised there were not more.

Throughout the two years I spent in the district I never tired of watching, in that hour before curfew stilled the city for the night, the double line of private rickshaws conveying to their homes the thousands of Sing-Song-Girls, or 'Shang-Dau-Dzoos' as they were known to the Chinese, along the broad Racecourse Road, against a circular and brilliantly lighted backdrop of shops, amusement places and restaurants which looked onto the racecourse. Shanghai and nearby Soochow were renowned for the delicate beauty of their slim, long-legged girls and it was generally acknowledged that collectively they could not be equalled anywhere else in the world. Taught from childhood all the traditional legends and songs to qualify as professional entertainers at business dinners, parties and other functions, the most popular among them could earn in one night more than a police sergeant was paid in a month.

Unlike the purely functional types of rickshaws that plied for hire, the girls' vehicles were finished in gleaming black cellulose with bodies mounted on

85

chromium wheels. The girls sat back in pairs in these expensive private rickshaws, a sure sign of the money they earned. Each rickshaw was pulled by a young coolie-cum-bodyguard strong and athletic compared with the sweat-soaked coolies pulling the rickshaws they rented to ply for hire in Shanghai's busy streets.

The girls, beautifully and delicately oriental, enhanced their slimness and their shapely legs by wearing long, tight-fitting gowns, usually black or dark blue, split at high-thigh level on both sides. Over the gowns they wore starched white jackets. They donned only a minimum of jewellery. Some of their elderly admirers were known to pay out large sums for the privilege of just touching their hands.

When the more intelligent girls sensed that their beauty was on the wane and they had not, like some of their number, squandered their earnings on a 'small white face', as a playboy friend was called, they formed their own businesses by grooming young girls from country families anxious to get rid of unwanted daughters.

Those who were less provident but who had not ended their days in abject poverty, as was so often the case, procured young virgins from the same country sources for sale to wealthy clients.

One such old lady, by then in her sixties, wandered into the station one day and plied Dick Ekin, whom she had known for a number of years, with a stream of questions concerning his health and general wellbeing and that of others she had met over the years. The final diffident but wholly predictable inquiry concerning Australian-born Detective Sergeant Jim Grant, whose uninhibited, devil-may-care disposition made him universally popular, especially with women, brought an involuntary glow to the wrinkling cheeks which terminated at Dick's next words, with an anguished 'Ha-yaw, I have left two girls from the country alone in my house.' This was followed by a swift emergence from the station to hire, it was safe to assume, the fastest rickshaw in sight.

Dick who had long known the story and, driven no doubt by his Geordie sense of humour, had merely commented on her bad joss at being absent from home when Grant called on her house, as he had stated he would, on leaving the station a few minutes before to investigate a case in her district.

No mean raconteur was Dick. According to him, years ago, Jim Grant had actually made an off-duty call at this woman's house in the hope of gleaning information, which she and her like often imparted unwittingly, to learn from two young girls he found there that the mistress was out. She had gone, he was told, to fetch the 'Have much money man' for whose pleasures they had been brought to Shanghai. Within the hour, aided perhaps by an overwillingness to accept from this charmingly handsome and obviously rich man that that person was he, both girls had been divested of their virginity and, in consequence, the old lady of a fat profit.

It was no consolation to her that her expenditure would be recoverable by re-classing the girls as 'slight seconds' and passing them on to a less discerning buyer whose tastes were restricted by his means.

On Christmas Day English officers were placed on half duty leaving the remainder to fill in on full duty. Similarly the Scots at New Year were given the same amount of time off work. The Russian Christmas, celebrated always later than the Gregorian festival, saw the White Russian officers with time enough to attend the deeply moving services at the Route Doumer Cathedral where the singing of the choir and the congregation in the responses was emotionally inspiring.

Yuletide provided every station a two-hour free-drinks party for station staff and friends. Officers' wives provided the food. That was the only time females were permitted to enter the canteens. They were, however, free at all times to go, unattended if they so wished, to the club bars and restaurants on the eighth floor at police headquarters and to the mat shed by the police cricket and tennis grounds on the racecourse sports complex.

For the Chinese their Lunar New Year was the greatest calendar event. It was interesting to note that the New Year festivities always provided a large reduction in crime. This was also evident during the Christian Christmas celebrations. Evidently the city's criminals gave the same amount of respect to the foreigners' festive season as they did to their own.

By midday all Chinese ranks from sub-inspector upward joined a large cosmopolitan collection of officers at the canteen bar to toast one another in convivial *bonhomie*. Most colourful were the Sikhs of the mounted branch in their sky-blue tunics adorned with chain mail. At waist level they sported scarlet cummerbunds. Indeed the Sikhs, tall and bearded and wearing khaki and blue turbans with sabres hanging from their highly polished belts gave the gathering such glittering splendour that I doubt if ever there was a more colourful spectacle anywhere east of Suez. A blind eye was turned towards those on duty who slipped in for the party.

The canteen was full when Inspector W C Wong, whose initials might suggest the nickname by which he was popularly known, arrived to be greeted by Chinese, Indians and foreigners alike. Fluent in English, he was soon amusing the ladies with stories drawn from his inexhaustible fund of amusing anecdotes.

Breaking off for the fourth time to be introduced to more wives and girlfriends he asked, in his usual inimitable way, 'Why all this formality? Mr Wong this and Mr Wong that', and then to the consternation of all present, he turned back to his attentive audience and requested that they call him 'Shithouse' as all his friends did. Only then did we realise that as this word did not appear in any dictionary, old Wong had not realised just what he had said. However, habit prevailed, and he acquiesced in its continuance to the end.

After the Scots had celebrated their New Year we switched to the daylight scene in the streets with hundreds of traders carrying their wares to market in baskets slung from bamboo poles. Butchers served their customers from high chopping blocks on stalls and in shops using razor-sharp cleavers capable of slicing pork as evenly and quickly as any machine. These same cleavers were the most favoured murder weapon in Shanghai.

Prospective customers gazed into glass tanks and with obvious difficulty pointed to the particular fish they wanted – one of many swimming seemingly in gay abandon seen and then unseen in the crowded confines of the tank. Foreigners toured markets seeking melons or other juicy fruits well aware of the practice of injecting typhus-infected creek water to increase weight and, thus, price.

Omnipresent in any market were the doctor-cum-dentist practitioners offering acupuncture as the cure for any illness while nearby their opposite numbers loudly extolled the virtues of potions made from powdered snakeskin mixed with ground tigers' teeth. These medicinal miracles, they claimed, would effect cures in half the time of the acupuncture process – and at half the price. Unbelievably to the foreigners from the West salvaged cigarette ends were being shredded and rolled on portable tables to be graded and sold to smokers anxious to save the higher cost of the factory-made Pirate, 'Hay-Dau', or Ruby Queen brands.

Street chiropodists carrying portable chairs and razor-sharp knives painlessly removed corns and callouses with remarkable speed and efficiency unknown in the West and at a fraction of the cost. One loud barker, who had been offering a proprietory brand of whisky which in reality was weak tea, made himself scarce before we approached his trading spot. There was an easily operated re-capping machine in the police museum, complete with supplies of Johnnie Walker caps, perfect in every detail, which police had seized from a more sophisticated operator of this particular swindle.

Hawkers and others found to be obstructing right of way were taken to the station and bailed in a sum less than twopence. When released, they usually returned to the same pitch, or near enough. There they began selling again on the well-founded belief that on showing their bail receipts they would be free to carry on trading for the rest of the day.

By early morning the flower sellers, who daily flocked into the city from up-country areas, were decorating Racecourse Road from end to end with tier upon tier of exotic oriental blooms as well as a profusion of European varieties perfect in every detail except one. Like those I saw later in Australia they had no scent.

Sandbagged newspaper offices, armed guards outside banks and commercial houses, British and other members of the Shanghai Defence Force standing guard on perimeters behind sandbag barricades, police armoured motorcycles setting forth on what could be hazardous trips along western-district roads – all these common sights told the story of Shanghai's daily confrontation with violent death.

In the French Concession in a high-walled house constantly patrolled by a small army of bodyguards there lived in luxurious style a smallish Chinese, Tu Yueh-sen, millionaire and gangster chief whose terrible power was wielded over an empire of crime that outranged in evil that of Al Capone in Chicago.

Opium, brothels, trade unions, hired killers, the slave-girl trade, protection rackets, gold smuggling, gun running and all kinds of crime were under the sole control of Tu, the head of the 'Ch'in Pang' – the Green Society, the Mafia of China.

According to a friend who remained in China until the late 1940s Tu remained as powerful as ever throughout the war years. After the war this gangster, in 1946, waged his own private war against Mayor K C Wu and the Kuomintang administration of Shanghai. This he won after he stopped all vegetables entering the city. Only the Communists could beat him. He retired, a very rich man, to Hong Kong where he died peacefully in bed.

Completely ruthless was the Japanese military puppet, Wang Ching-wei, whose underlings in all parts of China under Japanese occupation ran riot in a brutal campaign of political mass murder, torture, summary execution and, indeed other brutal and savage acts that shocked the world when the time came for revelation of the appalling record of one of the most cold-blooded, ruthless regimes ever seen in history.

Wang made his headquarters in Nanking, the former capital of Chiang Kai-shek, but he often visited a fortress home in Jessfield Road, a western outside thoroughfare over which the Settlement authority had jurisdiction. The road itself provided a route for Settlement public transport vehicles and SMP armed motorcycle patrols. On both sides of the road and others in the western areas the buildings were under the control of Wang's puppet regime known locally as the Ta Tao government. There were many attacks on the police and on buses and other vehicles from the Settlement proper. In all cases armed Ta Tao thugs retreated in perfect safety to buildings overlooking the road.

Odd bursts from Tommy guns mounted on the sidecars of Settlement motorcycle patrols manned by two foreign (usually British) sergeants were fired in reply to random shots directed at them as they rode up and down those outside roads. In the Bubbling Well station, which had jurisdiction over roads in the western district, there was a feeling of the utmost frustration as the puppets, from the security of their roadside buildings, caused two or more armed turnouts every day.

A crisis confrontation was reached when Ta Tao men, mostly recruited from village desperadoes, began to appear on both Jessfield Road and its near neighbour, Edinburgh Road. One of these gangs opened fire on a Sikh Settlement police constable on traffic duty and killed him outright. Within minutes the thugs had retreated to a building on the side of the road and a turnout of armed SMP men could only remove the body in sheer frustration. Yet that murder produced a show of force by the Settlement police and the order to the Ta Tao killers was, 'Get off the road or we open fire'. It had its effect in restraining any invasion of the Settlement roads but there was always the danger that the uniformed mercenaries of Wang, watching from concrete guard-houses erected on the broad walls hiding the extensive mansions and grounds accommodating the various departments of the puppet administration, could open fire on the police patrols from the Settlement or on public transport vehicles.

An attempt on the life of the chairman of the Shanghai

Municipal Council and head of a large British company was frustrated by a member of my squad, who shot dead a would-be Japanese assassin at a public meeting at which he was addressing a large crowd when the attempt was made.

In an effort to reduce such incidents on these streets, search parties, comprising a foreign and Chinese sergeant and four constables were increased during hours not covered by the nightime curfew. Three constables searched the more likely-looking and occasional attention paid even to the innocent in appearance. They were followed by the two sergeants, guns in right hands with muzzles pointing down to the ground, a regulation safety precaution when on walking search party.

All safety catches on the Colt automatics with which the force was armed (· 45s for foreign members and · 38s to fit the smaller hands of the Chinese branch), were firmly screwed down. This was to prevent an officer in an emergency forgetting to release the catch or fumbling in a night-darkened side street to locate it. An added safety measure was that no rounds were ever carried in the breech. Thus, any officer having occasion to draw his pistol to kill (shooting to wound was strictly forbidden on the grounds that a wounded man could still carry on shooting), all he had to do to put a round in the breech was to work the slide just once and the gun was ready for instant use. While in training every recuit in the depot spent hours practising what was known as the 'Quick draw and load technique' until he matched near-enough the speed of arms instructor Dan Cormie. Again and again Cormie drummed into us the importance of this proven fastest of all draws, especially when confronted by a man with a Mauser. Then speed was essential. Just one bullet fired from this high velocity gun could pass clean through three people and carry on to lodge in a fourth. Though unlikely anywhere else in the world it was a distinct possibility in densely populated Shanghai.

A constable in plain clothes always walked ahead of the search party to hold those seeking to evade search by turning around or crossing the road. When it became common practice to use girls to carry weapons before and after use, selected Chinese police wives were trained as female searchers and added to our patrols. Probably the greatest realists on earth, the Chinese submitted to these searches with good grace knowing from bitter experience that it was the only effective deterrent and done for the common good.

In the early days plain-clothes Chinese detectives performed this duty until the night a party from my station, proceeding along Yu-Ya-ching Road, the boundary with Louza District, returned the fire of a tough-looking party of five they had halted with the command, 'Veh-Yau-Dung – Li-Chi-Lay' – (Stop and raise arms).

Summoned from Louza by a shopkeeper's phone call Sergeant Johnny Weeks identified the five as one of his station's search parties, and succinctly observed on arrival of police from Chengtu Road, 'Proved your chaps were on the alert, and capable of recognising another bunch of rogues when they saw them.'

On one search I seized 19lb of high-grade Yunnan opium in one pound blocks from a car driven by a Chinese. It was one of the biggest hauls on record and I had visions of commendation for my vigilance. Alas, my hopes were dashed when a high-ranking officer of the Japanese Gendarmerie claimed the opium was the property of the Japanese military forces. It was handed over and driven away in a Japanese staff car.

A junior sergeant and two constables were sent out

each day to bring in the professional beggars, who infested the streets frequented by the foreigners and the wealthier Chinese inhabitants. Once caught they were confined overnight in the beggar cells and in the morning taken to a point some fourteen miles west of Shanghai where it was hoped we would be shot of them for a day in the city. Yet often before noon, for the price of a bus ticket, many of them were back in their usual spots to display hideous infirmities of their own or some deformed child bought or hired from real parents. These children always evoked generous sympathy. With the approach of police the children were quickly taken into the next district or into Frenchtown, whichever was the nearest. This was to prevent the children being seized and put in the care of one of the benevolent societies.

Ghastly open sores were flaunted daily by the beggars in the main shopping precincts. Lepers would approach passers-by knowing full well that to avoid any possible contact they would throw money into open hands. One man we sent for hospital treatment immediately after release was seen with the dressings removed and dirt from the gutter rubbed into the healing sores to worsen the infection again. Another with a diseased foot so revolting that at first it appeared to be faked, as some were, was found to be the possessor of a nurtured suppurating heel through which the actual heel bone was protruding. This was his only earning asset in a land in which war had produced indescribable suffering for millions in the cities and in the vast countryside.

Many classed as beggars earned a precarious living by picking up waste or cigarette ends which they sold to market traders. A dead cat or dog with a good pelt was a welcome extra. Not one of these beggars ever washed. One day I heard a member of a group being herded into the police van demanding a word with me. In excellent

English that must have been learned at some overseas university he asked if I could spare him the final degradation of being taken in and confined with the rest of the group. He claimed to be the disowned son of a well-known businessman. Pointing with obvious self-loathing to his filthy body and the rags he wore he told me he had come to this sorry state through addiction to heroin.

One unfortunate and totally different type lay for a year under a pile of mats from which he was never disturbed. The reason was that he suffered from the incurable tropical disease elephantiasis, which results in a gross swelling of the lower limbs and scrotum so that it enlarges to the size of a football. In the bantering tone he invariably adopted towards police, and people from nearby houses who gave him food, he told me one day that we would not be inconvenienced by his presence for very much longer. Noting his absence, and missing his cheery asides when returning to day patrol after a month on nights, the beat constable told me he had died with minimum fuss the previous month.

That I was taken aback would be putting it mildly when, after telling two coolies in heated argument in busy Taku Road to pack it in and go home, I was told by one in unmistakable cockney, 'Ah'm not standing for this geezer cloutin' mi kids.'

The string of vituperation which followed was pure Bow Bells. Inspector Moffat, whose knowledge of Chinese and Shanghai was second to none, explained that the man would be one of several time-expired naval ratings who had remained in Shanghai and merged with the Chinese so successfully at the end of World War I that by now they were indistinguishable from the coolies they had later become. Most had married former Chinese girlfriends and raised families.

Superstition was rife in China. Chinese New Year was always heralded by the noisy crescendo of sound as cymbal-clashing monks expelled devils from houses in the city. As it was well known that devils could not turn corners, the drive always began at the back door and ended at the front, where a stone slab in front of the door higher and wider in size prevented their re-entry.

Another superstition saw families placing a mirror at the foot of stairs tilted at the exact angle to ensure that the devil, seeing his own hideous likeness, would suffer such shock as to flee the house with all speed, taking his 'bad joss' with him. Many years later in London's Soho Chinatown I saw the self same mirror placed at the foot of the stairs in a Chinese restaurant owned and managed by two elderly Chinese. During New Year Shanghai Chinese wore their new clothes, visited friends, watched street entertainers and acrobats. Large numbers could be seen walking the streets with their pet canaries in ornate hand painted cages.

Superstition dominated the lives of most Chinese in those days. The belief that good luck resulted from touching the outstretched paws of the huge bronze lions outside the Hong Kong and Shanghai Bank building on the Bund was so entrenched that even the educated business classes crossed the wide road just to touch them. By the mid-30s the countless daily contacts had actually reduced by one third the original thickness of those huge paws. At some time in 1942 the Japanese Military removed the lions from their pedestals and shipped them to Japan where it was reliably said they were melted down for armaments.

There was also the belief that by touching the hump of a hunchback bad fortune could be kept at bay. Once, on patrol a senior constable drew my attention to one of these unfortunates who had been touched by practically everyone as he walked towards us on Yates Road, contemptuously remarking, 'They think it brings good luck.' Yet even this self-proclaimed sceptic could not resist leaning back with a rueful smile, and touching the hump a split second before it passed beyond his reach.

A man seen running across the road immediately in front of an approaching car was intent, not in suicide as most foreigners thought, but on ridding himself of the devil he believed to be on his back. The closer the shave the greater the belief that he had rid himself of his devil at last. This preoccupation with devils was so entrenched that anyone injured on the street no matter how seriously and regardless of broken bones, was immediately seized by well-intentioned passers-by and vigorously bumped on the ground to rid him of the devil always assumed to be responsible for his misfortunes.

On the eve of Chinese New Year two constables were detailed to take the van and pick up three victims of a fire and a suicide. Normally it was a welcome break as nothing more was entailed than directing two coolies to lift the bodies and place them in the van. Yet the couple pleaded with Harry Thomas on office duty to excuse them on the grounds that bad joss would inevitably follow any contact with death on New Year's Eve. He, understanding their deep-rooted fears, and after it had been agreed that any bad luck attaching to the job would automatically choose to settle on the most senior officer present, sent me along with them. When, as we approached the mortuary the sliding door behind the long front seat silently opened unnoticed by us in the front and the body of the suicide, mouth agape and blackened by Lysol, arms outstretched above his head in rigor mortis and propelled forward by an application of the brakes selected me for a stiff-fingered jab in the back, the constables humorously hailed it as proof of their beliefs.

The senior mortuary attendant obviously had no qualms about contacting death in any of its forms on New Year's Eve. We watched him take the bodies and drop them with a resounding thud into zinc-lined boxes which were lined round all four walls. He opened several boxes to show us the grim contents, leaving until last what he described as the worst case he had seen in forty years. With breakfast not far away it was a favour I could well have done without.

Status was extremely important in China. It was indicated by the length of the nail on the middlefinger of the right hand, the easily discernible indication that the owner was not a manual worker. Far removed from such folk as ordinary clerks, businessmen or even our Chinese language teachers, who were content with a mere half inch of growth, some of the people we met on patrol had grown their nails to such fantastic lengths that they had to be protected by sheaths with gold fastenings. With the palms held upwards the nails extended to the armpits. It still remains a mystery to me how these possessors of such high status managed to eat, wash or sleep.

Status or 'face' as it was commonly known was not much in evidence in back-alley family businesses which operated almost exactly as they had when they were started generations before. Labour was cheap and hard work was never at a premium in such locations. Laundrymen, with sinewy arms and steely back muscles, developed from a lifetime of wringing out sheets, blankets and blue cotton cloth, worked side by side with the next door baker, who spent hours shaping and stretching long frames of short, thick noodles into slim lengths.

Skilled sawyers with backs almost as wide as they were

high manhandled 40-foot cedar logs from the waters of the creek on which they had been floated from up-country. They set the logs upright in the many-platformed rigs from which they were cut into inch-wide boards with double-handed bow saws with a precision not bettered by multiple saws anywhere in the West, and at a fraction of the cost.

The grim realities of the agonies that war had inflicted on China were omnipresent in Shanghai but the two foreign areas, at least, provided balsamic amnesia, if only fleetingly, in the host of night clubs, cabarets, restaurants and the other diverting venues dedicated in the main to soft lights, sweet music and certainly a girl in one's arms – even if the romantic content was soured somewhat by female insistence on cash for charms. Still a girl had to live in a male-dominated environment and the signature tune that, willy nilly, set the pattern was that American popular favourite 'Ten Cents A Dance'. There was money enough in a male pocket to ensure a good living for the multitude of pretty girls in Shanghai.

Entry to the exclusive Russian night club, Arcadia, was possible only after careful scrutiny by a uniformed doorman peeping through a Judas hole in the vine-screened oaken door. The Arcadia recreated the gracious aura of Tsarist Russia with its traditional decor that might have been transplanted from an aristocratic salon in old St Petersburg. The musicians, all Russian, were dressed in the elaborate Cossack style uniforms that reminded the exiles of their greater days of glory before the October Revolution sent them into stateless and often penurious existence overseas. Dress was formal and old-style chivalry reigned supreme in the courtly kissing of a lady's hand and the well-bred deportment of all the guests. I have yet to hear that appealing melody we know in English as 'Black Eyes' played with such spirited

100

fervour as that displayed by the Arcadia musicians. Even non-Russians such as we could not escape the nostalgic lure of the music that recalled for so many exiles golden memories of halcyon days that were gone forever.

At the Renaissance, Vertinsky crooned in the style that had made him famous in pre-revolutionary Moscow and which was to send him back at the end of World War II. Romany music was played by a string ensemble to accompany the spirited agility of a troupe of mixed gypsy dancers. Tough and sinewy in black leather boots with scarlet silk blouses tucked into baggy black trousers, the dancers went through routine after routine of acrobatic Bohemian folk sequences.

It was at the Renaissance one night that, after an angry complaint from one of the dancing girls about the objectionable approaches of a tourist, her male partner followed the man outside as he left the establishment and knocked him cold into the gutter as he turned to respond to the light tap on his shoulder. The partner returned to his dancing with not a trace of anger or emotion in any form on his expressionless face.

In a different league, though not far away from the superior establishments in Avenue Joffre, was the Venus cabaret run by British Jew, Sam Levy. The Venus had been famous among seafarers in the dockland region of Hongkew in happier days but Japanese restrictions in their defence sector had forced the move to the French Concession where the lure of his taxi-dancers, mostly Chinese and Korean, assured him of a good living even if the pickings of the former Hongkew were no longer available. There was a second-class band of Filipinos, who had obviously fallen foul of drugs or booze, a gaggle of fairly toil-worn servants, who delivered the two local brews of beer, Ewo (a Jardine Matheson product) or UB (Union Brewery). The girls were willing enough to be bought out by randy customers and Sam, a genial chap always, could smile all the way to the bank at sunrise.

Over in the Settlement's Bubbling Well Road the barrel-like figure of former American Navy man, Joe Orapello, was reflected many times as he stood in the small, mirror-lined bar of his drinking establishment. Joe, beefy arms propped on the bar top, was forever the genial host, the New York Italian-American, well favoured by his main customers, British soldiers. It was an orderly establishment, unusual in Shanghai. Joe, squat and wide and gigantic of chest, took a philosophical view of life, an attribute garnered after years of service in the navy as a cook and, later, of adventuring in Mexico.

If he could be persuaded to venture into the kitchen Joe provided the best hamburgers in the city, certainly a shade more competitive than the excellent fried-egg-topped hamburgers served daily in enormous quantities at Jimmy's Kitchen in Nanking Road, an establishment that was making a fortune for Jimmy James, former cook in the American Fifteenth Infantry and a close friend of Orapello.

While Joe looked capable of holding his own against a Sumo wrestler he admitted that a weak heart would prevent him from tossing the bar cat out of the door let alone a bunch of noisy drunks. Yet he looked tough and his poker face showed no trace of this disability. Once asked why American marines did not patronise Joe's Bar he pointed to the British squaddies in the place.

'When trouble starts, these boys settle it with their fists,' he said. 'They only damage themselves. When the Americans start anything they go wild and break every mirror in the place using as many glasses as they can lay hands on.'

I was not an *afficionado* of Terpsichore. I had two left

feet when it came to ballroom dancing. Nevertheless, I often went from Joe's place to the Lido cabaret across the road to enjoy the rhythmic tangos played by the large Filipino band until the brilliantly illuminated rotating stage commenced its slow turn to fade the orchestra out and bring into view the big band for the quicksteps, foxtrots and waltzes. As the stage turned the band's signature tune heralded the start of a marathon, non-stop session of music that provided for the Chinese, Korean and Russian hostesses more dance tickets each night than any of their counterparts elsewhere could be expected to earn in a week. The Lido, which ran its own football team in the top Shanghai league, was a gold mine.

Further down Bubbling Well Road were the Little Club and the Majestic Ballroom, both providing relaxation and, often, battle scars for servicemen from the city's defence force. The Little Club, only a few yards away from the much larger Majestic, offered patrons the intimate atmosphere of a circular ballroom floor around which, fairly closely, tables were arranged. The hostesses, mostly Russian, sat on chairs around the ballroom floor. In the Majestic there was much greater floor space and around the walls the intimacy of alcove seating offered the seductive secrecy of the amorous wooing of the dance hostesses, mostly Russian and Chinese toughened by long participation. The alcoves also served as shields against flying bottles, in the frequent brawls between servicemen that broke out mostly after drunken rows over the affections of the hostesses.

It was at the Majestic that one of the worst battles took place between American marines and the Italian Savoia Grenadiers. The Majestic was completely devastated as the combatants used bottles, glasses, tables, chairs, anything that could be wrenched free to act as a weapon

103

as blood spilled everywhere and the hostesses, screaming in terror, rushed for the dressing room exits on each side of the stage. The Grenadiers, outnumbered at the start, brought in reinforcements by truck but they were too late to save the life of an Italian petty officer who was thrown clean through one of the first floor windows to fall on the overhead tram wires and crash to the ground. He was killed instantly. In time the military police of both sides, clubbing first and arresting later, brought order where there had been chaos. It was best that any lone Settlement policeman near enough to the violent scene should wait for the military police to handle the situation in their own rigorously effective way rather than trying to go it alone.

Despite the trials and tribulations ever present on the outside roads they did provide enjoyable distraction from the daily grind by offering a wide variety of night club entertainment. Several of the establishments had been opened by German and Austrian Jewish refugees, who had been able to escape the violent anti-Semitism of Hitler in Germany and, after the Anschluss, Austria. Among the most popular were the Ali Baba, The Hungaria and the Winter Garden, which was operated by Jimmy James and which provided first class New Orleans jazz for the enthusiasts. The music at the other clubs was less exuberant but professionally polished by musicians who had earned high repute in Berlin or Vienna.

Our favourite out west was the Eventail, a night club patronised mainly by Russians and by those married police and army officers who enjoyed its quiet and friendly atmosphere. It was at the Eventail one night that I suddenly emerged from the deep concentration that allowed me to keep step with my partner Jessie, on holiday from Singapore, to realise that she and I had the entire ballroom to ourselves. When we had started the floor had been well crowded but there had been skulduggery afoot. The band, the management, genial and certainly conniving Bill Carr, even my partner and everybody else had been in the swim. I cut short my demonstration dance amid the applause of the watching crowd. Admittedly I was no Victor Sylvester or Arthur Murray but when pressed hard enough I tried.

The Eventail served rainbow cocktails in four tiers. These were more the favourites of our lady friends than ourselves who paid for them. The method of serving was romantic. The head waiter switched off all the lights to leave visible only his seemingly disembodied head illuminated by the radiance of the blazing brandy capping the drinks. Amid a muted fanfare from the band the drinks were handed to each lady in turn with such courtly grace as to make them feel, according to one, like visiting royalty.

A short distance from the Eventail was Jock's Bar. Another of those legendary Shanghai bars which never closed its doors. Patrons seated in the large open alcoves were merely requested to lift their feet off the floor at 6am to permit the bar floor to be swept. Ex-seaman Jock MacKenzie established the bar at the end of World War One, and on his death in the mid-20s, the establishment was inherited by its present dour owner, Jock No. 2, the former Chinese head bar-boy.

Farrons, owned and managed by Shanghai-born Roy Farron was one of the most exclusive night clubs out west, so exclusive that guests were expected to wear evening dress as Roy himself always did. Drinks and service there were only for the wealthy – a punitive service charge on all drinks ensured that. On the outbreak of the Pacific War, Farron, claimed by the Japanese military to be a spy for the Americans, was taken to Bridge House by them, and according to witnesses therein at the time was, within two weeks of arrest, tortured to death by the Japanese Gendarmerie. (I saw Farrons several times on the way out to the Eventail, but as Bill Carr dismissed it as far too expensive for us police, I never once went in).

'For those critics of Empire' – Jessfield Park, out west, did not as they so often claim, have a notice board outside saying 'No Chinese and dogs permitted inside'. There was, however, an amusing notice outside all public lavatories to the effect that, 'Toilet paper is sold inside, but purchase is not compulsory'. At two cents a sheet I understand it sold quite well, but with a thickness and texture of a sheet of rough sandpaper the wonder was that it sold at all.

A letter written by an American lady and published in the *North China Daily News* expressed the belief that, after an overnight shipboard stay, the city's reputation for violence had been grossly exaggerated. I wonder if, on the following day, she had read in the same paper of two persons being killed and several injured in the sleazy Concession thoroughfare, Rue Chu Pao-san, known worldwide as 'Blood Alley', she would still have thought the same.

Blood Alley, out of bounds to all service personnel, was situated off Avenue Edward VII, which divided the Settlement from the French area. The short street, connecting Avenue Edward VII and the busy Rue du Consulat, was entirely dedicated to wine, women, song and lechery in its most flagrant forms. Hardly any of the cabarets – Mumm's, the Frisco, the Palais, the Crystal or the Parisian closed before eight o'clock in the morning. There was also the bars: the New Ritz, George's, Monks Brass Rail and the Rose. Like the cabarets they offered the sybaritic and most willing sensual cooperation of an

106

ethnic mix of females hard to find anywhere else in the world: Chinese, Russian, Korean, Filipina, Eurasian, Indochinese, Burmese and many others.

Out of bounds Blood Alley had to be. Booze and lust together had erupted so many times in massive riots that the former patronage of the city's multi-racial service-men had been banned. So the battleground was left to merchant seamen, civilians from all walks of life and such itinerants as thugs, thieves and pickpockets, the pick of the criminals. The mainly Russian riot squad of the French police quickly quelled most of the savage blood letting with Gallic-directed and Slavonic-hammered riot stick ferocity.

Shepherds in Kiangse Road, just off the main Nanking Road public transport route, easy to reach but hard to leave, was usually crowded. The reason was that, for the price of a beer, service personnel, mainly British, and off-duty police officers along with civilians in all walks of life, could fill the inner man off two large roasts on the bar counter presided over by middle-aged Nelly, the White Russian barmaid. Nelly, perhaps the most popular female in Shanghai, tenaciously defied the onslaught of the years in order to honour a promise she made the day the Japanese forces invaded and took over the Settlement. This was that when the Royal Navy returned after the war was over she would be back in the bar to serve them. She made it – but only by the most slender of margins. The night after serving the crew members of the first Royal Navy ship to sail up the Whangpoo Nelly died in her sleep of a heart attack.

Not far away in Jinkee Road Harry Webber, ex-Royal Navy petty officer and skipper of the P&O tug and lighter fleet on the river, offered English food and Indian curries.

Popular among British service units was Ma Jackson,

107

the Portuguese Eurasian widow of a former British sailor, who ran a no-nonsense bar in Bubbling Well Road resuscitated by Royal Navy and Royal Marine donations after the Japanese bombings of '37. Injured in the bombing were several Royal Marines from a British cruiser on the river.

Ma Kennedy and Maisie, both Americans, owned high-class brothels in appropriately named Love Lane which, due to their orderliness remained free from police interference. In this connection, no British girl was ever permitted to run loose in Shanghai. Police coverage was such that the few who made the attempt were handed over to the consulate within days, and returned home on the first ship. Similarly, in the interests of trade and goodwill, the British Chamber of Commerce never allowed a British firm to go bankrupt, and so preserved the good name and reputation British business enjoyed in China.

The Chinese besides being adept in business were an ingenious lot when they took to crime. Take the case of the couple of 'houseboys', dressed in normal servant's garb, who entered Louza station quarters and calmly removed the large silver badges from caps left outside the dining room by officers taking lunch inside.

Certainly just as bold were the three men in white overalls who, moving in and out of literally dozens of police officers waiting in the compound of the High Court, took away the ornate striking clock from the tower of the main courthouse. It was not until weeks later when the Public Works Department was asked when repairs would be finished that the realisation dawned that the clock had gone forever.

Similarly, a couple of 'electricians', authentic to a high degree, removed the dynamo on the White Horse Whisky sign, the largest neon illumination in the Orient standing on the Mohawk Road–Bubbling Well Road corner. On night patrol, Sergeant Ron Crouch asked the couple if they could speed up the operation so their ladders, obstructing passage on the pavement, could be moved. Showing a most praiseworthy desire to assist in speeding up the work Sergeant Crouch helped to steady the ladders as the couple brought down the dynamo which, they said, was faulty. It was only after the British firm, Mackinnon-McKenzie, the agents for White Horse, had noticed that the sign had been non-functioning for several nights that they sent maintenance men to investigate. It was then that Ron Crouch discovered he had been – unwittingly it must be said – an accessory to larceny.

Yates Road was the location for much affluence and, of course, it had become the scene of some of the numerous daily armed robberies that took place in Shanghai. I took part in an armed turnout there when one of our police party watching the descent down stairs of a Chinese gave him free and unmolested passage on the assumption that he must have been a family member because of the well cut charcoal grey suit, homburg hat and the *pince-nez* he wore. Mindful of Dan Cormie's repeated warnings never to allow anyone to pass unsearched, I stopped him. Despite his smiling and polite assurance in good English that he was the family lawyer I frisked him and found a loaded Mauser automatic in the briefcase under his arm. On the next three floors up we caught and disarmed two rougher types. A fourth man, even more harmless looking than the first was taken, Mauser in hand, from behind a chimney on a neighbouring five-storey house. All proved subsequently to be not armed robbers but professional killers sent by the Wang Ching-wei faction to murder a wealthy pro-Chiang supporter. The master of the house.

109

One of my colleagues, Sergeant 'Dutchy' Van Amerongen, a former second officer on a Netherlands Royal Interocean passenger liner, augmented his police pay by fattening pigs on waste from the Union Brewery with the help of a Chinese herdsman to whom he passed all instructions by letters bearing both his signature and the impression of a specially made chop. When the pigs had been sufficiently fattened the herdsman was presented with a letter seemingly signed and chopped by Dutchy and presented by a man to whom, the letter stated, the pigs had been sold. He was to be allowed to take the animals away, which he did. The entire operation was felonious. The letter, the signature and the intricate chop impression were forgeries – but perfect enough to convince the herdsman they were genuine. How, Dutchy wondered, had it been possible to copy the impression of the chop which he always kept on his key ring. That, alas, remained a mystery that puzzled him for many a long year, and still does.

Seated on the top deck of a bus travelling on Nanking Road I watched a well-dressed Chinese sauntering seemingly innocently on one of the tramway boarding islands in the road. A tram arrived and stopped to take on passengers. It was summer and the tram windows were open to cool the passengers on the inward-facing seats. Still watching, I saw the saunterer reach through the open window of the tram and take what he had obviously decided was the best hat in the row. Then, pausing just long enough to set the hat on his own head at just the right angle, leisurely walked across to the other side of the road. Meanwhile, the dehatted one, hands clasped to his head, looked from left to right then down to the ground before the window where he probably hoped the hat had fallen after being accidentally knocked from his head. By the time it occurred to him what had actually happened, the same thought must have come to him as had already come to me: by the time we had got clear of our respective seats and crossed the rush-hour traffic any hope of us identifying the thief or he his hat, amongst the scores of similarly hatted men streaming towards the Bund, would be considerably less than one thousand to one.

A member of a gang arrested one moonlight night with a silver collection burgled from a nearby house broke away from the rest, and it fell to me to give chase to this resourceful gentleman through a maze of high-walled gardens. With the distance between us closing, I arrived on top of the last wall I had seen him scale, and after quartering the garden beyond with my eyes, my gaze centred on the shadow cast by the wall immediately beneath my dangling feet which appeared deeper than the rest. Without much difficulty I traced his prone form, face flat against the wall and hidden under the turned-up collar of his coat. He had reasoned, he told me later, that in my haste to catch up I would leap right over him, and leave the way clear for him to double back the way we had come.

Detective Inspector Instone was an advanced Chinese scholar, who would never allow men to get suspects to talk by means other than patient questioning. Returning to the station office one day he found a prisoner lying deeply unconscious on the floor. Vehement denials by officers convinced him there had been no use of violence and his mind turned to a story he had once read in a Chinese book about a sect in a northern province who were capable of simulating death at will. A quick check disclosed that the prisoner came from that region. He ordered a smouldering spill to be inserted in each of the man's nostrils. In no time at all the prisoner was spluttering his way back to life. It was a matter of some

111

conjecture whether or not he would have emerged from the self-imposed coma unaided or died what would have appeared to be a natural death. Certainly there had been no visible sign of life in the man.

The career of one old con man, whose knowledge of human reactions under pressure brought him handsome returns, was abruptly ended when one of the essential elements of his stratagem, a queue of impatient customers behind him included an alert off-duty policeman. This old crook preyed on small-goods and money-exchange shops. Invariably he would produce a five-dollar note with the request that it be exchanged for singles. As the notes were placed on the counter he asked for a packet of cigarettes, offering a small note in payment but keeping in hand his own five-dollar bill. While the cigarettes and odd coppers in change were handed over he placed his five-dollar bill on top of the five singles and, with an apology for the trouble caused, asked for and received from the shop owner, whose mind had been diverted by the cigarette purchase, a ten-dollar note in exchange. His tricks came to a temporary end when the alert constable spotted him and took him into custody.

Poh-Tsloo, or Strip-the-Pig gangs as they were commonly known, operated from alleyways late at night. They waylaid and stripped passing females of everything down to their pants and vests. It was not out of consideration for female modesty that these items were not taken, but because of their trifling worth. Card girls from gambling clubs, bar and cabaret hostesses carrying the considerable sums they earned nightly were prime targets. Consequently, any off-duty policeman leaving any of these places as closing time drew near would find himself leading an ever-lengthening following of females – a sort of protective Pied Piper as the processions was joined by other girls working in establishments on the way to the station. All of them knew where the officer was going and that his presence would enable them to get to their homes with all their possessions intact.

One of the most popular sporting venues in Shanghai was the Canidrome in the French Concession. Here one of the fastest games in the world, pelota known in the city as hai-alai, drew vast crowds of gamblers to bet on the seemingly superhuman agility of the South American players. At the Canidrome also was dog racing which, again, drew vast crowds for the Chinese are inveterate gamblers. As at the racecourse in the Settlement the turnover in cash was vast but the prospect of winning was, for most, odds on against.

I was persuaded by Bill Carr to accompany him to the dog track. It was there I learned that the Canidrome clerks had an infallible knowledge not only of the dogs that would finish first, but also of those which would finish last. We saw the almost indiscernible shake of the head when we placed cash with him to bet on Bill's choice. Somewhat shaken by his action and the barely audible suggestion that we should change our minds and back his choice, we did that and cashed in threefold. All afternoon we followed his friendly and seemingly inside advice profitably. Then we decided against stretching our luck too far and, as a final bet, placed all our winnings on his next choice. The dog came in last. The result was that it was the clerk with our generous commissions every time we won, and definitely not us, who enjoyed the proverbial day at the races.

Political assassinations worsened throughout my service, and when Central Government-appointed judges were selected by the Wang Ching-wei faction as prime targets I was armed with a Tommy gun and made responsible for their safe transit to and from court each

113

day in a fast police tender. To this was added a nightly duty as plain-clothes bodyguard to the broadcaster, Carroll Alcott, whose satirical jibes against what he called the Tokyo-Pokio-Rome-Berlin-Axis had resulted in his twice being stopped and threatened by the Japanese Gendarmerie. With the Japanese not yet ready for an open brush with the police, three uneventful weeks of this was enough for me and I successfully applied for return to station duties.

Wealthy Chinese, similarly at risk, hired police-trained Russian bodyguards, all of them proficient shots and of heavy physique. These bodyguards gave protective cover to their employers from the time in the early morning they left their homes and stayed close to them until they were safely back in their high-security residences often late at night. In the care of these people at high risk of being shot or kidnapped the guards could be seen blocking every car window with their bulky forms. Those in the front seats kept eagle eyes always on the lookout for lurking gunmen. If a cinema performance was ordered then a line of rear seats was always booked in advance but never claimed until all lights were out.

To prevent armed thugs moving freely in and out of the Settlement, checkpoints were set up along the western perimeters, but after several cars had driven through at high speed with the occupants raking the police with automatic fire, the barriers were staggered at shorter intervals to force approaching traffic to reduce speed, thus making it easier for the police to stop and search suspect cars.

The Chinese puppets, who resented this new affront to their dignity, took reprisals against individual foreign sergeants whose numbers had been noted in passing the barriers. The wife of a puppet official, whose car had been stopped and searched by a young sergeant, returned within a few hours to enjoy the sight of this sergeant being shot several times through the stomach by a gunman crouching at her feet in the car. As the door was opened for the search at the barrier the gunman opened fire at point-blank range to hit the sergeant. The car then sped off at high speed.

Other police officers were shot dead on remote outer roads by gunmen who had concealed themselves behind hoardings or in derelict houses before curfew to wait half the night to avenge the imagined loss of face suffered by their puppet masters at the barriers. It was at this time that British women, easily identified by their distinctive passports, were being stripped and searched by the Japanese military at the barriers guarding the entrance to the British Concession in Teintsin. It was all part of the campaign being waged by the Japanese militarists to humiliate in every possible way the British under the banner of their 'Asia for the Asiatics' drive throughout China and other regions of Southeast Asia.

In the Japanese defence sector of Hongkew York-shireman Sergeant Tam Wimsett was stopped by an anxious American who had driven through the Japanese military barrier in the centre of Garden Bridge without stopping. He had not realised he was entering the Japanese area until his car was followed by a Japanese military truck. Wimsett, hoping that an apology to the Japanese would settle the matter, stepped on the running board of the American's car and it started to return to Garden Bridge. No sooner had he mounted the running board than the Japanese military truck followed and swerved inward so as to roll Wimsett between the truck coachwork and that of the car. The sergeant's rib cage was so badly crushed that he was still in pain eighteen months later when he returned to duty after specialist treatment in London. In retirement in his birthplace,

Halifax, in the 1970s Wimsett died after being knocked down by a car.

A most serious incident in the western area involved Jock Kinlock. He challenged a group of thugs and was answered with a hail of bullets. Though wounded and in great pain Kinlock with a sweep of his Tommy gun hit several of the gang. The following morning a good photograph of Kinlock giving his name and station appeared in all the Chinese newspapers printed outside the Settlement. In bold letters underneath the photograph was an exhortation to 'all patriotic Chinese' to kill Kinlock on sight. In hospital Kinlock was given a British military guard. This was believed to be due to a shortage of police officers, but the real reason was quickly made known when Kinlock in British army uniform marched out with his guards after recovery and boarded with them a ship bound for Hong Kong where, by prior arrangement, he joined the police force there. Had he remained in Shanghai he would undoubtedly have been killed.

Despite the fact that they patrolled what were known as the 'Badlands' in fours, losses amongst the Chinese members of the SMP were heavy. This was due to the courageous disregard for their own safety they displayed when on duty. In the depot, and again in the station, we were told that, come what may, we could always rely on them giving their full support regardless of the odds. Sergeant Dick Ekin, remarking once on the difficulty of keeping them in a backing up role, said, 'Give them just a quarter of a chance, and they're soon at the front.' The oft-repeated assertion that we were biased in favour of the Chinese may well have been true, due no doubt to the genuine respect and liking which, to a man, we had for them.

The sergeant on charge-room duty virtually ran the

station for the officer-in-charge and was answerable only to him. A Chinese interpreter-translator recorded in his own language even the most trivial report brought to the station to supplement the four pages the sergeant would normally fill in the thirty-two-line occurrence book during his eight hour duty. In addition, two English-speaking Chinese gatemen, as they were known, took fingerprints, locked and unlocked the grille leading to the line of cells, each twelve feet wide and twice as deep, constantly patrolled by a Sikh constable. There was an open grille for temporary detainees and adjoining were the detention room and padded cell. The entire section never held less than sixty and at times more than a hundred prisoners.

Checks were made at hourly intervals and a mental note was kept of gang members under interrogation, always split up and placed in different cells. Food sent in for prisoners was always searched to ensure that nothing was concealed in such things as rice or cakes. All chopsticks were recovered after each meal, a necessary precaution against suicide attempts. Suicidal prisoners would rub one end of a chopstick on the floor to a fine point. They would then mount the stone slab, which screened the urinal, and fall face down and stiff-bodied with the sharpened end of the chopstick held at a right angle to their foreheads. On impact with the floor their notoriously thin skulls would be pierced and their brains skewered by the chopstick. Others also suicidally inclined but more alert to the chance of being thwarted by the patrolling Sikh constable waited until he had checked their cell and moved on to the next. They then fastened one end of a rope already made from strips torn from their clothing to a crossmember in the grille less than three feet from the floor and the other end round their necks. Then, by stretching their legs fully and arching their backs to bring maximum pressure on the rope, they had every prospect of being dead by the time of the next cell check. In my early charge-room days I had my first experience of the seemingly omnipresent death wish among prisoners. Urgent shouts from a Sikh constable sent me rushing to the cells where I found him, arms through the grille supporting a prisoner who was going blue in the face after roping himself by the neck to the grille. Luckily we were able to free him and he made a quick recovery.

Another prisoner just released from the cells to be questioned by the CID officers took advantage of a momentary distraction in the station compound to break away from a Chinese detective escorting him and charge, head down and body bent double, into the wall opposite with sufficient force to kill himself. By the time we reached him his skull was a mere empty shell with his still pulsating brain on the ground underneath his head.

From 8am cases ranging from petty quarrels and fights to a mixture of more serious crimes such as murder and violence in all its forms, fraud and larceny, kept the office man working against time until he was relieved at 4pm.

Petty thieves, handbag and earring snatchers, sometimes accompanied by their victims with torn ear lobes dripping blood, were brought in several times each day. On patrol one day I heard the cries of an old Chinese lady, whose earrings had just been snatched. I joined a stream of men running in pursuit of the snatcher, whose identity beyond the scant description of the victim that he was young and dressed in black no one seemed to know. Drawing level with the head of the crowd, most of whom wore black clothes, I saw one make the telltale falter I had been watching for when he looked back and saw me. Taken back to the old lady she was so sure he was the snatcher that even when the beatman and I could not find the earrings she was still prepared to make a charge. More accustomed to close searching, the charge-room gateman did in one minute what we had failed to do in ten. He found the earrings concealed inside a tiny cut in the lapel of the man's black coat.

A question put to a coolie in Chinese by an office man invariably was met by a blank, uncomprehending stare until the clerk, from whom he was awaiting an interpretation, told him he was being addressed in the Chinese language. His first reaction to this was always one of unbounded admiration for the foreign office man, who could speak his language. By the time he had absorbed the fact that the foreigner was speaking Chinese usually it was necessary to ask the question at least once more before an answer was forthcoming.

This never happened when urgent messages were phoned in. It was assumed that whoever answered calls would be fluent in Chinese. Time and time again I've picked up the phone to hear an over-excited amah reporting in breathless and rapid Chinese that an armed robbery was in progress, then drop the phone before the already alerted Chinese charge-room clerk could request a repeat of house and lane numbers which often ran into four figures. This caused us much worry as officers from the station turned out, armed and steel-vested, to what we could only hope was the right address. It was always the old amah who had the sense to slip out and make what haste she could on her tiny bound feet to call the police. Such an old lady, feet crippled by the cruel bindings commonly applied to baby girls in the old days, stopped my search party in Yates Road to report kidnappers at her master's house in a nearby lane. It was her swift action that made possible the arrest of two members of a gang who threatened the delivery of first finger joints, and if that failed to produce the required ransome money, the ears also from selected children of no less than twelve children they had snatched from the wealthier families.

It was one of this duo who committed suicide by ramming his head against the station wall sooner than follow the example of the other and turn informer.

When hiring a ricsha the coolie expected the fare to either tell him in Chinese where he wished to go or direct him there. When however, as was the case with the lady tourist who could do neither, he looked out for a foreign policeman for help. Since leaving the Bund the lady had obviously been studying the scale of charges set out on the wing of the ricsha because she complained that despite repeated requests in good plain English that she be taken to Yates Road, the coolie had deliberately taken a devious route to increase the fare, and that after an hour in the ricsha Yates Road seemed to be as far away as ever. From the hostile reception accorded my amused explanation that if the man could speak English he'd hardly be pulling a ricsha, and the reason for all the deviations, I gathered that she was as little impressed with Shanghai's ricshas as she was with its police.

As another puzzled coolie seeking help was informing me in the usual laconic coolie jargon that the larger than usual Chinese sitting in his ricsha 'Veh-Shaw-Ta' – (didn't know). His fare intervened to ask if I spoke English, and then for directions to The New World Centre before going on to say that as an Australian born Chinese he had no knowledge of this impossible language. Relieved that he now knew where to go, the coolie was still shaking his head in perplexity as he joined the main stream of traffic at having to call upon an Englishman to interpret between himself and another Chinese.

The White Russians apart, very few outside the police had even a smattering of Chinese, preferring rather to rely on servants or clerks. The police Commissioner himself was an advanced Chinese scholar. One assistant commissioner could read and write Urdu, German, Russian, Japanese and speak French. Inspector Jan Ware, ex-matelot and deputy officer in Louza, always started the day by checking the occurrence book entries made the previous day against those recorded in Chinese by the charge room clerk. It was common to hear a charge room officer tell his clerk to leave out the embellishments and repeat verbatim what he had actually said. Many studied Chinese beyond the final pass stage to master the characters or learn Mandarin, Russian or Japanese. A London born detective who in jocular mood was apt to answer, 'Hi-Cock' to 'good mornings'. He was asked by a criminal court judge, when no interpreter was available, if he could present his case himself. He acquiesced first in the Shanghai dialect, and then in fluent Mandarin, to the delight of the Peking born judge who had not himself at that time acquired a working knowledge of the local dialect.

Following the return of Sergeant Wilson his boy, briefly employed by me in his absence, went back to him as previously arranged. When agreeing with probationer Ian MacDowd to share his boy, who was in need of some extra money, I was advised that to get the best out of him I should encourage him with the occasional kick in the rear. Months later, the discovery that he had absconded with every item of clothing from Ian's room but nothing from mine on the same floor, taught me the wisdom of not kicking boys' rears. Especially those short of money.

While there was some anti-foreign feeling it was not

apparent amongst the older people who realised that without the foreign military and police the Japanese would have taken over the whole city in 1937. The sole exception to the rule was the students. To them we owed the doubtful distinction of being the first police ever to be referred to as Pigs, but this feeling was secondary to their hatred of the Japanese. Always more reckless than the boys, the girls always wore scarlet ankle socks as a symbol of walking in Japanese blood. Many were arrested by the dreaded Kempati, better known as the Gendarmerie, and whenever knowledge of an impending arrest came to the ears of our special branch they blocked the move by arresting the subjects on any pretext that came to mind, and then holding them until it was considered safe to release them. None were ever given the reason for their arrest and detention as this might betray valuable informers, and this applied to two female students who were held in Chengtu Road for several months. At first, whenever these girls chanced to be looking through the glass section of the detention room as a policeman passed by, they withdrew from sight with expressions of distaste. Finally, however, with that perversity inherent in all females ignored by the male, and especially after observing the easy friendliness which existed between the Chinese staff and ourselves, the aloofness dissolved into smiles and requests for the English names of such things as the scissors and nail files they got into the habit of borrowing. Months later while out on patrol, a soft spoken 'Hello No. 110' drew my attention to a group of girl students and I recognised our two recent detainees, both smiling broadly.

The shocked surprise of their friends at the girls' temerity in speaking to a police Pig of all people made them impulsively withdraw at first but looking back, it appeared that curiosity had overcome prejudice to the extent that the girls were by then surrounded by the others eager to learn the reason for their odd behaviour.

Shanghai was built on mud flats on the bank of the Wangpu River when it was given to the British founders of the settlement under duress, and with the impression that nothing could be built on it. The present city with its multi-storied skyscrapers was built on piles driven deep into the mud as was illustrated in my time when Dorman Long spent over a year preparing the foundations for the Bank of China on the Bund. When built, entry into the fourteen-storey Metropole Hotel in Frenchtown was gained by climbing six steps from the street but since completion the whole building, fortunately maintaining an even plane, has subsided to a depth equal to twelve steps, and entry now is made by taking six steps down.

Fresh out from London where buildings with seven storeys were as high as they went, the Park Hotel, at the bottom of Bubbling Well Road, had much the same effect on us as it had on most Chinese countrymen seeing it for the first time – but with a difference. While we viewed its 23rd storey with necks craned to the limit from a safe distance, they unwittingly strayed across the pavement in tune with their eyes as they ranged upwards floor by floor and all too often, and at least once a month, over the kerb and under the wheels of a fast moving truck.

Sewage had always been a problem especially when high tides coincided with heavy rain until a solution was found by the British PWD in 1939. This was after the night I emerged from a dark alley on the flooded Taku Road as though on cue, to get a drenching of mainly human excrement thrown up by a motorist who failed to

123

see me in the black buttoned greatcoat worn at night to render us inconspicuous to would-be marksmen. The stench preceded me that night as I returned to the station, and permeated my room from the verandah where I discarded my uniform. The other policemen were all made apprehensive by accounts of the tactics likely to be deployed by the wives of families we were to evict from houses declared unsafe by the PWD. As predicted, the ladies were waiting about ten feet apart outside the houses in question, each behind her varnished Mo-dung brimming full with the conveniently liquefied night's accumulation of night soil, and all with scouring brushes held at the ready. Like miniature brooms made from stiff twigs these brushes were first dipped below the surface and then brushed upwards and outwards against the rim furthest from the woman with sufficient force to project a heavy spray over anyone who ventured within fifteen feet. The confrontation ended peacefully when the PWD prudently shelved their plans for the time being. As was usual in all like situations there was never a man to be seen, and if questioned later the stock answer was, 'Da-yak Dikeh-Dza-Tee, Ngoo veh-Shaw-Ta-Gah.' (About this affair – I know absolutely nothing).

A Chinese watchman with deep wounds in his head staggered into the charge room one night to hand in his gun and name his duty post. Then drop down dead. Subsequent enquiries revealed that he had previously agreed to admit a gang into the house of his wealthy employer after submitting to a light blow on the head to cover his own complicity in exchange for a share of the proceeds, but on the appointed night he had second thoughts and denied them entry. In retaliation the gang returned with butcher's axes and inflicted such deep cuts in his head that the police doctor could not say how he had managed the half mile walk to the station, let alone hold on to and safeguard his gun.

On receipt of a phone call from a foreign lady reporting the premature onslaught of a mental illness suffered annually by her son before the usual arrangements had been made for his admittance to the mental asylum, I was sent to the flat they shared to prevent him leaving as he had the previous year when inoffensive bystanders had suffered serious injuries at his hands before the police arrived. Knowing that a military pass required for an ambulance to enter the Japanese occupied area where the asylum was sited had been applied for only minutes before I left the station, it was with some concern that I noted the truculent attitude of the heavily built man who could only be our patient as he pushed past his mother as she opened the door at my ring. Immediately his mother closed the door he re-opened it to fix those below with a malevolent glare before I closed it and got him back to his room. This pattern was repeated every few minutes for what seemed an eternity until finally, as I ushered him back into his room for the umpteenth time he swung round with lightning speed and landed a punch to my jaw with sufficient force to rock me backwards and nearly black out. While dazedly pulling myself together I was suddenly pinioned from behind by the woman begging me not to harm her son who she said was normally friendly with everyone. It was only then I noticed a photograph of a boxing team hanging on the wall in which he figured prominently and I realised he had timed that near perfect punch by watching me through his wardrobe mirror.

When sub-Inspector Black arrived with the pass and asked what had happened to my chin he thought I'd been fortunate in gaining at one and the same time some valuable experience and a modicum of gratitude from the Old Man (officer I/C Chengtu Road) for preventing a recurrence of last year's debacle. The observation from the Chinese ambulance driver to the effect that the patient did not seem to like me when he came at me with bared teeth and kicking feet at the asylum, despite the straightjacket he was by then wearing, so closely parelleled my own that I went back to the police car and left Dick to it.

Returning the twenty dollars his expensive habits had obliged him to borrow early in the month, Henry insisted on buying a drink. My own preference for the station canteen was ruled out as not suitable for such an occasion as were the bars where the girls drank cold tea dressed up as brandy at a dollar a time. Only the European staffed Elite Bar on Bubbling Well Road where Ella the proprietress was, according to him, a personal friend, would do. Cries of welcome back Mr Wade greeted our appearance at the bar where the example of Ella's gracious acceptance of the most expensive drink she could think of was followed by everyone else in response to Henry's general invitation as he paused to bestow a nod here, and a handshake there before rejoining me at the bar. The air of bonhomie which started so spontaneously, gathering momentum through the band's fanfare and the toast acknowledged by Henry with a gracious bow ended abruptly when his request for a pen to sign the bill met with an emphatic demand for cash for, not only this bill, but for some old ones produced from the safe. When the lady remained unmoved by liberal doses of Henry's considerable charm and persuasive powers, his bow to the inevitable preceded my own by only so long as it took him to

request and accept the twenty dollars he had just
returned to me. When he appeared at the end of the
month as promised with the full amount due and
insisted once again on a celebratory drink he readily
agreed to my suggestion that we take this without benefit
of fanfares, toasts and blondes in the station canteen at a
fraction of the cost.

With rice in short supply as a result of the Sino-Japanese
war, the Council bought huge supplies from outside
sources, and sub-Inspector Jeff Coleman and I were
assigned at short notice to ensure that it went only to
authorised dealers. The first intimation of the transfer
came when I reported off duty at 11am, and was told to
move to Carter Road quarters that same day. My concern
about the reaction likely from my boy to the short notice
proved to be as unnecessary as it was short lived when he
told me he had made all arrangements for the move the
previous day. The impressive efficiency of the grapevine
which had supplied him with this news before even the
station officer was aware of it was first demonstrated in
the depot when a new recruit was told that the dignity of
the force was not enhanced by embryo police appearing
in public with doll's heads protruding from their
pockets. This alluded to a carelessly accepted gift from a
bar girl in Rue Petan eight miles from the depot, and the
recruit's first and only visit to Frenchtown. Nor was this
service exclusive to police. Of several ricsha coolies
waiting outside my favourite bar as I left it that night one
and all, with the customary pats on the seats of their
ricshas, called out Carter Road. Not one said, 'Chengtu
Loo.'
   The China coasters in which Jardine-Matherson and
Butterfield-Swires brought the rice to Shanghai were
fitted with spiked anti-piracy guard fences fore and aft of

their bridges to prevent pirates posing as deck passengers from seizing control of the ships on the high seas, and transferring their cargos to the junks of accomplices waiting in mid-ocean. White Russian guards, armed and trained in our police depot, where carried as an additional deterrent.

The rice was unloaded on the French Bund and carried into adjacent godowns, managed by an American, Bill Ried. Council-hired assessors carried out checks on bag weights and quality as this proceeded. Grit similar in appearance to rice and pellets of mud moulded into the shape of peas and all the different types of beans was mixed with all these commodities at source, but by stabbing spiked tubes with which they drew off samples from selected bags the assessors calculated the purity of the grain. Coolies moving the rice wore the usual voluminous blue cotton trousers which, tied at the knees were used as receptacles for the rice which they siphoned from the bags on their shoulders with bamboo replicas of the probes used by the assessors as they walked from ship to godown. When their trousers would hold no more they made for the back of the godowns and emptied them by releasing the knee fastenings while standing on the ever growing pile to be taken away later by truck driver accomplices for sale on the black market.

Knowing the utter futility of using orthodox measures to combat this pilfering amidst the confusion of hundreds of coolies engaged in loading delivery trucks both in and outside the gates the ever practical French police resorted to the cane as the most effective deterrent. The first offence merited four heavy strokes. If caught a second time this was doubled. Those reluctant to co-operate in this exercise were quick to extend their hands when asked if they preferred the loss of pay a prosecution would entail.

It was on one of these ships now unloading fruit grown up country that the large snake which cast its skin every year in the main godown had probably come to Shanghai. Eventually, alarmed by the size of the sheddings, Bill Ried arranged for its destruction, but after noisy objections from his coolies on the grounds that this would bring unlimited bad joss, not altogether reluctantly in view of the considerable contribution the snake made to the large number of rats killed daily by the scores of pi-dogs enticed by weekly offerings of meat dropped through the floor gratings to live under the godowns, he cancelled the arrangement.

Large sea-going junks manned by their family owners tacked up and down the river with such superb seamanship that full advantage was taken from every last breath of air as they went about a mere hand's breadth from the wharf before beating back on the return tack. It was common to see this difficult feat performed with a kindergarten-sized girl at the tiller while the rest of the family raised and lowered the heavy sails without so much as a glance in her direction. Once, drawn by loud cries and the sight of running men carrying hooked fending poles across the decks of nearby junks, I was in time to see the half drowned man they pulled out of the water dropped on deck. Then, without a single enquiry as to whether the immersion had been accidental or intentional, his rescuers used their hastily reversed poles to give him a severe beating for wasting their time.

This turned my thoughts to the warning implicit in a story concerning the sodden young recruit whose report that he had just pulled a would-be suicide out of the river was met with a curt order to take a hot bath, report for typhus and typhoid injections, and never do it again.

All the effluent from the Settlement, the Concession, Chapei, Nantou and Pootung representing some six million people plus all the towns upstream was discharged untreated into the Wangpu, and it was from this due to political necessity that the Shanghai Water Works drew their supplies. The drinking water that was produced from what was recognised as the worst source in the world, at least for a major city like Shanghai was due to the ingenuity of the British engineers of the Water Works Co.

A month later my temporary transfer to the licensing squad which kept a check on eating places, hotels and all forms of entertainment was humdrum for the most part but enlivened by the unusual. It was in the Eastern Areas I saw a Buddhist holy man doing penance with rows of miniature lead weighted meat hooks deeply implanted in the bare flesh of his back. Since these drew no blood as they were forcefully jerked down by their own weight with every step the inference was that they had been there a long time. But as the man was totally oblivious of his surroundings and curious lookers-on, the question of whether the hooks were removed or stayed in position while he slept remained known only to him.

The New World near the racecourse which provided entertainement for the average Chinese was also a tourist attraction. Early morning before opening hours were the best times to visit. You could see trick cyclists ten to a bike, tightrope walkers by the dozen shouldering double their number, each balancing chairs and tables on their heads, sword swallowers and dancers, conjurors and acrobats all doing the impossible. They filled every space and the air about them with the tools of their trade. Similarly at practice, the most trivial mistakes made by boy acrobats going through complicated routines were corrected with cuts from a cane, while flawlessly executed seven tier pyramids were acknowledged with the curtest of nods but with the threat of the cane should the next not please. Beetle and cricket racing addicts were catered for in another room where each contestant was placed in a separate channel for guidance to the finishing line. To prevent punters offering any inducements such as food, blowing or prodding, the courses were enclosed in glass cases. Tension increased and bets doubled as first one and then another, after making good starts, stopped to comb their whiskers while a third made a sudden rush forward to stop tantalisingly close to the finishing line, then pause maddeningly combing away to permit another a foot behind, his toilet completed, to rush forward and finish a mere whisker ahead of the favourite.

The CID maintained an efficient informer system which was supported partly by a general fund, and partly by themselves. It was customary for a Chinese who had received any kind of favour to redress the balance by giving the person concerned ten per cent of its value. By this he gained face, and effectively relieved himself of any indebtedness or requests for favours in return which might either be at a greater cost, or involvement in something inimical to his own interests. Accordingly, subject to the offer being voluntary, the CID were permitted to accept ten per cent of the value of any recoveries, and with this were able to maintain informers in every street. The very high proportion of successful prosecutions under this system placed us third in the world league.

Its effectiveness was demonstrated once when on mobile patrol one informer waved me down to report that a Chinese detective was being held at gunpoint in a nearby house. Another who had seen an unmarked truck leave a local cotton mill after the night foreman had satisfied himself that the beat men had passed out of sight resulted in some useful arrests. In line with his

131

reminder when sending me to stand outside a new Japanese Gendarmerie-owned gaming club to deter the entry of wealthy Chinese, as the Japs knew full well that England would not go to war if I got myself killed, Inspector Moffat, with Dick Ekin and I, was obliged to leave the old Chinese gentleman still suspended by his thumbs with feet just touching the floor, when the thugs previously seen by our informant rough handling him in his own house proved to be Japanese Gendarmes in civilian dress.

The day I left the licensing squad in Central the constables on night duty staged a two-hour strike. They, with the Japanese, were the only ones not subject to King's Rules. Wind of this had filtered through in the early hours and no arms were issued to the early day duty which remained in the compound to mingle with those coming off duty and still armed. Streets were patrolled by Sikhs and Britons on motor cycles, but the few shops which had opened had closed doors again within the hour. The strikers listened quietly when addressed first by the station, and then the divisional officer, but a White Russian Inspector noted as an unnecessarily strict disciplinarian was chased with a blood chilling howl to the sanctuary of the armoury. Over in two hours during which time shops and businesses well beyond the confines of Central had put up shutters was, if they were needed, an indication of how quickly a busy city could be brought to a halt when its police ceased to function even in part.

A pretty mixed crowd, the police could have filled a bookcase with interesting accounts of their earlier lives. Ralph Hocking told of shipping as a deck hand from his native Sydney to Canada during the depression years. Of 'riding the rods' (travelling free on the bogies of freight trains) in search of the non-existent work he had gone

132

there to find. Of the cold nights he and others had spent hiding in marshalling yards night after night until the train they sought was ready to leave. Of watching out for the good guard who checked his wagons before the start as opposed to the bad who waited until the train was passing through an unpopulated area at high speed before checking and throwing them off.

Then there were the ex-Cossacks who had fled Russia on horseback during the revolution. Several of the younger Russians had spent years as trappers and wild horse dealers in Manchuria. Some had travelled the world as ratings in the Royal Navy. One in particular was a ship's officer whose back was still deeply scarred from a flogging he had been given while working in the salt mines of Siberia. His release had been secured by pressure applied by the nearest British Consul acting on information supplied by a Russian who had witnessed his arrest. Two had served in the police along with Errol Flynn in the then little explored dependency of New Guinea.

A timely warning to young probationary Sergeant White that he was treading on dangerous ground in continually ribbing the diminutive table boy during meals was proved, when a promise that the teasing would cease was followed by another from the boy that he would in that case stop spitting in Mr White's soup.

6

JAPAN

Ex-London policeman Roy Clore, Dick Buxton, Tom Brooks and I twice took our annual twenty-four days' leave in Japan. On both occasions we stayed at the traditional national-style Tokiwaya Hotel in Katsuza. The first time we travelled in the Clyde-built Japanese shuttle liner, *Shanghai Maru* and returned to Shanghai aboard the *Nagasaki Maru,* a Japanese-built replica of the *Shanghai Maru.*

As we boarded the *Shanghai Maru* we were handed glass bowls in which we were to place a stool specimen by eleven o'clock. Long before then the same stewardess appeared at the cabin door to be told that all would be well with delivery before the deadline. At ten o'clock the same lady, after a completely unselfconscious demonstration, invited us to accompany her to the surgery and bend over for an enema-type extraction. This was declined with a request for patience and another assurance that given time we would oblige without aid. The obvious pleasure with which she accepted the four bowls, each containing equal parts of Tom's earlier production on her next call was exceeded only by our own at not having to expose our rear ends in the sick bay.

To our relief this operation was dispensed with the following year when, no sea berths being available, we applied to the finest English-speaking Japanese military commander in the Yangtze area to obtain a flight by Japan Air. His permission in writing was a concession never before accorded to police nor, as far as I know, any other non-Japanese person or group.

At the flight assembly early the following day we were the only passengers not wearing heavy coats. Wrongly we assumed that our Japanese fellow passengers wore the coats to observe the strict formality always observed by Japanese males. It was when the unheated plane gained height and the temperature dropped to near freezing that, for four long hours, we shivered in teeth-chattering discomfort and wondered if we would reach our destination without frostbite.

At Nagoya airport some twenty miles from Nagasaki we were searched by gendarmes to ensure that we had no more than the permitted hundred yen obtainable in Shanghai at the rate of two for one. An unusually attractive air hostess-cum-interpreter asked us why we had come to Japan and what would be our final destination. Finally, the girl was instructed to take us to the buffet and then to see us aboard the right train for Nagasaki. The girl maintained the customary respectful few paces behind us until we were clear of the gendarmes. Then to our dismay in view of her presence during the stripped-down searches she pushed unceremoniously into our midst to exclaim, 'Gee, it's nice to hear English spoken again.' Over steak and coffee she told us she was a Nisei, a Californian born Japanese-American, sent by her parents to their homeland only three months previously.

Any doubts about the girl's American background were dispelled when I rejoined her and the others after visiting the toilets to which she had directed me. Convulsed with laughter she asked if I'd found it. While the novelty of joining the ladies as it were in these places where no partitions exist between the facilities for males and females had worn off for us the year before, they were still new to her.

Remarkably, my case and new Burberry raincoat carelessly left in the station booking hall were just as I'd left them two hours before.

On arrival in Nagasaki we rejected both the train and ferry services as too long and opted instead for what must have been the most suicidal taxi ride in the east. The taxi was a Japanese-made replica of an American tourer. Its driver a suicidal maniac or so it seemed to us seated behind him as we careered across the city at top speed. The only intersections we did not race over at full speed, ignoring the probability of being hit by cross traffic, were the occasions when we stopped bumper to bumper with an oncoming similarly driven vehicle a split second before what seemed inevitable collision. The two occasions this happened both drivers alighted and advanced on each other not to start the fight we at first expected, but to bow to one another. The first back in his seat then politely drew back to permit both to proceed with all speed to the next encounter. The relief with which we left Nagasaki lived only so long as it took our driver to demonstrate again and again how he could hurtle us round winding hairpin bends high on the narrow road overlooking the coast at a speed that never slackened. He shaved past oncoming vehicles with inches or less to spare. Yet, miraculously it seemed to us, he got us there all in one piece.

The two-storey Tokiwaya Hotel, flanked by tall trees, faced the beach at its extremity which was furthest from the village. We met the manager, who had been a cook in the United States Navy, and his wife, a former housemaid in a British home in Shanghai. Although lunch always began with half a lobster its main courses followed the

English style of cooking which suited us. The maids, known as nan-sans, were simple country girls who were temporarily employed during the summer months. Most of the hotel's guests were Shanghai policemen taking their annual leave. They were the mainstay of the place and often the only guests.

Afternoon tea was served on the beach where we lazed until the pre-evening coolness sent us walking over the nearby hills, all neatly terraced and cultivated to the last square inch. After a shower and change of clothes we visited the village illuminated only by the diffused glow of oil lamps filtering through slatted shutters. Amid the pleasant pine-scented air we reached the aromatically spice-scented village shop to drink beer if they had it, and if not, we went on to the larger of the two geisha houses in the area. There was always a plentiful supply of beer there but, as the head girl did not like us or, for that matter, any foreigners, we kept our visits to the barest minimum, particularly after the night when our attention had been focused longer than she liked on a Chinese-speaking Formosan nan-san. Without considering that she did not speak English and we could not converse in Japanese but that the Formosan girl's Chinese provided the communicative interlocution that we needed, she took affront at what she considered to be our failure to bestow on her the dignity of her position in the house. She put her umbrage into unpleasant action by introducing a party of soldiers into our midst. Thus obliging us to drink the nauseatingly unpleasant hot saki they favoured for the sake of economy.

As was customary at these gatherings, only one small glass served the entire party and this was passed at random with a small bow to any member of the group seated circular fashion on the floor after being refilled by the last one to drink. Inevitably, there had to be one amongst them imbued with sentiments similar to those held by Madam, and he, a coarse heavy-shouldered bullying type repeatedly passed the glass to Tom with an aggressive leer that was an insult in itself without the derisive bow that went with it. Whenever the more moderate soldiers denied him the glass the girl gave him another. Tom's threat, uttered head down in his umpteenth bow of acknowledgement, through the grimace of the smile he had maintained throughout, that he would 'Pan this bastard soon', would have been amusing at any other time or place, but knowing the dire consequences that would follow any assault on a representative of the Emperor, we urged caution and restraint. When Madame had extracted maximum enjoyment from our discomfort she took the soldiers away, presented us with the bill for the saki, and hoped we'd call again.

We never doubted the sincerity of the welcome extended to us by the two sisters who owned the other geisha house about a mile down the road. Though the warmth of their welcome was genuine, we could not rid ourselves of the thought that their fondness for free beer was the activating agent. Even before we entered the place our order for four beers had been anticipated and placed in six glasses, two of which the ladies had already half emptied themselves. Two of the six cushions on the floor were for the owners to sit on. Ostensibly to enable them as our hosts to recharge our glasses as necessary but in reality to enable them to empty any of ours unguardedly put down within their overlong reach. The amusement of Roy as he watched the glass of one unsuspecting customer being emptied by one of the sisters was short lived when he reached for his own to find it had been drained dry by the other.

The sudden request from Sergeant Jim Salisbury,

whose guests we were at the Katsuza family hotel, not to move our feet, drew our attention to the puppy-sized ball of black fur under the table which he identified as the giant spider good-luck mascot of the hotel. Any doubts about the authenticity of his remark were dispelled when the girl bringing our coffee quickly changed direction to give this monstrosity free passage from under our table to the long window drapes which it agitated strongly as it crawled quickly to the sun-warmed pelmet above.

Since return passages could be booked only from Nagasaki the toss of a coin decided that Roy and I should make the one-night visit for this purpose. As the old-fashioned hotel favoured by most of the Shanghai police was full, we secured a room in a nearby, newly-opened hostelry. Back in our room before dinner we ordered beers and told the nan-san who brought them to save herself a long walk up the stairs by bringing four the next time we rang. Aghast at the very idea, she made it clear that protocol demanded she should pour the beer and as it was impossible to pour four at one serving she would continue to bring them two at a time. A few rings later, however, there was noticeable hastiness in the pouring and her leaving the room. From the time of the fifth ring protocol went by the board. Thereafter, the door was opened just sufficiently wide to permit the entry of bottles from which we were left to pour the beer for ourselves.

Accustomed to the disastrous after effects of as little as two bottles could have on the average Japanese male, the entire staff had assembled in the hall as we arrived at the head of the stairs in response to the dinner gong. Our first idea was that the assembly was there to welcome some celebrity but it soon became obvious that the reason was to see both of us, filled to the gills, tumble head over heels in a drunken stupor down the stairs. Our stately descent did much to raise our prestige among the hotel staff.

On a walk through the Yoshiwara, the brothel district, after dinner we joined a dozen or so others in appraising the attractions of the overpainted kimono-clad girls sitting back on their heels in three rows in the large open windows. Incredible as it seemed to us, they were earning the dowry they would later hand over to their respective fiances, many of whom paid them regular visits before their 'paying guests' would book them for a night's pleasure.

We viewed with great pleasure the profusion of multi-coloured flowers, miniature trees, shrubs and fairy lights adorning the facades of bars on the cherry tree-lined avenues along which hostelries were placed. Our pleasure was dissipated quickly enough once we had entered a bar. In the frowsy, inelegant surroundings the only saving grace was the attractiveness of the hostesses. Quickly they left their Japanese male companions when we entered to ply us with questions about our nationality and the reason for our visit to Japan among seemingly countless other inquiries. It was then that it dawned on us that we had not seen a single foreigner since we left Katsuza. No wonder then that we were more than usually interesting to the girls.

Far removed from the cherry trees and the fairy lights of the bar district were the women we watched bunkering ships on the wharves behind the shipping offices. Each woman, stocky and muscular and bent almost double under the weight of coal carried in panniers on their backs, ascended gangways one behind the other in a human chain to reach the hatchways high on the decks to discharge their loads. They did this with an economy of movement made automatic by constant repetition and then they returned to the wharf to repeat the process over

140

and over again. We watched some of these women taking their noonday meal and were astounded that the small bowl of rice garnished only with a spoonful of vegetable soup containing a sardine-sized piece of fish provided sufficient nourishment to keep them muscled enough to carry out the back-breaking toil which was their sorry lot day after miserable day. For a European or American that bowl of rice would have been the small sweet accompaniment to a meal the gargantuan size of which these women would never see.

On the train taking us back to Katsuza a seemingly harmless drunk opened the coach door probably to give him a better view of the countryside. Soon tiring of this, he lurched down the otherwise empty coach to deliver a finger-wagging monologue at Roy and me. This went on until the guard arrived and slid the coach door shut and did some finger-wagging himself at the drunk probably on the subject of annoying foreigners travelling on Japanese trains. He then escorted the man back to his seat in the corner behind us. Immediately the guard had left, the drunk reopened the door and stood by it as he had done before.

It would be impossible to say just how many times in the intervals between the guard's visits to close the door that the drunk opened it again. On one occasion a lurch of the train deposited him flat on his back inside the coach instead of, as seemed inevitable a second before, out on the track. Eventually we lost interest and returned to our reading until the agitated guard came to us and asked if the drunk had passed us on the way to the front of the train. We assured him he had not and hurriedly he went back to look under and behind the seat the drunk had been occupying. Then he went into the toilet and finally took a long look through the open door down the track along which we had just come before sliding it closed for the last time. Turning to us with a down-in-the-mouth expression and with hands upturned as if to say 'There's nothing we can do about it now,' the guard picked up the bag at the corner seat, made a note in his book and made his way back to the rear of the train.

The reason for the extra attention on us at the hotel became clear when mama-san announced the imminent arrival of a concert group from Tokyo and the girls' desire for escorts to the show in the village hall.

When we arrived at the village hall with the nan-sans we saw that four chairs had been placed conspicuously in the middle of an audience seated on the floor. We took a long look at the chairs not knowing whether to occupy them or try the floor like the remainder of the audience. Roy solved the problem by pointing out that if the nan-sans had been good enough to cart the chairs from the hotel then we should be good enough to sit on 'em. So we perched on them just long enough to show our appreciation of the nan-sans' kindness before passing them to one side and joining the others on the floor.

Despite the fact that while we had sat on the chairs the view of the audience behind us had been impeded there had been not one expression of annoyance from one of them. Just one more example of the inbred politeness always displayed by the Japanese in their homeland.

The conjurors and comedians who adopted the appropriate postures before blowing clouds of white dust from the seats of their pants stole the show. So far as we were concerned the highlight came when a troupe of Tokyo cabaret girls drew shocked gasps from our nan-sans at the sight of so much female flesh. Roy, born actor that he was, commenced to delight the nan-sans with his imitation of a man who though deeply shocked at the exposure of so much female flesh could not tear his eyes from the shapely legs of the girls on the stage.

142

Bobby Tate, a police colleague, was a late arrival at the hotel as a result of his having to take his second thirty-day course of anti-rabies injections in two months. He had tackled an infected dog in Frenchtown which was savaging a girl. Tate, who had left the Hong Kong police to join the SMP paid his first – and what was to be his last – visit to the geisha house. He asked the madam the price of a large apple-pear in a basket of fruit. Twice the size of a large Bramley cooking apple back at home these apples crossed with pears were hybrids grown only in Japan. He was told by the madam that if he wanted the apple-pear then he would have to buy the entire basket for five yen since the contents could not be sold separately. Tate, a brash Londoner, after weighing up that with only 200 yen in his possession to cover the entire leave the fruit was beyond his reach, grabbed the apple-pear and took a huge bite out of it. After throwing one yen to the woman he jumped through the window to the garden below to evade her teeth-and-claws attack as, infuriated, she leapt at him. The ensuing police visit to the hotel to identify Tate as the one responsible for the disturbance and damage to her flower garden, together with a similar incident later, put the mark of Cain on him so far as the management and the geisha houses were concerned.

There was an air of melancholia during the last days of our stay. This was not caused so much by our imminent departure but by the realisation that we, as juniors, had been obliged to take leave late in the season and that we would be the last police guests of the year. It could well have been the memory of mama-san's foul-smelling herb tea or the application of oils applied back and front to cure his recent cold plus many other kindnesses from her, that impelled the normally insensitive Roy to ask as we made our way to the ferry whether or not if he kissed the old girl goodbye we would do the same.

The following year we fell in with a suggestion from the staff that we should prolong our stay by taking the eight-hour train journey instead of the ferry trip that took six hours. Our departure coincided with the onset of the monsoon rains which dripped incessantly down our necks owing to the inadequacies of the small umbrellas held at full-arm stretch over us by the tiny nan-sans throughout the long walk, knees bent to get as much cover as possible, to the railway station. Whether it was the dismal weather, our departure or the prospect of an early return to the family farms, or a combination of all three, the fact was that tears streamed down the faces of the nan-sans as we took that final walk. Truth to tell, we felt just as dismal ourselves but without the tears.

Shortly after arriving back in Shanghai every policeman who had spent his leave at the Tokiwaya Hotel received a letter to say how much the management had enjoyed his patronage and expressing the sincere hope that he would come again. In due course the four of us each received the conventional letter but Tate's, arriving at the same time, was written on slightly different lines.

'Dear Mr Tate, we hope you enjoyed your stay at our hotel and sincerely hope that you will never come again. Signed . . . Manager.'

Memories of those happy times in Japan still remain fresh in the mind. Paramount is the contrast we found between the Japanese military forces in China and the polite and hospitable people with whom we mixed on the most harmonious terms when on leave in Japan. From July 1937, Japan had launched a full-scale military attack on China and had occupied a large part of that country's vast coastal region and some interior territory. The barbarity of the Japanese forces had produced worldwide condemnation but it had small effect on the military government back in Tokyo which had allied itself with Hitler's Nazi Germany and Mussolini's Fascist Italy. This had produced in China a long succession of anti-Western inimical actions which included the sinking of the American gunboat, *Panay* and the wounding of the British ambassador, Sir Hugh Knatchebull-Hugessen. Yet, in our holiday resorts in Kyushu, the warm friendliness of all the locals and the genuine sincerity of their welcome have, I'm sure, left with all of us happy memories that reflect the basic decency of the Japanese people.

7

HOSTILITIES

Within weeks of Prime Minister Neville Chamberlain declaring war on Nazi Germany in September 1939 all Britons in the SMP received a letter from Foreign Secretary Lord Halifax asking us to remain in the police where we would be far more useful to the country than in the armed forces. He strongly urged us to remain where we were. Despite this, many left to join the Royal Naval Reserve (the 'Wavy Navy') in Hong Kong or, hopefully, to pilot Spitfires. Reports coming back from earlier departures, however, indicated that the volunteers had been taken off their ships in Hong Kong or Singapore to fill any government vacancies which could not now be filled from the United Kingdom. For instance, Canadian-born 'Snowy' Whittaker, who had served in the Gordon Highlanders and was intent on joining his old regiment, was pressed into customs service in Singapore. Another SMP officer, Reg Bloor, anxious to rejoin the London police, had taken a Dutch ship bound for London, via Java. When the vessel was diverted to Singapore he suffered the same fate as Whittaker.

The Canadian recruiting officer at the consulate eyed Dave Orme and me with renewed interest when we said we did not wish to be officers in Hong Kong's Wavy Navy or pilot Spitfires, but merely to join the army. On his assurance that this would soon eventuate we submitted our resignations to be effective in three months' time.

Dave and I expected to be leaving the police in November, 1941, but headquarters decreed otherwise. As we were both full sergeants we were told the date for leaving the force would be extended by six weeks and that I would immediately be transferred to Bubbling Well, the well-known trouble station out west. I heard later that the reason given for my transfer was that if I was so damned keen on action I might just as well get into practice there as anywhere else.

Shanghai, still neutral and with two British battalions and ancillary units stationed in the Settlement as part of the defence force, was still the social capital of the Far East. Its hospitality was renowned far and wide. I cannot count the number of times I returned to the station around midnight in the sports jacket and slacks donned for a quiet beer in a nearby bar after being wined and dined lavishly by some American, Russian or other host casually met on the way. Blanket invitations to dine in Chinese homes were sent to the station at least twice a month.

In contrast to the obvious hostility of Japanese officialdom to all foreigners the open-handed and seemingly genuine hospitality of Japanese businessmen in Shanghai was demonstrated when Ron Crouch and I in light summer suits joined a throng of tail-coated Japanese at the opening of new showrooms in Hongkew. We had been taken there by Superintendent Igaki, a former schoolmate of Ron's whom we had met by chance on the street. Not once was there any sign that our informal dress in the midst of the strictest formality had caused Japanese eyebrows to rise. Indeed, our glasses were constantly refilled with imported beer or Johnny Walker Black Label whisky before they were half empty and we were plied with more food than we could eat in a week. As a final gesture our hosts pressed on us the

147

services of the loveliest Japanese girls I have ever seen in or outside Japan.

Tragically, a week before the birthday party Igaki had invited us to attend as we left the showrooms, he was gunned down and killed outside his house in Japanese-controlled Hongkew. No arrests were ever made by Japanese detectives investigating the murder and it was anybody's guess who the killers were. That Igaki was extremely pro-British was well known. His murderer or murderers could have been anti-Western Japanese, Chinese puppets, the Chungking underground of Chiang Kai-shek or criminal elements. We shall never know.

Russian Easter gave us the opportunity to witness one of the most spectacular and deeply moving celebrations in cosmopolitan Shanghai. Thousands of devout Russians converging on their cathedral in Route Doumer in the French Concession with lighted candles in their hands. To the strains of glorious Russian Easter music sung by an excellent choir the congregation, which flowed into the packed cathedral precincts, in loud voice told the world 'Christ had risen'. After the service there were parties in most Russian homes and for us there were invitations to the Russian police club where excellent traditional dishes were served to the accompaniment of over-many glasses of vodka. Police officer John Weeks had a Russian wife, and she cooked and served all the traditional Slavonic fare in their quarters. We drank the vodka served in shot-sized glasses in one gulp at agreeably short intervals to help the food down and to toast in the happy, convivial atmosphere our host and hostess, their friends, our friends, and anyone else who came to mind. Happy memories that will never fade.

It was after one Russian party that events appeared to

support Mike Harman's oft-repeated assertion that we British, accustomed only to our less volatile females, should never marry Russians. Idly at first, but with mounting interest, we watched a Russian watchman approaching us on Bubbling Well Road. Stoically he pushed his bicycle with one hand while with the other he warded off a noisy and bellicose female. His reaction to her onslaught with feet and fists was to prop his bicycle unhurriedly against the kerb and then deliver a swift punch to the jaw which sent her somersaulting across the pavement before resuming without so much as a backward glance, his measured pace up the road. The woman, after focusing her eyes with obvious difficulty on the retreating figure of the man still pushing his bike, set off in hot pursuit to fling her arms round his neck in rapturous adoration, and to hold them there until they passed from sight. To Mike's quizzical remark, 'Which of you fellows would have had the sense to do that?', we had no answer.

There was another Russian watchman, who was warned by police officer Paddy Duffy of the dire consequences that would follow any future tardy timekeeping. When the watchman drew his pistol and levelled it at his own right ear, the Yorkshire-born Paddy told him not to be so daft but to put the weapon back and go and relieve his long suffering mate.

The Russian looked at Paddy and softly said, 'So, Sergeant Duffy, you think I am acting silly and that I am only fooling, eh?' He pulled the trigger.

'By hell,' said Paddy afterwards, 'the bugger wasn't fooling.'

On another occasion I was warned by the wife of a Russian drug addict with a reputation for extreme violence that he had just been sedated by his doctor prior to his being taken in on a larceny charge. I placed him in the padded cell for his own safety. At midnight I handed the office over to Duffy. The man was still sedated and in a deep sleep.

At about 3am he awoke and went berserk so much so that Paddy, an unbeaten boxing champion of Shanghai for twelve years, had difficulty in restraining him. Of slight build and medium height he had torn out three of the tough rubber panels that lined the wall of the cell. He had pulled down the metal guard from the centre light fitting which I, with an advantage in height and with longer arms, could only reach with my fingertips. As the bed and table were still secured to the floor in positions beyond reach of the light, even the police doctor could not fathom how the man had done so much damage during the period that started with the first sounds from the cell and Paddy's entry only seconds later.

It was in 1940 that British forces in the International Settlement were evacuated to Hong Kong and Singapore and the Americans to the Philippines. The Savoia Grenadiers, marooned in useless exile in the Settlement thanks to British sea power, stayed on with the two gunboats in the Whangpoo river. While Japan's envoy Nomura was said to be talking peace in Washington, unbeknown to the world at large and to us in the Settlement the decision to strike had been made in Tokyo.

In November 1941, I was summoned to the consulate and told that the ship that was to take us to India on our way to enlist in the army had left Bombay for Shanghai. We were advised to dispose of all our heavy clothing. So we prepared to say goodbye to Shanghai.

On December 8, 1941, I was on night office duty. The phone rang at 12.40am and Jeff Coleman with whom I had shared the rice-control duty, speaking from central desk told me the Japanese had come over Garden Bridge from Hongkew and were deploying artillery field pieces along the Bund to cover the British and American shallow-draught gunboats on the river.

The British gunboat, *Petrel,* was asked to surrender. Immediately its commander refused and it opened fire despite the overwhelming odds against it. Firing with pom-poms, its only armament, the *Petrel* was raked with fire from the Bund and then by heavy shells fired by the Japanese cruiser, *Idzumo,* anchored in Hongkew. The *Idzumo,* originally sold to the Russians by Britain, was captured by the Japanese in the Russo-Japanese war of 1905 and was placed in Shanghai's river as a permanent naval command post. Quickly the *Petrel* was hit many times and set ablaze. It sank and left a large patch of oil over its grave in the Whangpoo. The American gunboat, *Wake,* was captured intact by the Japanese.

Strangely, Japanese police officers, normally scarce on the ground on night duty stayed close to the station in their entire strength. The sound of heavy gunfire from the Bund acted as a signal for them to make a concerted rush to mount station motorcycles without obtaining the customary permission and make for the Bund.

After the firing had ceased one Japanese officer, not noted for his friendliness towards us, returned to the station and, ignoring me now as of no consequence gave the clerk an account in Chinese of the hard fight put up by the *Petrel,* which had resulted in heavy casualties on both sides. As a pensive sort of afterthought he said: 'They fought just like the Japanese navy.' From then on until stopped by the Japanese I was kept busy answering phoned enquiries by stunned British residents who had firmly believed that Japan would have stayed neutral to prosper by making armaments for sale to both sides in the war.

On December 9, members of the Japanese naval

landing party took chocolate and other confectionery they had taken from a British godown to the Japanese naval hospital where, exceptionally, survivors from the *Petrel* had been taken. There could be no doubt that the gallant fight of the crew of the *Petrel* played a significant part in influencing the Japanese towards adopting, initially at any rate, a softer line towards British nationals left in the city than they would have done otherwise.

A cable from the British Government in London instructed us to remain on duty and do all we could to help at least 10,000 British nationals converging on Shanghai. In the interim between the start of the war in the Far East and the time of our dismissal from the police we made every effort to fulfil our task.

Within days of the Japanese military machine taking over the Settlement area there came fearsome indication of the intention to stamp out crime. In Gordon Road rioters were strung up by their thumbs for several hours. In an adjacent area a large block of buildings in which a shot had been fired was completely sealed off. As food stocks there became scarce a hole sufficiently large to permit a man to squeeze through was cut in the barbed wire denying exit or entry to the area. Sadly, the hole was well within the view of a concealed rifleman and the first escape attempt was the last.

On the third day of a similar enclosure elsewhere, British Detective Sergeant Frank Guess responded to an appeal by telephone from a British woman trapped in the buildings surrounded by the Japanese by suspending a bag of baby food between the legs of a long-gowned volunteer Chinese detective to take him, handcuffed, into the woman's building on the grounds that he was a suspect in a case under investigation. Had the deception been revealed there is no doubt that the detective would have been shot. Heaven alone knows what would have happened to Guess.

Similarly, when I left the station after signing off at midnight on what had been an exceptionally cold day, two elderly British women, who had been trapped on a narrow traffic island for more than two hours, were permitted through the intervention of one of the better-type Japanese officers, who had relieved me, to sit in the station until stand-down came nearly three hours later.

During another area closure Inspector Bradley found himself standing in front of a crowd cut off in St George's Square. Suddenly he heard a voice addressing him in perfect English. Nonplussed, he looked round. Behind him was a line of Japanese soldiers. He could hardly associate the impeccable English with anyone in that group. Yet within a few seconds one of the soldiers, *sotto voce,* was telling him fluently that only recently had he been recalled as a conscript from London where he had been on the staff of one of the leading Japanese newspapers.

A former member of a top London club, this unwilling conscript, by reason of his background and education, was rejected by the lower ranks brutalised by such savagery as distending the stomachs of Chinese women to bursting point by fastening their mouths over village pumps. He faced the ever-present threat of being abandoned to suffer the revenge of Chinese women when and if seriously wounded or physically incapable of continuing the long march forward. Despised especially by the upper echelon, he was a most unhappy man. This background came from a Japanese policeman who had served three years in the Japanese army in China.

A Japanese sergeant, who noted my interest when five Japanese brought in for disorderly behaviour grovelled at his feet, explained that he had threatened them with corrective treatment at the Bridge House in Hongkew from the Kempetai, the Japanese Gendarmerie. The five could well have been members of the same gang that, a few nights before, had boarded a tram on which I was travelling from the central area to Louza. They pushed their way roughly through the dense throng of standing passengers as far as the driver's platform and then turned back to reach the rear of the coach. Three girls, obviously members of the gang, pressed themselves against me so hard I had to reach up and grab the handrail to avoid being shoved off my feet. As they were Japanese I thought they were engaged in horseplay just to show everyone which was the master race. That was until I reached into my hip pocket in the Louza canteen to pay for my beer. Two dollar bills which should have been there were missing and could only have been taken by the girls. Today of course, we all know that Japanese innovations are followed almost everywhere. Certainly, that tramway incident could well have been the world's first case of 'steaming' now prevalent on London's Underground transport system. Gangs of steamers rush their way through crowded trains to steal from passengers in exactly the same way as that gang robbed me and, obviously, others on that Shanghai tram.

Certainly the Bridge House and its occupiers, the gendarmes, had established such a reputation for torture and brutality of the most savage kind that the mere mention of the place and the gendarmerie would cause instant terror in the stoutest of hearts. I remember the much-decorated Japanese army major I once saw standing rigidly to attention before a private of the gendarmerie who, seemingly propped up by his long cavalry sword, was lounging at ease, obviously a fearsome character instilling terror in the officers who, in their turn, brutalised the men under their command.

On one occasion on the Bund I met a white-haired man, who stopped to talk to me. Even after he had made himself known to me I could not identify him as the robust manager of rice godowns in the French Concession I had known a year back. He told me he had been arrested by the Japanese Gendarmerie on the outbreak of the Pacific War and had been incarcerated in the Bridge House. His account of the savagery inflicted on him night after night by his gendarme captors during interrogation sessions made the blood curdle in absolute horror. This brought to mind the young English girl who committed suicide after spending four months in Bridge House. Rather than face life with memories of brutal, subhuman tortures she had been subjected to at the hands of the gendarmes she drank the poison Lysol. Medical opinion was that no sooner had escorting gendarmes taken her to her flat and left that she ended her life.

Such was the Japanese reputation for Draconian treatment of criminals that, within weeks of the Japanese takeover of the Settlement, there was room and to spare in what had previously been the packed confines of Ward Road Jail, the world's largest prison. Warders, for the first time in their lives, found themselves able to twiddle their thumbs in an effort to relieve the complete boredom that the new era of Japanese rule had thrust on them.

One afternoon as I left the British Consulate-General in civilian clothes I was asked to escort a young British girl over Garden Bridge in the forlorn hope that my presence would avert a repetition of her misfortune the previous day when she was made to stand for hours in the hot sun by a Japanese sentry standing on the bridge which gave access to the Japanese dominated district. The sentry had knocked her hat off because she had not

155

bowed low enough to him. Even when British sentries had stood close to the Japanese in the centre of the bridge up to 1941 all Chinese passing the Japanese sentry boxes had been forced to bow. For many who had been accused of not bowing low enough to give due prestige to the Emperor's representative, there were beatings and men, women and even children were severely assaulted. After the takeover of the Settlement the sentries extended their reign of tyranny to include such enemy nationals as Britons, Americans, Netherlanders and other members of the Allied powers. They were recognisable as they wore red armbands which bore numbers and an initial letter denoting a nationality – B for British, A for American and so on. Registration of all enemy nationals had been carried out early in 1942.

A European man brought in by a Sikh traffic officer for ignoring a hand signal delayed his departure from the office just long enough to tell me in no uncertain terms just what he thought of British policemen. Three weeks later that same European appeared at the station to ask if I could help his wife, who was being held at a barrier under circumstances similar to those under which the English girl had found herself, and for the same reason. Through the intervention of the same officer, who had helped the two old ladies on the traffic island, she was freed by the time the man got back to the barrier. With a diffidence oddly at variance with his former anti-British antipathy he came back later to thank me for effecting what he considered to have been a near miracle. Under the impression that I had not recognised him he identified himself and told me how much he regretted the derogatory remarks he had made previously.

Shortly after this, seventy of us were discharged from the police as our presence was considered to be no longer conducive to the good order and well-being of what the

Japanese called the 'New Order In East Asia', propagated under various slogans including 'Asia for the Asiatics' and others meant to inflame Asian feeling against Britons, Americans and other empire-builders.

In the case of ex-Grenadier Guardsman Tam Wimsett from Halifax in the then West Riding of Yorkshire who was well known for being the smartest man in the force, the grounds for his dismissal were that he was too slovenly. That was comically unbelievable to all of us –yet another indication of the warped, inimical antipathy, certainly born of an inferiority complex, to members of the white races and the British in particular.

Dave Orme and I, of course, had resigned from the force earlier in the hope of joining Britain's armed forces. We had from time to time called at the British consulate and had been assured after the outbreak of war in the Pacific that we were on the list of people to be repatriated on what later became known as the *Wangle Maru,* a Japanese liner, the *Asama Maru,* brought to Shanghai under the terms of an exchange of Japanese nationals in Britain and British nationals in China.

Spirits buoyed up by the prospect of sailing home we kept in touch with the consulate to ascertain the date of departure of the repatriation ship. Two days before the sailing date there came the sickening news imparted by a consular officer that our names had been removed from the list to make way for what he said were more deserving cases. For a long time there had been general disgust as choices were made known. Certainly there were deserving cases such as those Britons who had suffered in Bridge House. Yet it soon became apparent that a large proportion of the repatriates were middle-aged or even elderly business tycoons whose contribution to the British war effort would be practically nil. Thus came the appellation, born of universal disgust the *Wangle Maru,* which duly set sail carrying a load of consular personnel, high court judges, torture cases and a conglomeration of big business personalities many of whom had never set eyes on the United Kingdom and its leaden grey skies.

For us left behind there had been successive heart-breaking episodes when the Japanese with spectacular parades celebrated the conquest of Hong Kong, of Malaya and Singapore and the sinking of the two battleships HMS *Repulse* and HMS *Prince of Wales* off Singapore. Yet not one of us left to face whatever the Japanese had in store for us as enemy nationals believed that victory could be theirs. We knew that no matter how long the war lasted final victory would be ours.

We had a long and testing time to wait.

My test arrived early one morning when in the pre-dawn darkness I was arrested by members of the Japanese Gendarmerie and incarcerated in a large assortment of old and elaborate Chinese buildings that had been occupied by the Fourth Regiment, United States Marine Corps, as members of the Shanghai Defence Force. Surrounded by high walls and containing several compounds in traditional style the ornamental woodwork of the buildings had become the home of thousands of bugs, a blood-sucking army that was going to defeat our every attacking sortie and strategic ingenuity in trying to rid the place of their bloated, blood-filled bulk.

Also arrested during the early-morning roundup were seventy-three other members of the police force as well as civilian Britons, Americans, Netherlanders, Greeks and a few prisoners of other nationalities that included Canadians, Australians, one Belgian and a Russian Jew who had acquired Norwegian nationality.

We were the very first enemy nationals to be taken prisoner. Unlike other enemy nationals later, who were interned in several camps as family units under the control of the Japanese Consular Police, we were removed from families and guarded by the Japanese army under gendarmerie control. With the arrival of men tortured in the Bridge House, of which we were an annexe, our numbers rose to 350 or so. We were told by the Japanese there was a charge against everyone arrested and imprisoned within the high-walled complex.

The camp commandant was a grey-haired Japanese reservist officer, Colonel Odera, whom we called 'Old Handlebars' because of his elaborate moustache. He was only occasionally in the camp as he was also in charge of prisoners of war, mainly American marines from the Legation Guard in Peking and from the embassy and consular guards left behind in Nanking and Shanghai. From time to time we received bread baked by the prisoners in their camp at Pootung across the Whangpoo river.

Second in command and the officer regularly in charge of daily discipline in the camp was Lieutenant Honda, who spoke American-accented English fairly fluently. Under him was a young sadist whom we called Dogface, typical of the brutal officer class that had been spawned by the militarists in Tokyo and who had spread their savage inhumanity in China, Korea, Formosa and Manchuria and who were left in the process of extending pitiless oppression throughout Southeast Asia. There was also a young trainee doctor.

So far as our backgrounds in Shanghai were concerned there was no doubt that we embraced many echelons of life from taipans to tattooed members of the 'vulgar herd', executives of the great China business empires such as Jardine Matheson, Butterfield & Swire or the American-owned Shanghai Power Company to former American Navy sailors, who had married Chinese wives

159

and who, on retirement, had stayed in China. Many of them had become bar keepers. Indeed, Joe Orapello was only one of many ex-sailors or marines in the bar business who had been rounded up by the gendarmerie and placed in Haiphong Road camp. As we were all in the same Catch-22 situation class distinctions went overboard pretty quickly and we soon got used to such sights as a bank manager scraping vegetables alongside a former private in a British or American unit.

At the start of our imprisonment we were, naturally, a robust lot, having lived off the fat of the land as privileged Westerners. Then came the shocking contrast with the pitiful wretches brought in to join us from Bridge House by the Kempetai inhuman torturers.

Torture, alas, is still with us in what should be an enlightened and civilised age. The Bridge House in Shanghai was a hell-house of horror, an obscene excrescence in which the Kempetai brutes inflicted on men, women and children atrocious agonising torments on prisoners thrown into crowded cages, male and female together, for periods of eight months or more. The pitiful wretches, dragged out usually at night, to suffer indescribable pain from a wide variety of tortures, were kept alive on a meagre rice diet. Under constant beatings and the bestial destruction of the human body it was no wonder that many people failed to survive the sadistic savagery of the Kempetai. Those who did survive were left with psychological scares that could never be cured during an earthly lifetime.

In Haiphong Road there was from time to time the entry of a wretch, who had been delivered by the Kempetai from the Bridge House. Immediately there had to be medical treatment and delousing. With bodies bruised from the beatings and minds afflicted by the terrors they had suffered, the Bridge House prisoners

160

often failed to recover from the mental agonies inflicted on them. Most of the men, however, recovered physically and managed to join in daily camp routines.

Not one of the men would talk about their Bridge House experiences. They gave evasive answers to questions about how they were treated. We received an Australian journalist, a freelance writer, whose condemnation of the Kempetai and the tortures he had undergone there was lurid in the extreme. He spoke out fearlessly and with vivid descriptions of the suffering of the victims of Japanese savagery. It was a tragic mistake. Within a few days of his arrival he was taken back to the Bridge House by Kempetai officers to suffer again the barbaric tortures he had managed to survive previously.

How the Japanese in charge of us had managed to learn of the Australian's outspokenness remained a mystery for some time. Then all was revealed. Obviously someone had passed on to the Japanese the man's comments. A revealing discovery was made when ex-policeman Ian MacAulay was set to work carrying supplies to the Japanese quarters. Knowing that it might be a trap set by the gendarmes he courageously picked up a letter addressed to the commandant from a former up-country businessman who, five years previously had been decorated after sustaining an injury going to the assistance of police in a shoot-up. That letter, dropped on the floor of the passageway to the Japanese quarters, was brought by MacAulay back to the store from which he was carrying boxes to the Japanese quarters. Just before he found the letter he had seen a one-armed camp inmate, Berry, hanging about the passageway to the Jap quarters.

Continuing his story, MacAulay said: 'I was carrying a

box in both arms but it was not too heavy. I saw the letter on the floor of the passageway and not a Jap in sight. I slipped the box on my left hip and with my right hand picked up the letter.'

Back in the store MacAulay opened the letter just as Yorkshireman Bill Wright, serving with Hugh Collar, the Imperial Chemical Industries representative in China and chairman of the British Residents Association in Shanghai, as senior leaders of all personnel in camp, entered the store. He read the letter which contained accusations against J R Huxter, manager of the Mercantile Bank in the Settlement. It was decided that the contents should not be divulged to anyone else. Had the news been spread around camp there is no doubt that the informant would have secretly communicated with the Japanese and MacAulay would certainly have been taken to Bridge House. So far as we knew there were no other 'traitorous' revelations passed on to the Japanese.

As for the Australian journalist, it was not until five months later that he was returned to camp, emaciated and haggard. This time he made it known that he had been treated well by the Kempetai – a palpable lie that must have been a condition for his release from the Bridge House.

Sixty-year-old Eric Davies, a Welshman from Swansea who was the agent in Shanghai for Lloyds of London, was also brought into camp from Bridge House. He possessed indomitable courage. Others in Bridge House had heard him telling his torturers night after night that they could do their worst but he would not talk. He was deposited, badly beaten, from his own green Humber saloon car that had been taken from his garage on the night of his arrest the previous year.

I can never forget the fearful tension we suffered as

Kempetai cars passed through the camp's fortress-like entrance and names were called out by Honda. These unfortunates were taken away as we waved them goodbye and we selfishly thanked our stars that it was them and not us. One never knew, however, any one of us could be the next.

Looking back on those experiences as helpless captives of a brutal war machine shining examples of real courage come easily to mind. Usually Kempetai removed men from our camp in groups of four and they remained in the Bridge House for long periods. When they returned they were full of praise for Sikh prisoners with them who, they said, were tortured every night but who remained loyal to the British Crown. Similarly, exceptional courage was displayed by officers of the Clyde-built Lloyd Triestino liner, *Conte Verde*. The officers had been seized by the Kempetai after the Italian surrender in the war. They scuttled the ship in the Whangpoo river where it had been forced to remain since the outbreak of war in Europe in 1939.

Life in Haiphong Road deteriorated as the Pacific war took its toll of the necessities of life, particularly food. China had been aggressively overrun by the Tokyo military machine since 1937 and fighting still continued throughout the land with the government of Chiang Kai-shek established in the wartime capital of Chugking in Szechwan province. Famine had spread through many parts of the land and the excesses of the Japanese war machine had left thousands of areas of farmland totally destroyed by their scorched-earth policy. Thus, in our Shanghai imprisonment the rigours of war soon took their toll of the human frame. Rations were short. Medical supplies were almost exhausted. Our main source of protein was cracked wheat sent in by the Swiss Red Cross at the start of our incarceration. The sacks, dwindling rapidly in number, unleashed louse-ridden grains among which an army of grubs wallowed in luxury, fat and squelchy as our 'vegetable squad' set about the impossible task of freeing the cracked wheat from its squirming predators.

In the courtyards, in our rooms, everywhere, hordes of outsize bugs dropped nightly on our sleeping forms and sucked our blood. We were invaded by myriads of mosquitoes. Rats emerged, large and fierce from sewers. There followed the inevitable toll as the human frame weakened under the different assaults – blackouts. On the morning countdown parades there would be among many a sudden loss of consciousness and a heavy fall on the ground. Malaria laid several of us low. Among the worst sufferers was journalist Ralph Shaw, night editor of the *North China Daily News,* and correspondent of the British national daily, *News Chronicle.* With him in the same room was police Sub Inspector Ben Williams. On three separate occasions they were both delirious for days on end and could not be roused even to eat. When they came round they were wraiths of their former selves and were unable to stand unaided. Throughout these periods of illness whenever Honda or Dogface took the nightly count they remained outside the door of room four which I shared with Williams and Shaw. The young Japanese army doctor, patently a learner if ever there was one, was sent into the room where he took the most cursory glance at the inanimate forms of Williams and Shaw on their camp beds before making a hurried exit.

Though far from pleasant, our sufferings were as nothing when compared with the hardships suffered by the Allied (mainly British) servicemen taken prisoner after Singapore fell!

One of the worst cases of savagery by the Japanese

came when stalwart Scot Bill Hutton, an inspector in the Shanghai Municipal Police, was taken from the camp by the Kempetai after receiving a swordstick beating from Dogface, an officer who had earned the hatred of his own soldiers because of his brutality. Dogface – the name bestowed on him by his own men – we had seen many times inflicting on young soldiers not long out of school full-pack marches for three hours or more and then, during drill sessions, savagely kicking in the stomach and groin any one of them who had incurred his displeasure. One soldier told Bob Tate, who had a smattering of Japanese, that if they had to go into action, then Dogface would certainly get more than one bayonet through his back.

It had to be Dogface who sadistically beat Hutton after the Scot had been accused of attempting to get a message out of the camp by one of the Sikh guards. The Sikhs, former members mostly of the police, had joined the anti-British Indian National Army of Subhas Chandra Bose and were marched into camp to augment our Japanese captors. Some, of course, were solidly loyal to the British Crown but in a region totally controlled by the Japanese any display of opposition to Japan's decision to control them could have meant barbaric treatment and possible death. In the case of Hutton it was evident that the Sikh who had reported him to the Japanese was a willing follower of Chandra Bose. Bose, incidentally, died in Japan at about the time of the Japanese surrender in 1945.

I still vividly remember Hutton waving goodbye to us as his two captors marched him to the Kempetai car. It was the same pair of brutes who brought Hutton back ten days later. The first sight we had of Hutton was when his head and shoulders heavily hit the ground as the door of the car carrying him on the floor was opened. Obviously his unconscious form had been propped against the door and he had partially fallen out when the Kempetai opened it for us to carry him into our medical room in what once had been the American marines' recreational hall.

Hutton's terrible physical condition shocked and angered us. The fine white dust that clogged his eyes, nostrils and mouth was an indication of the extensive amounts of electricity that had been applied to his body and which had completely dehydrated his entire frame. Dogface saw Hutton's unconscious form burst half-way out of the car. He laughed as he booted the inert body clear of the vehicle. He indicated, still grinning at the sight of the Scot on the ground, that we could take him away.

It was soon clearly evident to us and later to the Japanese that Hutton was incurably insane and incapable of any coherent mental activity. Our camp physician, Dr Sturton, had Hutton removed to the camp hospital where valiant efforts were made day and night to restore him to health. A hopeless task. Finally the Japanese took him away for treatment they said. The next day we were told that he had died. A lethal injection without doubt.

With great courage Hugh Collar led a small delegation to the Japanese administration building to protest to Colonel Odera, Honda and Dogface over the treatment inflicted on Hutton. Time and again Collar protested over the harsh tortures which had been the lot of each new arrival brought in by the Kempetai. He was well aware that by reason of his own presence in Haiphong Road he was himself a candidate for Bridge House. A braver man I have yet to meet. The protests, of course, fell on deaf ears. The Japanese made it plain more than once that not one of us would live to see the end of the war. In other words, why should they worry.

One of the strongest – if not the strongest – men in camp was Greek seaman Spiros Noofitos. He could lift a large wooden table with his teeth. Broad and hugely muscled he was set on one day by five Japanese guards who savagely beat him to the ground with their rifle butts. For several minutes they rained heavy blows on his back as he lay on the ground shielding his head with arms kept brawny by regular food parcels sent in by Greek friends outside. Once they had finished we were permitted to pick him up. The reason for this assault? Simply a massive inferiority complex. We did not need a psychiatrist to tell us that Noofitos was so much physically superior to them they had to launch their cowardly attack in what they felt would be a demonstration to all of us that the massive Greek had lost face in being felled by Japanese might. Not one of us doubted that Noofitos could easily have taken on his five captors and five more and clouted the lot to kingdom come. In camp any retaliation by him would have meant a quick trip to face much worse in Bridge House.

After the attack Collar and the Greek leader, Captain Calafatis, a Greek Merchant Navy master mariner, complained to the Japanese. It was, as usual, a useless exercise. Lieutenant Honda, who was virtually the number one since Colonel Odera was rarely on the scene, listened stony faced without comment. Indeed, many of us felt that the attack and similar occurrences were instigated by him.

My job in camp was that of storeman. It almost landed me in dire straits with a gendarme. That was the occasion I had stopped a Japanese private soldier from stealing some of the half-rotten meat that was a part of our meagre rations. Within minutes the private brought a gendarme to the store certain in his own mind that the gendarme would give me a severe beating. So he lingered on to watch what he expected to happen. Instead, the gendarme assisted him out of the store with a hefty kick in the rear. While all gendarmes are bad some are better than others. As this particular one, cheeks bulging with at least six men's meat rations he had stuffed in his mouth slouched out of the store I thanked my lucky stars that he was one of the latter. Had it been Dogface now . . . .

I inherited the storeman's job from Bill Carr, who had been forced to quit only a few weeks after taking over from a Shanghai accountant. That well-bred Englishman had found himself unable to cope with the Japanese quartermaster, a crony of Dogface and just as nasty. What forced Carr to hand over the job to me was the onset of violent headaches due solely to the weakness caused by a diet bereft of any real sustenance.

I had control of what was left of some Argentine corned beef and sundries sent to us, the first civilians to be imprisoned, by the British Residents Association from its emergency stocks held in store since the 1914-18 war. The food was still edible – at least for those not too fancy about what they ate. We had been getting twice weekly some army-baked loaves made of near-black maize flour but, in time, there was a severe cutback in this ration and this did cause some arithmetical problems when supplies became unpredictable. My problem came when I had to decide how to share the loaves – one loaf per man or two between three men or a greater slicing to make the supply go round. I had to work with the quartermaster which was a trial of my powers of self control. I had to tell him of our total requirements but this mattered little to him. He invariably held back until the last minute an announcement of when the loaves were coming and how long they would have to last. So, rushed almost to total despair, I had to work out – no computers then – my estimate of what we needed. The total had to agree with the quartermaster's estimate. I never did see that figure, probably because if the quartermaster had erred in our favour he did not want us to know. Once the loaves had arrived the quartermaster watched carefully as I began my single-handed count with room captains peering anxiously and certainly hungrily through the store door waiting to collect their rations.

Thrown into trays made for a gross but five times the size of our ration it was a formidable task to shuffle the bread tray by tray into countable groups, detect and request replacements for any stolen by hungry Japanese soldiers on the way in. To reach the exact figure week after week to give every man in camp his full quota was a herculean test of mental capability. I paid tribute to my old school headmaster many times – and to his much-used cane.

Dr Sturton, an English missionary working amongst lepers up-country, had earned the admiration of every man in the camp by his courageous resistance to practically every order of the Japanese that threatened our wellbeing medically and mentally. The wretches returned from the Bridge House owed their recovery solely to the doctor's constant care and his incessant demands to the Japanese for whatever medical supplies he could drag from them to keep his daily clinic operating with the help of British and American former medical orderlies in the armed services. He had organised a small hospital in which serious cases of illness could be treated with what drugs and other supplies could be obtained.

It was a great day for him when the half-trained Japanese army doctor was replaced by an older and obviously better qualified physician, who spoke good

English. Much later we heard from American marines imprisoned in the camp, in which he served as a doctor, that he had earned their gratitude by his many acts of kindness. For instance, bowls of meat stew were given by him and his wife to each of six prisoners detailed weekly to carry coal up to his second-floor quarters.

After the Japanese surrender on the evidence given by the prisoners of his great humanity he was not imprisoned with members of the Kempetai and other service personnel charged with war crimes but sent back to Japan a free man.

Dr Sturton was, after the war, one of the chief witnesses at the trial in Hong Kong of Japanese gendarmes accused of the brutal murder of Bill Hutton. Prison sentences were imposed but most people felt that the death penalty was the only punishment that fitted their inhuman crimes.

The reason for the unprecedented gift of a large cong of brown soya sauce from the Japanese to flavour our otherwise tasteless vegetable stew came to light months later when the well-preserved body of a long-haired brown sewer rat was scooped up from the dregs at the bottom of the large earthenware cong. Ex-matelot Harry Webber, in charge of the cooks and I decided to keep the discovery a top secret if only for the sake of the more squeamish amongst us. What the eye doesn't see the heart doesn't grieve. That old adage certainly fitted the bill as far as Harry and I were concerned.

Authentic news was scarce. We existed on rumours – of doubtful veracity let it be said – but some relating Allied victories, German defeats and Japanese losses did cheer us up. Certainly we never doubted the eventual defeat of the Axis powers but we were never certain that we'd still be in the flesh to celebrate the final victory.

Early in 1944 a Sikh policeman, a member of the

squad of camp guards, gave us heartening news. The Sikh, whom I'd once brought back to the police station when he had collapsed in a Japanese-controlled area one bitterly cold night, courageously in view of the Hutton tragedy smuggled in a copy of the Soviet daily, *Pravda.* Detective 'Tiny' Pitts, probably the largest man in camp, who was fluent in Russian, translated the printed words for us and they told of Soviet victories on wide fronts in Europe and of the once-victorious Nazi legions retreating in disorder with enormous losses over the icy wastes on which their frozen bodies lay in many thousands. This was the retreat of Napoleon in 1812 repeated but in far greater triumphal significance than the Czarist victory.

Then came the shock of a Japanese order that we were to be moved from Haiphong Road. Where to? We were not told. We had no idea of our destination but we at least knew that we would be going north by rail for the younger ones amongst us had been taken to the North Station to load wagons with what belongings and supplies we were carrying with us.

The day quickly came when we said goodbye to the former American marine camp at Haiphong Road and we were assembled on the grass in front of the main building to be taken in trucks to a point near the station. From there, in what was certainly intended to be a show for the Chinese to let them see the humiliation of the former white masters, we were marched for a hundred yards or more past huge throngs of Chinese residents gathered to see us depart. We could see and feel the compassion and sympathy of the crowd as they watched us enter the station. We learned of a protest made on our behalf by some consular official. Many believed it had been the German consul but we never knew.

We were herded into coolie coaches with seats of four

widely spaced bamboo slats from which the straw cushions had been removed. The order to remain seated was rigidly enforced by clubbing with rifles throughout the five nights and days we spent in excruciating physical discomfort. Lower limbs of prisoners were severely swollen and painful. In some the skin from ankle to knee had split open, leaving wide gashes and open sores. I was lucky as were five others. We managed to remain free of the swellings but our leg muscles stiffened and ached intensely.

On the second night, after we had crossed the wide Yangtse at Nanking on the train ferry at Pukow and had headed north again, I saw Ralph Shaw, delirious with head slumped on chest, being held on the seat only by the elbows of those next to him. Former police sergeant Malcolm Morrison, shaking with malaria and the effect of two weeks torture in Bridge House just before we left Shanghai, was also close to falling on the floor as, with herculean effort, we kept him on the seat. Fortunately, Lieutenant Honda, passing through the coaches, gave us permission to place their inert forms on the luggage rack. In their emaciated state it required little effort on our part to lift them as we would have done six-year-old children.

The Japanese, who had plundered most of the British and American Red Cross food parcels sent to us in Shanghai, issued each man with a parcel, either British or American. We were told we would get nothing else until the end of the journey. We still had no idea where we were going but in this crowded and cramped train we prayed that it would not be far.

I was given a much depleted British Red Cross pack which still contained a long-opened tin of bacon that had almost totally mildewed. This I carefully rationed with Bill Carr and we were still eating it when the train stopped at Fengtai, a large railway freight marshalling yard near Peking. We left the train stiff and weary, many the worse for dried blood which had congealed on their split-skinned legs. The Japanese soon had us moving stores and baggage in seemingly endless forays to large godowns in the bays of the marshalling yards.

We pushed baggage trucks to huge godowns in which we established our new quarters. Shaw, Morrison and the other casualties of the journey had been placed on top of the baggage trucks on stretchers. Perilously they scraped under electrified wires which the Japanese had placed round the godowns to make a prison in a region of more than twenty British godowns formally used as stores in the soya bean trade. Sentry posts had been built high at strategic points and these were manned either by Japanese soldiers or by conscripts from Japanese-controlled Taiwan.

The Japanese quarters were situated about 300 yards from the godowns in which we established our spartan living quarters. We were lucky that we had arrived in Fengtai in the summer. A winter in northern China would have seen most of us frozen stiff in the cavernous enormity of the unheated godowns. We did not have the clothing to withstand the below-zero temperature of the ice-bound north. Still, we knew that Fengtai had not been our final destination. Most of us believed we were on the way to Japan, via Manchuria, or that we were destined to end the journey and, perhaps, our lives in Manchuria.

One thing was certain and that was that American marines, prisoners of the Japanese in Shanghai, had passed through Fengtai earlier. Indeed, we found messages scrawled on the walls of the godown and I was surprised to find that a Major Quigley had previously occupied the same floor space as that now allocated to me.

I must say that we were a resouceful lot. No sooner had we landed at Fengtai and established ourselves in the bare and forbidding confines of the godowns than the organised operation that had served us so well in Shanghai was under way in our new surroundings. The cooks, seemingly miles away, brought us food by rail – a miniature track on which they pushed small wagons laden with steaming stews made up of anything they could find. We had, for the first time in our lives, camel stew. Whether or not the animal had more than lived its span of years on earth we did not know. Nor did we care. There was sustenance enough in the meat. Alas, camels were not plentiful or within reach. Our diet deteriorated quickly and all the ills of near starvation beset many of us, particularly the older members of the camp.

When August came we were still in Fengtai and it seemed obvious that Japanese plans to continue our journey northward had been thwarted by events about which we knew nothing. Day after day, night after night, we had got used to the incessant noise of steam locomotives and the clang-clang of wagon or coach buffers meeting during shunting operations. Then suddenly there came a deathly stillness after one day of much increased activity as we heard trains departing in rapid succession. Soon enough, the reason for the silence became clear when the unusual quiet in the Japanese quarters gave way to raucous shouts from both officers and men as they passed in and out of their saki store. A Taiwanese conscript, who had come over from the Japanese area, told us that two unusually powerful bombs had been dropped on Japan and that the Emperor had ordered all Japanese forces to end hostilities and surrender. We also heard from the same source that the Soviet Union had entered the war and that there was heavy fighting in Manchuria. This explained the heavy activity in the yards and then the silence as trains left for Manchuria heavily laden with troops and war material.

Unbounded joy swept through the camp but for us the war lingered on. About nine o'clock that night a party of drunken Japanese soldiers flung open the doors of our godown and trained two machine guns on us. Intervening Taiwanese conscripts pulled the self-appointed would-be executioners from behind the guns and pandemonium reigned. As fast as one drunken soldier was pulled from his gun another took his place, and when he in turn was pulled back a staggering third made for the gun. Finally, about midnight the noise subsided and we managed to get some much-needed sleep.

*　　*　　*

Soon we were free men again. American officers, who had been dropped by parachutes over Peking, entered the camp to tell us that the war was really over and the cause of the Japanese surrender had been the atomic-bombing of Hiroshima and Nagasaki that had left enormous casualties and almost total destruction of both cities.

For us there was the pleasure of seeing Colonels Odera and Honda having to obey the orders of the Americans, cowed and clearly hating their humiliation visible to all of us. We were told that we would soon be leaving the godowns to move to new quarters in the city of Peking.

We were moved at night in Japanese military trucks, a ragged army of white men of different nationalities. As we drove through the long tunnel in the massive city wall we emerged into the brightly lit streets where thousands of Kuomintang flags flew to celebrate the defeat of Japan and the triumph of Chiang Kai-shek. At that time the war effort of the communists under Mao Tse-tung had not earned worldwide recognition and it was Chiang in the wartime capital of Chunking, who was given the accolade of the triumphal warrier.

We were divided into sections, one taking over the Japanese Sui Mei So Hotel where the sleeping facilities were provided by hard tatamis, the mats on which every Japanese then slept. The other section established itself in the luxurious ambience of the internationally famous Wagon Lit Hotel. A hospital was established by Dr Sturton in the Peking Hotel where he and his medical team from the camp treated our own sick and prisoners found in various states of physical and mental deterioration in the city's jail. Among the prisoners released and treated were members of the crew of the planes commanded by Major General James Doolittle which had bombed Japan from an aircraft carrier early in the Pacific war. They had crash-landed in China in Japanese-occupied territory and had been savagely tortured. They survived and were sent back to the United States.

It was during a visit to the Wagon Lit Hotel that I was introduced by my former police colleague, John MacAulay, to a tall, slim girl whose face seemed vaguely familiar. She carried on a somewhat hesitant and disjointed conversation with MacAulay and into my mind there came a picture of a much younger girl whom Ron Crouch and I on police duty in Shanghai had often seen leaving the Yates Road apartments at about 8am most mornings and then being taken in a private rickshaw towards the Bund.

Suddenly there came the realisation that this young woman was, indeed, the same person we had admired

176

for her poise and well-dressed allure in Shanghai. The change in her appearance was shocking. Her face was lined and yellow, her hesitant speech was indicative of some damage to her reasoning process. Her entire manner clearly showed she had at some time been under great stress. She would move away from us and then return almost immediately. At times she forgot what she had said only seconds before and then suddenly proceed on a totally different line of conversation. Obviously this young woman had gone through a time of trial and tribulation.

MacAulay, whose humanity was well known, had appointed himself as the girl's guardian. She asked him for a few cents to buy chocolate. MacAulay had taken all the money sent to her by her former employers, a London-based firm, for safe-keeping. Forgetful, and obviously not in control of all her faculties she had left money lying about the hotel. From what she had told him in her more lucid moments MacAulay told me her story. As he spoke, the young woman, eyes cast down, would nod in agreement. At other times she listened without a speck of interest.

She was a German national. Before the Pacific war she was private secretary to the manager of one of the larger companies engaged in the China trade, she spoke and wrote four European languages in addition to perfect English.

When the Japanese had taken over the Settlement she found herself without employment as all British and American firms were immediately closed by the Japanese. She turned to the German consul in Shanghai who provided sufficient money for her to live on. Fearing that life in Shanghai would become intolerable under Japanese control and having been advised by the consul and friends that, as a single woman living alone, she should move to the safer haven of Peking, she took their advice. In 1943 she moved to Peking.

She found a room and settled in. Her arrival had been noted by the Japanese military and several gendarmes entered her room ostensibly to check her papers. From that time on her existence in Peking became a veritable nightmare. She could not remember the number of times the gendarmes had taken her away at night to rape her, beat her senseless and then drop her half naked on the street outside their headquarters to be covered in rain or snow only to suffer the same bestial treatment by the entire gendarmerie personnel a few nights later. Small wonder that this talented young woman was almost completely destroyed by the inhuman brutality the gendarmes had inflicted on her, alone and defenceless in a strange city. Certainly the move from Shanghai had been a tragic mistake. She was in desperate need of medical treatment and this was finally arranged in Peking. The last time I saw this once beautiful woman she was travelling aboard ship for home in the care of an older woman. Her passage and the urgently needed medical treatment was paid for by her former employers. What happened to her after that I do not know. All I could do was wish her well.

All the Red Cross letters written to us from loved ones which the Japanese always denied every having received were found opened and read in their former administration building in Fengtai.

In Peking at the Sui Mei So Hotel, formerly a Japanese military guest house, the irrepressible Londoner Bob Tate, who before joining the police had served in the Royal Ulster Rifles, augmented food supplies by removing and selling as many of the Japanese furnishings as were portable. The home government provided a weekly allowance of three shillings and

178

sixpence (eighteen new pence) to buy toilet requisites – a small piece of black-market soap, a razor blade or toothpowder the next week. Jack Liddell, a prominent British businessman in Shanghai who had been imprisoned with us, and the French Banque de l'Indochine each made loans of five American dollars to all police personnel.

An American propaganda film shown for the benefit of Chinese officials made a prominent display of the flags of the United States, China and France during a victory parade. Unless the hardly discernible flutter of a banner at the side of the screen bore the Union Jack insignia our flag seemed to be non-existent. This led to several American officers, who had flown in the Royal Air Force prior to America's entry in the war in 1941, to walk out in disgust. The Americans clearly were set to take over the former British predominant position in China and the large influx of their pre-war China businessmen, including several repatriated from our camp in 1943, in military uniforms guaranteed that no time was going to be wasted in assuming the predominant political and commercial role.

Jock Bain, police colleague and former Seaforth Highlander, and I decided that the only way to cure our inability to sleep in the softness of our beds in the Hotel de Peking to which we had been transferred from the Japanese hotel was to bed down on the thick carpet for some time before tackling the beds for a second attempt to avoid insomnia.

Shortly after this we heard piercing screams and the thud of running feet along the corridors of the four floors below. The realisation dawned that the violent rocking of my bed before and after waking had not been a dream but stark reality. There had been an earth tremor. I switched on my bed-lamp and more prolonged tremors

179

followed to set the large centre light in the room swinging like a pendulum gone mad. Our beds rocked wildly but the three of us in the room tacitly agreed that we would not join in the panic and the tremors having subsided we returned to our slumbers. Half-asleep we were dimly aware of the sound of the panic-stricken assembly returning to their rooms. At breakfast later the assertion of an Old China Hand that there had been too much ado about nothing would have been more convincing had the room he shared with other old men been on the fifth instead of the ground floor.

When it seemed likely that we were destined to spend a bleak northern winter in Peking we received the glad tidings that an American troopship would take us back to Shanghai. So in October we set sail from the nearest port, Taku, escorted by a British frigate which cleared the way through several minefields laid by the Japanese. Understandably we did annoy the American cooks aboard the troopship when our fat-starved stomachs refused to accept the huge and generous helpings of bacon, eggs and the accompanying trimmings of what they considered to be a normal breakfast. In time, of course, they cut down the helpings and gave us extra rolls in lieu of the solids we just could not take. Five days later we were back in Shanghai.

We were accommodated in the high-rise Embankment Building close to the river and the Soochow Creek. Shanghai was no longer the foreign administered city it had been for more than a century. In 1943 the Allies had returned the treaty ports to the government of Chiang Kai-shek and China's largest city was, for the first time, completely administered by a Chinese council headed by Mayor K C Wu. All police duties and all other services were now carried out by the Chinese. Foreign-owned businesses such as Jardine's, Butterfield & Swire, the

Shanghai Power Co., the Shanghai Tramways and the western banks continued to operate as before but there was no place for former personnel of the Shanghai Municipal Police, the River Police, the Customs and other law-enforcement units. There was a large presence of American naval and military personnel along with a much smaller British services contingent. There were security jobs on the docks and elsewhere and former SMP men and other westerners found temporary employment. In 1949 and 1950 the defeat of Chiang and the total conquest of the mainland by Mao Tse-tung saw all foreign-owned businesses nationalised and practically all former treaty-power nationals expelled from China.

In the Embankment Building I found a note addressed to me by the China director of a large British firm, who had flown back to Britain after our release in Fengtai. He asked me to meet him at the Palace Hotel in Nanking Road and that evening he confirmed that the permanent position he had offered me before he flew home had been approved in London. He paid for the meal of soggy chips and leather-sole meat plus four beers with notes amounting to a quarter of a million Chinese yuen. He left an almost equal amount for the waitress as her tip. The Chinese currency was at that time practically worthless. Wages had to be carried in kitbags with notes tied in bundles of half a million each. A trip to the market would cost more than two million yuen. It was no wonder that the American dollar, the world's strongest currency, was the most powerful financial unit in the city and that nearly all business deals were conducted in that medium.

The job was in China. I didn't take it. An old police friend was employed in my place and he lasted about five years before Mao booted out the foreigners. I offered myself at the British consulate as a potential member of a police force being recruited to administer law and order in the former Italian colonies in Africa. The job was on offer through the consulate which registered my application. I took temporary work with other ex-policemen making out manifests for air freight with the American forces. Illiterate or semi-illiterate for the most part, the GI hillbillies loading the planes relied entirely on us to indicate what and which went where. They were a likeable lot generous to a fault. They kept us well supplied with strong American Air Force coffee which only they could buy.

On many occasions Britain's fall from predominance in China was brought home to us. It was during my visit to the Palace Hotel shortly after our arrival from Peking that I met a young woman, thin and pinched of features, whom I remembered as an extremely attractive hostess in the bar of the hotel. I had last seen her throwing wine glasses in fury at the retreating figure of her latest boyfriend. Like many others she had suffered under the Japanese heel when work of any kind was unavailable and starvation faced her and many others in a similar plight. Her pleasure at seeing me lasted only so long as it took her mind to adjust to the mistaken belief that I was going to buy her a meal. When it reached the point where I realised that she was incapable of absorbing the fact that the once all-powerful Britisher she had known had not so much as the price of a bowl of rice in his pocket, I left her. The look of hurt bewilderment in her eyes haunted me for days afterwards. It still does whenever I think of it. On one occasion as I was on the point of greeting an American ex-policeman with whom I had worked in Chengtu Road he broke off his conversation with a trio of American relief officers just long enough to say, 'Nothing here for you fellows,' before pointedly turning his back.

Similarly, a White Russian, Petchenuk, with whom I had passed through the depot, informed us with evident pleasure that our country had lost all its former influence and would never again be a world power. So far as the Russians in Shanghai were concerned this was an isolated incident. While the Settlement police force was almost totally a British-administered and manned unit both the American and the stateless White Russian, locally enrolled rather than on contract from a home country, enjoyed the same status as the British members. After the war most Russians in Shanghai opted to settle in Australia. Petchenuk decided to go to the Soviet Union. In common with those who had chosen the Soviet Union previously, Petchenuk solemnly promised that he would write and advise the Russians he had left behind on conditions in the Soviet Union. Like them he never did. Petchenuk vanished in the immensity of Russia.

I went into a shop owned by two sisters on Bubbling Well Road with Malcolm to buy a kimono as a present for his sister back home. The younger English-speaking sister asked the elder if the usual charge of 200,000 yuen would be all right. She was told to double the price to 400,000 because as American marines we could well afford it. The first appeared hesitant and told her sister that she thought we were not Americans. The other insisted that because we were tall we must be and to demand the top price. Still insisting she was right the first complied and told Malcolm in English that the cost would be 400,000. Amused by this exchange we told the first girl that she had been right in her guess, and could we please have the gown for 200,000 yuen. Doubled with laughter she told her sister we had understood the dialogue whereupon she ran from the shop in blushing confusion while the other, still enjoying her sister's discomfiture and loss of face, handed over the kimono at the lesser price. Settling aside all ethics, they could hardly be blamed for getting all they could from the highly-paid GIs.

Back in Britain Winston Churchill's Conservative government had been defeated and Clement Attlee had become Labour Prime Minister. This caused some difficulty for Russian-speaking Tiny Pitts acting as interpreter for Soviet air force crews landing in Shanghai. All of them expressed high regard for Churchill and wanted to know why an unknown politician such as Attlee had been able to unseat him. Pitts, usually eloquently fluent in quick expositions on many topics, found himself as puzzled as they were.

Finally, the day arrived when many of us said, sadly, our farewells to Shanghai. The British ship, *Highland Chieftain,* had berthed in the Whangpoo and this was to carry me back home to start a second police career – this time in Africa.

As the *Highland Chieftain* moved away from the wharf to start the homeward voyage strong surges of emotion gripped us as we watched a large crowd of Chinese, many with tears in their eyes, wave their last goodbyes. Lifelong friends, still staying in Shanghai, wished us godspeed and a happy landing in the old country. Slowly we reached midstream and the ship moved slowly down river to enter the Yangtzse at Woosung. We looked over the ship's rail at the vanishing skyline of the Bund, for many the last time.

As we watched the familiar skyline and busy scene at the wharves where a British Blue Funnel freighter was loading the selfsame eggs that we ate every Sunday morning in my youth, there came a sudden confrontation with the Americans that could have had more serious consequences than it did. A landing craft was overtaking us at speed.

With a peremptory hoot on its siren it told us, 'Get the hell out of my way!'

We watched its downriver course, too fast, erratic. It was obviously out of control as it collided side on with the much bigger *Highland Chieftain.* So far as we were concerned there was no alarm. Our vessel had hardly budged one inch through the impact. The American landing craft, however, was not so lucky. There was a large gash in its side, its guard rail was severely buckled and a row of soldiers went unceremoniously head over heels down into the lavatory pans over which, bare-bottomed, they had been squatting at the time.

The next day I counted myself lucky that Dr Sturton, our camp physician, was sailing with us. His Chinese experiences had fitted him with the knowledge of the disease pellegra, a form of beri-beri which produces acute inflamation of the gums, tongue and throat and makes eating difficult and later impossible. Immediately Dr Sturton diagnosed my condition as even cold water scalded my mouth and throat like liquid fire. Although he was a sick man and visibly dying of cancer he injected me with a new drug from the ship's medical supplies called penicillin. In two days I was eating again. Once again we had cause to remember the selfless heroism of this missionary doctor without whose Christian humanitarianism our plight in camp would have been very much worse. I remembered the time in camp when Dr Sturton, bedridden and suffering painfully, had continued with the help of an ex-American navy sick-bay attendant whom we affectionately called 'Doc' Craddock, to tend every sick prisoner either in his makeshift surgery or in the camp hospital. If ever sainthood was the reward for selfless service to suffering mankind then the name of Sturton must rank high in the heavenly roll of honour.

In Hong Kong, our first port of call, efforts were made to recruit us as replacements for police force regulars then on a seven-month recuperative leave after internment during the Japanese occupation of the colony. Bill Carr, who had joined the force earlier, was given the day off and an extra ration of Scotch to help to persuade his old Shanghai police pals to join the force. Sadly, Carr was killed some weeks later in a traffic accident in Hong Kong. I refused the bait and continued on to England.

For the first two weeks on the *Highland Chieftain* we found our stomachs could not cope with the generous breakfast offering of bacon and two eggs. Loath to waste the eggs we tried hawking them around the ship only to be met by others making their various ways to our quarters in the hope that we could help them out by taking theirs.

We slept in hammocks or, at least, for the first night we curled up banana fashion in hammocks. From the second day onwards we found the steel deck, warmed by the engine room below, far more to our liking. Long war service had run the ship down and accommodation was crowded. Still all of us looked forward eagerly to setting foot in the old country once again.

Seven weeks later the ship berthed in Southampton. We who had applied to join the police forces of the ex-Italian colonies in Africa were taken by train to a now almost empty Army transit camp in Clapham to await the call from Whitehall to take the required examinations. In the meantime, some of us submitted applications for permanent employment in the Hong Kong police. These, we were informed, had to be turned down, since our three years as prisoners of the Japanese counted as eight. Thus we were too old.

186

8

THE NORTH AFRICAN POLICE

From Clapham we were sent to an old army camp near Kidderminster to await the outcome. A stay enlivened on one occasion by a question from an old soul obviously under the impression that we were Chinese. He wanted to know why we didn't go back to where we belonged.

We all passed the exams and the air of near melancholy at the prospect of still another separation from the wives with whom they had but lately been reunited after the prison camps was very apparent in the sadder and wiser demeanour of most of the other eleven ex-SMP (Shanghai police) fellows I joined in Southampton. This was in marked contrast to that other party of young SMP recruits imbued with the spirit of Empire who had touched briefly on this port *en route* to China those many years ago. Even the sight of all the ATS girls, whose officers overlooked our lone table in the first class saloon of the P&O *Strathnaver,* heading out for Port Said did nothing to dispel that despondency –heightened no doubt, by a sobriety enforced by lack of funds.

A young BMA (British Military Administration) police officer returning from home leave advised us to plump for postings to any of the five ex-Italian territories under offer except Cyrenaica which due to its war-ravaged state – lack of police quarters, amenities in general and strict police commandant whose promotion exams few ever passed, was staffed only by volunteers.

Two quiet weeks at sea enforced by our lack of funds brought us to Port Said from where we went by train to Cairo where the non-appearance of the official we had been told to expect put us in the hands of bag-grabbing 'Show you cheap hotel Johnny' hotel touts who found us rooms for the night.

Reporting at the British Military Administration HQ at Kasra-El-Nil next day we were collectively told that every effort would be made to send each man to the territory of his choice. The first of the single men to get an official account of the hardships to be endured in Cyrenaica I was agreeably impressed by the Administrator who could see in me a sensible, mature character who would under no circumstances insist on going to Eritrea when this would condemn a married friend to living in Cyrenaica under conditions fit only for the single. And since, he pointed out, all the positions in the other territories had now been filled by my married friends he was sure that I would volunteer for Cyrenaica. The example of my acceptance was followed by Fred Wells, always a realist and the others followed without demur.

Accommodation had been arranged for us at the New Zealand Club. Ensconced in comfortable rooms at the club for the duration of our five days in Cairo, we complied with official instructions to purchase from the officers' shop the £20 worth of uniform kit listed and paid for by them. We also visited Groppy's, famous for its ice cream, to drink our first local-brewed beers, and took taxi trips out to the pyramids and the Sphinx. On two of the nights lured by the bright lights, we tried vainly to recapture the inimitable and for us unforgettable atmosphere of Shanghai by visiting some of the several night clubs in the city with woeful results. In all truth the girls were just as attractive as those out East but even they, and the beer which was superior to that in Shanghai, could not dispel that funereal atmosphere which pervaded these places at night. The commercialism subtly played down in the East was as obvious here as the cold managerial appraisal afforded us on our arrival could make it – and the apathetic welcome of the hostesses who peeled themselves off in strict rotation from a line of chairs near the wall in an exact ratio of one for one and who, without reference to ourselves, were served soft drinks which were placed on our bills.

Following a disturbance at the door where a party of police had appeared on our first night we turned back to the table to the discovery that our beers had mysteriously vanished. Then, at a discreet signal from the girls we sat tight until after the police had gone, when the girls drew up their gowns and produced beers they had held nipped between their legs. The reason for this unusual charade, which was repeated on a second visit has always eluded me as the clubs were licensed and it was not after hours.

On our last night at the New Zealand Club when Malcolm incautiously agreed that we hear a brief *resumé* of a book written by an officer sharing our room for the night, I resolved that in the unlikely event of my ever writing one I would refrain from inflicting previews on others. Propped up in bed, the laddie in question ran us through a lengthy volume of adventures pertaining to those parts of the Middle East with which he was familiar for sixty long minutes. The final judgment from Malcolm whose fixed smile of polite interest had remained constant throughout, despite an early realisation of the enormity of his *faux-pas,* offered in response to the expectant pause at the end was: 'Quite good,' followed by a pointed good night – and a still more pointed request to the writer that he be a good fellow and turn off the light.

We returned to Port Said by train to board a small troopship for Benghazi where Inspector Jock Finlay took us to the warrant officers' mess which faced onto the harbour, and where the police occupied the entire ground floor section of the building. The quarters were spacious – even to the bathrooms which were furnished with outsize baths and toilets of such throne-like proportions that the account of the nurse accustomed to finding the seat on one in the permanent down position and who had hastened to the toilet last used by a male guest at their staff party and become wedged stern down is credible. She swore it was true.

From Jock we learned that we would be honorary members of the WO's bars and clubs, but as civilians without ration entitlement would eat at the town cafe where by arrangement we would be given breakfast comprising eggs heated in ghee (goat fat), and dark Arab bread at 6.30am.

Over pots of strong beer brewed by the army in Tripoli we met Alec Longland an ex-Palestine policeman who had an enviable record as a wartime saboteur in the Balkans; Alec Stewart the animal management officer, Tony Peake, accounts and Ken Edgington an ex-Grenadier who was president of the mess. The mile long walk along the harbour front and through streets of derelict buildings to the cafe in the main square that night was broken only twice by dim lights from the houses occupied by the only two Britons who had their wives with them. Apart from the dim glow from first the WO's club and another from the shuttered officers' mess the city was in darkness.

At police HQ next day we learned from the deputy police commandant, Major Gander, that while Arab

190

Palestine policemen were in charge of all police stations and did all police duties, we would be confined to stores and administration work. Following the departure of Fred and Nobby Clark to take these jobs in Oberdan training depot and Derna, Malcolm and I were left in Benghazi very much like spare cogs in a car without wheels. The Palestine and Rhodesian police officers who had organised the force from its inception on lines familiar to themselves were not much impressed with our scant knowledge of office procedure. For that matter neither were we. Additional to office duties the Inspectorate as we were known acted as duty officers at night when we dealt with any emergencies which might arise – like a mess running out of beer during curfew.

How to spend our off-duty time was easily decided. We could swim in the warm Mediterranean, walk over the dry salt flats outside the city or along the beach on which lay the hulk of the *Shanghai Moller* whose one-time wealthy owner was one of my fellow prisoners in Shanghai and later in Peking. By night we could drink at the bar above the mess or go to the club. Many of those evenings were made memorable by clever impromptu songs and recitations put over by the men accustomed to providing their own entertainment in the old days of Empire with an easy professionalism seldom seen now. I have still to see anything to equal Ken Edgington's skit on the myth that life in Libya was synonymous with hardship.

'Hardship,' he would bristle through his waxed moustache as he stalked solemnly to the open window to shade his eyes, while slowly sweeping the sea beyond the harbour – 'I see no hardship,' and his ensuing skits on these lines were so hilariously funny that we never tired of the act. There were songs like Galway Bay from Danny the Irish tenor and the old army marching songs played on the mouth organ of Big Hughy the farrier – a veteran of the North West frontier. Strong army brewed beer at eight cents for a large bottle undoubtedly played a large part in our enjoyment of these unforgettable nights. But without this dying breed, life in Benghazi would have been grim indeed.

Malcolm and I were seen a second time by Acting Commandant Major Gander. We were told that Malcolm was to become assistant paymaster and I was to familiarise myself with admin work with a view to eventual transfer to a district at a later date. The startling recommendation made by an unhappy Malcolm, dismayed at the prospect of becoming a paymaster, to the effect that I, being remarkably well endowed with brilliance in all things mathematical would have been a better choice for the pay job than he, was, to my intense relief, dismissed by the Acting Commissioner with the contempt I thought it deserved.

Detailed to escort bullion from Tripoli by road the question of food for the two days came up. A letter from our HQ requesting rations from the NAAFI was rejected. As a civilian they said, I was not entitled to them. A further plea from the same source resulted in my being handed a twopenny packet of biscuits and two ounces of cocoa. On the morning of departure floods on the Tripoli road forced cancellation of the military bus, but deck passages on a tiny Israeli coaster were secured in lieu. After an amused look at my rations when offered the use of the galley, the skipper invited me to share the four-man crew's mutton stew. Next day I met ex-Shanghai Police Sergeant McLennan now in the Tripoli police and in the bright light of a full moon accompanied him on his duty tour of the city. Here, the brown sandstone government buildings set in ornamental limestone gardens with their sunken pools surrounded by the night fragrance of fig and grape vines were in pleasing contrast to the harsh white and the marble replicas in Benghazi. My – by now – hazy recollections are of a Moorish city, little affected by the Italian occupation.

A day in the old Barbery port of Sirte by the Tunisian border with Ginger Brown last seen standing at the rail of the troopship we had left in Benghazi, and I boarded the military bus for the return trip, this time with a packet of meat sandwiches kindly prepared by the Italian mess caterer. Back in Benghazi I learned that I had been transferred to Benghazi District as Administration Officer and that the warrant officers' mess had accepted us as honorary members on payment of a monthly contribution to be utilized in the purchase of foodstuffs now being brought in from Tripoli.

The necessity of paying constables at an isolated oasis gave me the first sight of the desert proper. The oasis was about 120 miles inland from a point about 120 miles along the Tripoli Road. It being the only habitation between there and Chad two camel men who made six yearly trips to Siwa Oasis, 600 miles away on the Libya/Chad border, accompanied me as guides. After hours of running inland over stretches of unbroken sand the clear outline of a large town appearing unexpectedly on the horizon led me to wonder whether we were on a true course – but a glance at the guides staring stoically ahead without apparent interest, reassured me to the extent that they saw nothing unusual in the view. I considered it advisable to keep my doubts private for the ten minutes I estimated it would take us to get there, before airing my ignorance, with premature inquiries. So, I concentrated on the scene ahead once more, to see a second town taking shape in the far distance while the first, much nearer now, appeared to be blurring at the edges and floating in a hazy vagueness which commenced to shrink in size until we reached that point where the angle of light and shadow which had created the illusion of a town, dispersed to reveal the formation of stones which, standing in the bright sunlight only inches above the flat desert sand, had formed the substance of my first mirage.

Towards late afternoon the guides showed uncertainty making frequent stops to scan the horizon for a tree-capped hill which they said should now be near. Later, I realised that to these men accustomed to the flatness of the desert, the low mound topped with scrub we eventually came upon could just conceivably fit their description of the landmark we had been seeking. The apologetic guides, who were accustomed to picking out landmarks in leisured sequence over a period of five days from the backs of slowly moving camels, told me they were confused by the speed with which the truck passed from one marker to the next. But they got me there eventually.

The headman of the oasis escorted me to a hut in which his servants were erecting his most treasured possession: a huge iron bed complete with canopy and brass knobs on which, despite my protests that I could manage under the truck, he insisted that I sleep that night. He also gave us food, a sheep roasted in its own fat over two hastily gathered wood fires – by the light of which we sat cross-legged on the ground – to eat at leisure. Early next morning I witnessed the saga with which the dates we had for breakfast were harvested from the oasis palms. One man simply grasped the two ends of a short rope looped round the rough bole of one of the most prolific palms – all were slightly off the perpendicular and a good forty feet high – and literally walked up the trunk aided by sharp forward pulls on the rope which he raised a foot at a time in tune with his rapid

194

ascent. The trip back with dates still in the clusters in which they had been dropped from the trees into the body of our truck was simplified by driving back along our own tracks which in these hard red sands would remain clearly visible for years to come.

I was thankful that there were no women living within sight of the mess when, perhaps in need of an early lunch the day I got back, whoever was responsible for water economy turned the cock prematurely and forced me thereby to take a running dive from the mess into the harbour to remove the soap covering me from head to foot at the time.

As the truck taking me on transfer to the Jebel two months later left the lower sea level plains carpeted now by the tiny multi-coloured flowers produced by the recent rains and climbed up the steep Barce Pass there was a drop in temperature I would not previously have thought possible in Africa. Despite the heavy coat I was wearing I was shivering with cold when we reached Barce. My new quarters comprising four rooms and kitchen with a wood fired stove, formed part of a fort-like police headquarters. The whole was set behind tall cypress trees close to the town centre.

The four large European farms in the district developed by the Italians which had fed practically the whole of Libya before the war were controlled now by two BMA majors – Paddy Bell, an Irish farmer who had held a similar position in West Africa, and Tom Reece a farming engineer from home. The popular Senior Officer and District Magistrate was Major Alec Stuart, professor of Arabic in Cairo University before the war whose fluent command of the language was so widely respected that his every edict was obeyed without question. These three officers, the police headed by the huge ex-Rhodesian policeman, Tiny Tantum, Captain

John Pestell also police, Dr Magdellany and the Custodian of Enemy Property were the mainstays of our small club bar which was the sole venue of our social activities.

When the German POW-driven water bowser omitted one or both of its twice-weekly calls we were obliged to confine tea making to the minimum amount of water the horses could spare from their troughs and resort to soda water from the club for shaving.

Throughout my first year hurricane lamps provided the only illumination available, and it was by this means that I studied for the impending examinations. But consequent upon the arrival of an engineer from home, the town's war-damaged generator was restored to supply light until a warning flick gave five minutes' notice of the impending switch-off at 9.45pm. This often put unwary visitors to the town in the dark. I was awakened one night by bewildered cries of 'Where the hell am I,' which I realised came from Big Hughy who was sleeping in the guest bed in my room while conducting a short farriery course in the police stables. I groped round the house made darker by the shade cast by the tall cypress trees outside the window, until I finally located him inside the large wardrobe he had mistaken for the toilet.

To my immense relief, district storeman, Sub Inspector Fred Spragg returned from leave in time to organise the annual police feaster. Arab police constables' wives were called in to hand-roll the tiny pellets of wheaten couscous to be served with the meat. Our spirit rations, supplemented with bottles of cheap Cyprus brandy and gin, were placed on the long dining room table on the night of the event. Two eighteen stone, give or take a few pounds each way, belly dancers who chanced to be passing through Barce *en route* to Cairo that night, were engaged to perform for a fee of £5. Intended as a pleasant surprise, the two were smuggled into the dining room before dark and requested not to show themselves until called.

As darkness fell we welcomed the colourfully dressed sheikhs and notables as they arrived and saw them settled with at least one Briton in attendance on the cushions set in groups by each of the half dozen fires lighted to illuminate the compound. It was after the food had been generally enjoyed and the sheikhs, notables and such members of the off-duty force who had been able to attend were sitting in relaxed enjoyment, listening to the last of the performances spontaneously provided by the police singers and story tellers with which the Jebel Police was so richly endowed that Fred gave the signal which should have brought the girls out dancing. But didn't.

It did, however, cause the girls' agitated manager to appear at the half-open door. When we got a view over his shoulder of his two Amazon dancers gulping down without pause what remained in the two initially full bottles – one each of the cheaper gin and brandy they had taken from the sideboard – we resigned ourselves to the loss of our £5 – and began to think up ways and means of removing two drunken females from the house with the minimum of fuss.

The necessity for this was negated by the appearance of the girls themselves carrying their eighteen-odd stones in graceful gyrations towards the circle of guests. They put up a twenty-minute performance which amazed and delighted everyone present. For our part, our fascinated gaze remained rivetted throughout on their swiftly moving feet – willing them not to decimate the ranks of the notables by falling in their midst. Offering our thanks when it was all over we were met with timid requests for farewell drinks. The two bottles, one of Cyprus gin and one of local brandy, handed over by Fred in admiration of their performance and capacity for strong drink, were emptied without effect in even less time that the first.

The return of Colonel George Lavel, the Police Commissioner, from leave presaged the imminence of our compulsory participation in the Force's confirmatory examinations. In due course we assembled in the old mess for the traditional reunion with old friends afforded by this occasion. This was anything but conducive to the clear thinking desirable for the ensuing three days we would spend in the Commission's office.

Taking a Guards-trained squad of Chinese police, fully conversant with all English words of command in foot drill is hardly the best preparation for passing out in foot, arms and ceremonial drill in Arabic in the main Civic Square in Benghazi. Especially when under the direction of a keen new examining officer who switched from the time-honoured procedure of permitting the examinee to call the commands in whatever sequence came most readily to his mind – provided he covered the whole repertoire in the manual – to one requiring him to translate into Arabic, and transmit to the moving squad a sequence of commands selected by the examiner and conveyed to the examinee in English. However, despite a lapse of memory which afforded amusement and some derisive laughter respectively from the mixed civilian and military lookers-on when, following an 'About turn' in my ear, my mind dredged up in rapid succession the Arabic for right and left wheels and inclines – any of which would have turned the squad implacably marching forward, but failed to bring up the required 'Kelf-dor' before they were in an ornamental flower bed – from which I extracted them with what dignity I could. Despite this I did get through – if not with honours at least with a pass.

The belief that all army NCOs are out and out bastards was hardly borne out on one of these nights by the pre-prandial interrogation of the German POW cook conducted by Ken Edgington in the mess kitchen as we sat down to dinner.

'Where's your dinner Albert? Oh, you've just had it, have you? Then show me your dirty plates.'

Pause for an inaudible reply from Albert. 'Ah, you've just washed them up have you? Albert, you're a b....y liar. You and your mate have had no dinner, that is, apart from spuds and gravy. Now don't lie to me.'

A pause, then 'Who's still to come? Let me see. Seven police, WO Smith and myself? Right, put those nine plates on the table.' Pause. 'Now bring two more plates.' Pause. 'Now split the meat from those nine plates between the eleven, and you and your mate take a plate each, and in future,' in sarcastic tone, 'no eating beforehand. I want to see the police rations, yours and your mate's, and our two on the table when I get back here every night at seven o'clock. You can't live on spuds and b....y gravy.'

Attempting to re-establish his tough image after realising he had been overheard, his 'Silly bastards, impossible to find cooks like those two,' fooled no one save possibly Ken himself.

As a result of my immediate upgrading to full inspector after passing the examinations and the cuts successively imposed by the Foreign and Colonial offices as they took control of Libya, Fred's duties were added to my own.

On his handover to me we left HQ with bedrolls, a billycan made from, in the absence of anything else, a large jam tin scrounged from the army and goat meat sufficient for two days in our only saucepan in our three ton ex-army truck which judging by its appearance had survived but only just, the whole of the Western Desert Campaign. Our route took us along the south road still liberally festooned with booby-trapped vehicles left by the retreating German Army to pay police at posts on the way to the one-time Italian Administration Centre in the sub-division of Cirene – now known by its Arab name as Shahat.

Completing our check of the station in Shahat early the following day gave us time to see the mosaics in the ruins of Cirene at the foot of tomb-honeycombed hills of this ancient monument to the early Greek and Roman civilisations, recently uncovered by archaeologists from the British Museum. The climb up a seemingly endless series of stone steps in gathering darkness brought us to the former Italian Administration building – high above and a mile outside Shahat – to the sleeping quarters used by police when visiting Shahat.

It was like entering a huge marble hotel bereft alike of staff or furnishings and peopled only by the unseen ghosts of the cremated remains of the long-dead early invaders – contained in row upon row of marble urns in the crypt-like chambers beneath the main hall from which – by a shallow-stepped marble staircase of exaggerated width flanked on both sides by menacing sculptures of massive proportions which dwarfed us both – I followed Fred through the upper chambers to a small room in which the wartime RAF had covered the white marbled floor with packing case timber and built a small bar.

On none of the many cold winter nights listening to the receding sound of my departing truck as I climbed those stairs under the sightless gaze of first Apollo and then the larger-than-life Hercules followed by others unknown, each appearing briefly in the flickering light of my oil lamp before merging with the darkness behind, before settling down on this small bar floor with one blanket folded three ways under and two on top, did I ever dispute Fred's assertion that there was no warmer place in the Jebel.

Descending the Apollonia Pass to sea level next day we stopped to swim in the pool cut out of solid bedrock which if there is any truth in the legend, and I think there is, was created by Mark Antony for the use of Cleopatra, about twenty by ten feet by eight feet high and sited to fill with the rising tide and empty with the ebb – the perfect symmetry of its walls and the steps leading into it, with its attendant labour costs, ruled out any possibility of its having been created at any time other than in Biblical times.

It was while Fred and I were rising replete from a meal cooked by the wife of one of our station officers at the next stop and agreeing that the lady in question had been well worth the twenty-odd camels paid for her by way of the traditional dowry, that a grinning staff sergeant Adbel Rahim – aware of the adage that good relations must always take precedence over personal considerations – announced that a local notable had invited us to a second lunch. Despite being helped by the sympathetic sergeant when our host was not looking it was only after a two day tea-only diet that we got back to normal eating habits.

In answering the query put to the villagers from whom I bought my monthly supply of half-addled eggs – reminiscent of the cheap China eggs of my shooldays – as to why some were more addled than others it was explained with that air reserved for answering questions put by fools like me. The good eggs they said, had been laid and collected during the month of my last visit. The semi-addled ones had probably been laid before my last call and not found at the time. The darker ones which exploded at the touch of a knife must have lain out in the surrounding scrub for months before being found and sold to me.

A possible reason for the dearth of small birds in the Jebel presented itself one afternoon when an African starling – losing all fear of man in face of an attack from a large hawk – dropped like a stone to land between my back and the stone wall against which I was sitting, and from there to my knee, where he crouched for a full minute until quite certain that the sky was clear before taking off in low level retreat.

When, in ever increasing numbers the town's pi-dogs fell to harassing those on foot and their night-long barking added to the high pitched howls of the often rabid jackals and hyenas which came in from the desert at dusk it made sleep impossible. It was time for the periodic kill. With the memory of the many donkeys, those ill fed, ill treated and always overladen little workhorses of the Middle East seen daily in the army veterinary hospital at D'Annunzio with their under-bellies torn open by the pi-dogs, always in mind this was almost a pleasure. With a shotgun used in the town for the sake of safety I killed all but those endowed with that uncanny sixth sense which warned them to retreat beyond its short range who then turned to fix me with that same skulking malevolence they displayed when threatening at close quarters those walking in town not armed with a thick stick. These, picked off later with a light target rifle were replaced within weeks from the same source: the open desert.

Though he was not able to give us the whys and wherefores, it was from an unreported bite from one of these dogs that an Arab boy suffered the same fate as the boy I remembered in Shanghai. He, like the Arab boy, failed to report a bite from a strange dog. The father of

202

this boy, a city businessman who detected the first signs of rabies in the boy while the family were at breakfast, willed himself to act normally until his unsuspecting wife and daughter left the table at the end of the meal. He then enticed the boy to the locked room from which he was later removed to the isolation hospital in which weeks later he died a horrible death.

In Shanghai a person bitten was given stomach injections daily for thirty-odd days if the animal was not found or killed at the time. A painful bruise resulted from each injection and, as I was to find out myself, such exertions as sneezing, coughing, laughing or even any movement produced such pain as to be not easily forgotten.

In my case, I had seized a dog that had bitten a Chinese girl. The animal in its turn bit me. My anti-rabies ordeal then began.

Luckily, there was a happy half-way ending of the injection distress when, after two weeks, the dog that had bitten me was found to be free of rabies. Three police colleagues in Shanghai, however, who had been nipped while playing with a stray puppy discovered to be rabid, had to undergo the full course of injections.

At Barce hospital, after a large family dog I had been asked to shoot, and thought to be rabid, had taken advantage of the sudden appearance of the small son of the house in the line of fire to lunge forward and fasten its teeth in my leg I was relieved to hear that the old lengthy course of injections had now been reduced to just one.

A lesser menace, but a nuisance for all that, was the rubbery camel fly whose erratic flight made its movements difficult to follow or anticipate just where and when it would strike. On spider-like legs it alighted so softly that its victim remained unaware of its presence until a stab like a red-hot needle made him oblivious to anything else. Impervious to hard swatting, the only sure way to deal with them was to trap and roll them under the hand until legs and wings were entwined and then crush them between two hard objects before they untangled themselves to return to the attack. Attacks at night were the worst and betrayed only by a barely audible hum of wings when they passed close to the ear. Any defensive slapping at bare arms, legs and neck in the hope of trapping them was rarely successful in the darkness. They simply stood off to assess just which limb was getting the least attention, and then unerringly homed on to that.

There was a very strong belief that the house I occupied was haunted. So much so, that when Alec Stewart the Animal Management Officer and his wife Mary (a direct descendent of Ferdinand de Lesseps, the French engineer who built the Suez Canal) lived there. Mary insisted that she and Alec sleep on the back verandah within days of moving into the house. Under no circumstances would she sleep inside the house. It was rumoured that years before, an Italian officer in the Carabinieri had been murdered in the master bedroom in which I slept, and it was he who haunted the house.

At least twice a month during the more than three years I slept in that room I was awakened by violent shakings of my bed during the night. Fearing at the time I was heading for a heart attack I took the opportunity, after Dr Magdallany had made the annual medical check the Foreign Office insisted we take, to ask the condition of my heart.

'Strong as a bell,' he said. These periodic awakenings continued throughout my long stay in the house, but ceased from the day I was transferred back to Benghazi and have never recurred since.

Passing through Beda-Littoria, the scene of the unsuccessful attempt on the life of Marshal Erwin Rommell we called on Major John Briggs, a former Scots-born Canadian wheat farmer presently handing over management of the Barce wheat plains, and his small house to his Libyan successor. After the usual black coffee had been served, ours in the customary small glasses and his in a cracked tooth glass, he started a long discourse about the combine harvesters he had introduced to Barce. Twice he broke off to ask if we would like two cognacs but failed to produce despite our eager acceptance. Finally, with that touch of impatience reserved for the gormless he asked if we thought we were in the Waldorf and if not, and we still wanted the bloody drinks, would we kindly empty our glasses so he'd have something to put them in.

The barman's shame-faced admission to those of us still in the bar after his and Fred's combined farewell party, that he could not make a rainbow cocktail, prompted Fred to try for himself. From all the ingredients lining the shelves his every effort produced, with all the concentration of a scientist breaking new ground, mixtures suggestive more of something in which a navvy had washed his socks than something to drink. These, inspired no doubt with the need for economy urged on us all in those days, he passed to each in turn with a request to 'drink up'. Our willing compliance was the probable reason why I was the only one there early next day to see Fred off and the only one to whom the harassed officer responsible for the convoy due to meet the troopship at Tobruk could ask the probable whereabouts of a major named Briggs whose bags were already on the bus.

An inspired guess from Fred took us down the Barce Road where we found him by a line of working harvesters, oblivious alike of the time and the enormous personal expense which could accrue should he miss the bus, giving out last minute advice to all and sundry. A subject he continued nonstop all the way back to Barce and resumed, if facial expressions were any indication, in the ear of the unfortunate Fred from the moment he boarded the bus, caught only by the skin of his teeth.

While a bogged-down truck lost most of the first day of one desert pay tour it earned for me the unique experience of sleeping rolled up behind the roofless mud-and-reed windbreak two friendly nomads called home. And the unforgettable sight of the rain-washed desert slowly emerging as far as could be seen in the dawn light of an orange-red sun.

By late afternoon the unbroken vista of flat desert and sky gave way to sparsely vegetated ridges in the sand dotted with the scores of grazing camels tended by Ali for those more affluent than he. As I studied his lean sunblackened face and perfect teeth the town Arab's strong belief that a few months in the desert on a camel milk diet was the absolute cure for every imaginable ailment appeared less of the myth than I had previously thought. For that was all he had, fresh in the morning and curdled at night. After I'd paid the four mounted police constables whose duty it was to ride herd on the roped together camels at night, to safeguard them from theft by desert wilderness-based tribes, whose night rustling habits were well known, we parted next day with mutual thanks. We for the petrol-flavoured milk he had tipped into our emptied jerry can, and he for the welcome gift of the stale, coarse maize bread crusts Hassan, our driver, had salvaged from our meals on the way out. This would be his only variation in diet during the three to four months which would elapse before the grazing gave out.

Our bi-annual pay and inspection party comprising the district police commander, the district farrier sergeant, storeman, armourer and myself stopped to stretch our legs at a point four hours' drive from home. The last leg of a two week tour of the district. The farrier seized the opportunity to make a fire under the impression that someone in the party would still have tea. The water was boiling before he discovered that in line with my usual custom, I had handed mine to driver Hassan before leaving HQ. The DC had done the same, and as his fellow NCOs had none left the question of tea was dropped. That was until one of them noticed a lone camel man approaching from the direction of Barce. Speculation as to who he might be ranged from one to the other until he was identified as Ali Tahir, last seen by one of them serving six months in Barce Jail. Returning now, it was assumed, to his family, and camping out in the desert with supplies which would include, they knew, the last three months' tea and sugar ration from the government. My objections to a truck-borne police party heading for home – and the source of all supplies – cadging from a man making a three day camel journey into empty desert were dismissed with polite amusement. The remarkable good grace with which Ali parted with the tea appeared to support their view. But a noticeable disinclination on his part to accept their invitation to join in the tea drinking could have been motivated I thought, by a wish to be as far away as possible when, and if, a similar deficiency in sugar came to light.

This came to mind when Hassan emerged from my house with all the tea-making impediments as we prepared for an all-night patrol to an outlying grain farm where water was in short supply. Feigning shock that I should imagine him so selfish when I made it clear he was not to scrounge water from our troopers on all night watch for the Bedouins who cut and carried away standing grain by the camel load, he asked me to wait and see. Hours later, guided no doubt by gossip picked up in the suq he homed on to, and then followed, the deep wheel tracks made by a heavy tractor during the rains to a place where it had bogged down. There, with all the showmanship of a conjuror producing his first rabbit he pointed to the few inches of muddy water still in the hole. With that same disregard for economy which would have applied equally had it been his own, he added four, as opposed to the two cupped handfuls of tea he considered the bare minimum for two, to the scooped up engine-oil flavoured water to make tea as good as any I could expect this side of the next home leave.

The Russian member of the four man United Nations fact-finding commission had a tendency to stop every Tom, Dick and Ali encountered on their tour through the Jebel to ask his views on the British Administration. This seemed to the 'seen and heard it all before' French and British members such a waste of time, that by mid-morning they ceased to take part in it. An example quickly followed by the American when one small group being questioned about what form of government would best suit Libya asked the Russian, through the interpreter, where Libya was.

Just as I was becoming vaguely aware of an alien drug-dominated music rising and falling in the near distance while on my way home from the club one night I met police relief driver Ahmed. He, after identifying the music as the accompaniment to dances staged annually by temporary harvesters from his native Tripolitania in celebration of the end of their contracts, and exiled from home, invited me to be the first European ever to witness the event. Chairs were placed on the verandah of a long-empty colonial bungalow inside which ten men were squatting in the glow from a large wood fire. As we sat down two with flutes and three with drums set up a throbbing low key rhythm. After kicking the fire into a wide circle they started a jerky stiff jointed movement round the fire which quickened in tune with the music until what had been a simulated action, slowly developed into a series of movements dominated entirely by the hypnotic beat of the drums.

At this stage, like so many somnambulists with no will of their own they repeatedly advanced and retreated through the red-hot coals in their bare feet without a trace of emotion on their sweat streaked faces. Meanwhile, a scarecrow-thin greybeard, unsheathing a long knife attached to his belt emerged from the fire in front of my chair. With a superb showmanship he cut the skin under each of his eyes, the end of his tongue and several times in quick succession the air so close to my face that I felt the wind of its passing. In the absence of any reaction from me he then stepped back, placed the point against his stomach and slowly pressed until the blade was almost buried. Then, eyes seemingly sightless in their dilated opaqueness withdrew the knife to point wordlessly to the flow of blood from the cut.

Visibly nervous after the knife-slashing incident Ahmed's whispered request that we leave precluded any chance of discovering the secret of the knife trick at first hand. That the fire dancing was genuine was generally accepted, but none of the Arab officers who had seen it before could offer a reasoned explanation of how the trick, if it was a trick, was done. One theory that the blade retracted into the hilt was feasible only if the retraction started in the blade itself, as the hilt was far too short to take the whole blade. Another that the blade was flexible and conducted round the waist inside the belt of the loin cloth was too difficult for an old man to undertake with only the glow from the fire to see by.

There appeared to be two conflicting factors. No one in a truly hypnotic state could have made those knife slashes with such controlled precision as to avoid contact. But if he was under no such influence, the question of how he contrived to pass through the fire only seconds before the event without any sign of discomfort must, since the performers left Barce at first light, remain for me at any rate, the mystery it appeared to be that night.

Eventually, a half-formed decision to chance my arm in Australia sooner than take a third tour hardened when Arab officers took over the Jebel and I was returned to Benghazi where movement was restricted within the confines of endless salt flats, led me to reject the contract when offered.

Months later, a plaque in the bar of the P&O crewed *Empire Fowey* I had boarded in Tobruk told me that I was in the once oak panelled saloon of the ex-German ship *Potsdam*. Now refurbished in formica, but still the same ship on which we had joined the Americans for drinks in Hong Kong those many years ago.

9

AUSTRALIA

In 1950 the large-scale emigration to Australia of Britons under the assisted passage scheme greatly reduced my chances of securing a passage. However, I was fortunate in being offered a cancelled passage to Melbourne on the Glen Line motor vessel, *Dymas,* a twelve-passenger cargo ship, the only one of the many vessels I have known to accommodate its passengers two to a cabin in beds instead of bunks. All stewards and galley hands on board were Shanghai Chinese. Hal, the first mate, was still recovering from injuries sustained in June the previous year when his ship the *Anchises* was bombed by Chinese Nationalist planes while proceeding up the Whangpoo to Shanghai. The *Anchises* was a 9,000-ton cargo ship of the Liverpool based Blue Funnel Line. How is it then, I asked Hal, that he was sailing under the Glen Line house flag; because, he said, the Glen Line, being a wholly owned subsidiary of Blue Funnel, was merely a small extension of the Blue Funnel Line. The *Dymas* was making her last voyage before being broken up in Hong Kong. She called briefly at Port Said before berthing at her terminal port, Melbourne.

An announcement by the ship's purser at Port Melbourne that he only had sufficient Australian currency to cater for the families aboard worried me little until I discovered that sterling could only be changed at a

bank but as we had landed on a public holiday every bank
in the city was closed for the day. Even then I saw no cause
for concern as I had adequate sterling on my person to
last a week. I soon discovered that while sterling was
readily accepted wherever else I'd been, it was not
acceptable here in Melbourne. Most hotels were full and
those with rooms would not look at my British pounds.
Eventually, a well disposed policeman made a physical
swop of three for three Australian pounds and with these,
and with the help of a friendly Hungarian-born taxi-
driver, liberated and rehabilitated by the British after the
last war, I got a room at a pub close to Flinders Street
Station, the busiest railway terminus in the world.

In the dining room next morning the waitress asked if
I'd like an egg with it. My guess proved correct when a
rare, near inch-thick steak the size of the dinner plate on
which it was served, topped with an outsize fried egg, was
plonked on the table before me. A glance round the
tables revealed that 'with or without', this was the most
favoured breakfast or there was no alternative.

I stayed a week in Melbourne and then left for
Australia's largest city, Sydney, by the new diesel train
running under the name of *Spirit of Progress*. At the border
of Victoria and New South Wales we changed to the wide-
gauge, steam-hauled train running from the border
station, Albany, up to Sydney.

On boarding the train at Albany I was conscious of the
early-morning cold made worse by the failure of most of
the footwarmers in the compartment to provide even
minimal heat. An elderly couple with whom I shared the
compartment, amused at the belief common to all new
arrivals that it was always hot in Australia, lent me a
blanket to drape over my shoulders.

We were well on our way to Sydney when a man I
guessed to be in his thirties joined us after the train had

stopped at Katoomba in the Blue Mountains. We were soon in conversation and I quickly realised how different were the Jones and Browns and Smiths of Australia from their counterparts in Britain. Casually the man mentioned that he had just sold a hamburger shop in Katoomba to buy a pig farm near Sydney and that, without any prior knowledge either of hamburger enterprise or pigs, he had in both instances risked every penny he had.

The New South Wales capital, Sydney, was a teeming metropolis of pure Australian milieu with its infamous Kings Cross ten-shillings-a-time street girls, Paddington and its reportedly convict-built terraced houses, its pubs and hotels with their delicately enscrolled wrought-ironwork verandahs restored from the decrepit slums they once were and, most impressive of all the sights, the Sydney harbour bridge running from Dawes Point on the south to Milson Point on the north with a then world-record main span of 1,650 feet (503 metres) and clearance of 170 feet (51 metres) for vessels in the harbour. Today Sydney has a population well over three million. It was rapidly nearing that total when I arrived there.

The tacit and improbable-sounding alliance between the churches, brewers and landlords, aided by the arrangement whereby most firms completed the forty-hour week by 4pm on Friday was the direct cause of the frenetic Friday evening and Saturday morning drinking which was endemic in Sydney. The churches favoured the measure for obvious reasons, while the brewers and publicans could hardly be blamed for supporting a system which ensured high returns at low cost in restricted hours. Between four and six on Friday evenings and from 10am to 3pm on Saturdays they did their level best to ensure that their customers always six deep at the bar with eyes set on the clock, drank enough in those hours to set speed records in emptying glasses never equalled anywhere else in the world. Uncarpeted and seatless, the bars with their white-tiled walls were steam-hosed with detergent at 3pm on Saturdays. A hint no doubt to let customers know it was time to drink up and leave. That was the time the police in their Paddy Wagons, as they were called, roamed the streets picking up the incapables and, according to onlookers, some who were not, but had been drinking in the morning's five-hour long swill. All those arrested were held in the station until deemed sober enough and were released on payment of a fine. These fines, it was said, went some way to offsetting the high cost of police wages at the end of the month.

Since drinking Australian so-called beer served ice cold was not to my liking, I saw little of this, preferring rather to enjoy a few shots of Corio whisky with ex-Shanghai policeman Tom Rossington and his wife, Eileen. They had given me a room over their corner shop in Earlwood, a quiet Sydney suburb that looked less like a typical Hollywood Wild West township than most of the others I'd seen.

The old Shanghai connection was nostalgically recalled when the Rossingtons and I joined former SMP officer Johnny Weeks and wife Lolla, in visits to the Shanghai Russian Club in Strathfield. We could well have been back in a Shanghai night club so redolent of that great city's *joie de vivre* were the entire surroundings and the cosmopolitan crowd.

Among the floor show acts there were the Russian ballroom dancer and his wife, whom I had last seen in the Casanove night club in Shanghai. Now, as then, they finished their act standing one on each side of the buffet table stacked high with bottles of beer, vodka and food to acknowledge the applause of the audience that swelled to a deafening crescendo as the man reached over the table to lift his wife bodily over it, hold her briefly above his head as he saluted her with a kiss before setting her gently back on her feet by his side. A prodigious feat of strength for a man who fourteen years before in Shanghai had been already in his prime. Even the slimmest of professional dancing females do not come light as I recalled when I performed a Sir Galahad act in Shanghai and carried three of them across a deeply flooded road. It was with some relief that I set the last one down high and dry on her own two feet.

A newspaper advertisement was instrumental in my investing A£2,000 in a fisheries partnership being formed to troll for the giant Spanish mackerel off the coast of northern Queensland. While waiting for our mother ship to be fitted out I took a job making low-grade furniture the like of which was never produced even in the meanest English Midlands sweatshops during the depression years of the 1930s. Had I known from the outset of the many delays we were to face finding component parts for the fishing vessel I would have followed the example of many before me who had left the deadly monotony of the job the same day they had started but as completion was always just around the corner I stayed where I was. At that time work vacancies filled six pages of the *Sydney Morning Herald* every day. I wondered how the many Australians who comprised the main workforce, and described by one as a 'heads-down-and-arses-up-from-the-word-go-job', had endured these mind-numbing repetitive functions despite there being much better jobs on offer. I could only assume that it was the devil they did know as opposed to the one they didn't. In the opinion of one, who left the job within hours of starting, a rack should have been placed at the entrance on which our brains could be hung to be retrieved at the end of the day.

The Australian part of the workforce was varied. I had as workmates (but not for long) rough and tough men who were sheep shearers, outback station riders, gold and sapphire prospectors and kindred spirits who had forsaken the wilds for short spells of city life. To them could be added a handful of British immigrants, Poles, Czechs and other ethnic groups bent on accumulating enough funds to set up their own businesses. Last but not least there was the always half-drunk, part owner of a city night spot passing the time until his partner had apologised for accusing him, not without reason I suspect, of always being under the influence at the club.

As soon as our 112-foot twin diesel-powered Fairmile with three powered trolling boats on deck was completed we left Sydney for Townsville with all partners on board save one. Bill Davis, formerly of the China Maritime Customs, was to join us at Townsville. The skipper Ben, John Baldry and Cedric Pickering were Australians. The British element comprised Scottish farmer's son Tommy Lang, ex-Indian Army man Arthur Davison and White Russian George Novikov, an engineer engaged in Sydney. I made up the full crew.

As soon as we had sailed through the narrow channel flanked on both sides by high white cliffs and known locally as The Gap, the sole ingress to and egress from Sydney harbour, we each in turn took over the wheel at two hourly intervals to master the art of steering a ship at sea. When I took over this task at midnight I had no knowledge of the fact that to counter any sea or wind deviations from course, one had to turn the wheel in the opposite direction to the swing of the bows but not so much as to require much greater counteraction to bring a vessel back on true course. That way we learned, not only wasted fuel but left a wake like a dog's hind leg. Unlike a car, a ship under way runs at least, or more, three times its own length before it even starts to respond to a twist of the helm, all unkown to me then.

Two ships approaching at a fast rate worried me somewhat and deciding to give them a wide berth I pushed the wheel to starboard and in a sudden panic when the vessel showed no quick response I turned the wheel a full half circle. I had no desire to be responsible for the loss of a vessel that cost A£16,500. Alas, the result was disastrous. Instead of proceeding on course to Townsville I had the ship heading straight back to Sydney. In great alarm our skipper-instructor rushed up from behind, seized the wheel and expertly spun it the other way to set us back on course, and politely refrained from calling me the damn fool I felt myself to be.

There was a total lack of meat on board, so for us it was the red-fleshed bonito we pulled aboard, the only fish fast enough to hook itself to the long line we kept trailing in our wake, with scones baked by Jimmy, an Australian cook hired by Ben in Sydney, that we addressed ourselves to day after day. By the time we reached Townsville the condemnation of our diet of bonito and scones would have shocked any ears less delicate than ours – as well they might. We were to hear later that bonito was generally considered not fit for cat food, a fact that our by then queasy stomachs could not possibly have agreed with more. Nevertheless, we did reach Townsville after hugging the coast from Sydney past Newcastle and then Brisbane, state capital of Queensland, and on to our destination past Bundaberg and Rockhampton.

Shortly after noon of the eighth day we passed Magnetic Island, five miles from Townsville, crossed the breakwater and up a river narrow by Australian standards and finally tied up at the fisherman's wharf under the hostile gaze of those fishermen drawn there by the beat of our twin diesels. Not a very happy landing.

At that time Townsville was a quiet business centre with its main street running parallel to the coast from the fish wharf to the docks some one and a half miles distant. It was lined on one side with shops, hotels and offices and, apart from the Vestry-owned meat plant with its large abbatoir and cannery, the docks, a small shipbuilding yard, an open-air cinema and the fish-freezing plant, there was little else of note.

The first shoals of the mackerel, which started their annual northern journey between the mainland coast and the Great Barrier Reef in April, were beginning to appear off Townsville. As we anchored off a headland just south of the town we found that while the fish ignored our brightly coloured lures brought from Sydney, they readily bit at the lines baited with long-beaked garfish by the locals. One of the locals, who had been fishing with outstanding success all day, was invited aboard for a talk. The upshot was that Bill Porteous of Gladstone just down the coast, took over as skipper and head fisherman of our outfit. He made it clear – and we agreed – that his would be the last and deciding word in any decisions to be made as far as fishing was concerned.

Ben received our vote as a sleeping partner and he and his cook returned to Sydney. Bill's quick appraisal of our gear saw us quickly head back to Townsville to equip us with what he said would make us fishermen instead of 'bloody amateurs'. So by a stroke of good fortune we bought a flattie for as little as A£5. A flattie is a flat-bottomed boat with six inches draft essential for netting the garfish with which we'd seen him baiting his lines. We also acquired what he called debbies in which to seal the garfish as they were caught and wire and nylon lines to replace those on board contemptuously dismissed as useless by Bill.

After taking on fuel under the supervision of engineer George and stores bought by Arthur, doubling as cook and company secretary, we were initiated that night into the art of net-fishing deep in shallow water in two large bays south of the town. What garfish we caught were wedged in the mesh of our newly bought net made to hold nothing smaller than regulation size. The rest of the catch was made up of inedible star fish and the bottom-hugging sting rays roughly the shape and double the size of a dinner plate. Their tapering rat-like tails sheathed a spine so incredibly sharp that with just a flick over its back a ray could sever the top tendons of a foot placed unwittingly on it.

All were back on board by 4am. Bill then showed how to secure the garfish on our double-hooked lines in such a way as to make it appear they were still alive and swimming when being drawn behind our unwieldy double-manned dories each given an even share of the thirty garfish we had netted. After the mackerel had removed from our lines all those garfish allotted to us without loss to themselves John and I discovered that Cedric and Tommy had two to their credit while Bill with Arthur in the third boat had taken a mackerel for each of their allotted twenty garfish.

To John's aside to me that we'd better start pulling our socks up, Bill suggested that if we were going to pull up anything then he'd rather it was fish as the Board was authorised to buy nothing else but fish.

When we heard that the hobbling gait of Dave Williams, formerly a navy heavyweight boxer was due solely to his having stepped barefoot on the upturned spines of a stone fish while netting at night, there was a concerted rush to buy rubber-soled canvas shoes. The only stone fish we ever saw was found by Bill in the stomach of a fish he was gutting. Only slightly deteriorated by gastric action the poisonous spines that could cause an agonising death or permanent lameness were still closely packed in the shape of the brown stone the fish appeared to be when lying on the sea bed.

Catching mackerel was not, as we had been told in Sydney, simply a matter of trailing a line behind a boat and pulling them in two at a time. Mackerel, as we quickly discovered, were resourceful and hard fighters. Unlike their vulnerability in earlier times they had matured, according to Bill, to have become college-educated in the art of evading their human predators.

Emphasis was placed on the ever-present danger of being caught by neck or limb and pulled overboard to strangle or drown in the grip of the wildly lashing loops in a line uncoiling at speed as it was drawn over the stern by a fast swimming fish. The incredible velocity at which this could occur was demonstrated when a loop in a line held by an experienced elder fisherman stripped the skin from the back of his hand, in his own words, like a tattered old glove. This made him unfit for work for the remainder of the season.

Never working less than a 20-hour day we fished by the Island of Magnetic, Palm and Innisfail, and netted at night until we had nearly enough garfish and a fair catch of mackerel. By then we had learned to stand with the line in the right hand at waist level to take the initial shock of a strike and brace the right leg by the stern seat to avoid being pulled over by a hard-striking fish and to pay out lines free of kinks after losing hooks and up to two hundred feet of expensive piano wire too often for Bill's liking. We also rid ourselves of some of the fear of being too close to 12-foot sharks clearly visible in the

220

phosphorescent half-light, the most ferocious of its species, when netting at night. We always followed Bill's advice to keep the net between the sharks and ourselves. Had we not we could only guess what the consequences might have been.

That we were not a welcome addition to the fishing fleet was made clear by every fisherman on the wharf. Not one would give us so much as a glance or speak to us as we went about taking on stores. These included half a bullock from the meat plant at an average price of fourpence (1½p in sterling) for all its prime cuts, steaks and offal. We then adjourned to the wharfside pub to savour the hostility of the locals directed at people such as we who had bestowed our unwelcome presence where it was not wanted. This silent ostracism was attributable less to our being predominantly a Pommy-staffed outfit but rather to a distrust of, and aversion to, anything that had its origin outside the state of Queensland and worst of all in Sydney.

Every fisherman on the coast was in Townsville for the start of the season and the pub was packed with them. Greetings were passed from one cobber to another round the bar but there were none for us. Questions about the state of health were freely passed from one to the other but no one was interested in ours. Conversational gambits were directed across our fronts and over our heads but never at us.

The pre-dawn ritual of casting off and picking our way clear of the fleet was done the following morning in the spirit of 'bloody glad you're going and hope you don't come back'.

As we pulled out not even the office girls, who had rushed to their windows as we arrived the previous day, had appeared so early to give us a wave. The Great Barrier Reef to which we were heading is submerged to a depth of from three to nine feet depending on tides. Our early departure was timed to enable us to anchor off Rib Reef while the sun still clearly defined the reef's otherwise indiscernible underwater outlines.

The Great Barrier Reef is the world's largest chain of coral structures stretching 1,250 miles (2,000 km) along the continental shelf off the east coast of Queensland. The barrier reef proper is the outermost set of coral reefs beginning at a point near the coast of New Guinea northwest of Cape York and extending in a southeasterly direction, with breaks, to a point east of Bundaberg. The distance of this barrier from the coast varies greatly; it is about 150 miles (240 km) in the south and 100 miles (160 km) in the north. It narrows to as little as twelve miles (19 km) in places between. The shallow lagoon formed between the outer barrier and the coast is filled with subsidiary reefs, coral cays, and islands of igneous rock with fringe reefs. The lagoon is open at the south and north and has two main channels. These are navigable with difficulty as Captain James Cook discovered in 1770. The term 'Great Barrier Reef' usually includes the whole complex covering an area of about 80,000 square miles (207,000 sq km). It is an area of great scientific interest, owing to the enormous range of its geological features, birds and marine life. These are the tropical jungles of Hinchinbrook Island which rises to a height of 3,650 feet (1,800 metres), the 60-foot deep (18 metre) pellucid waters of the lagoon channels and the 6,000-foot (1,800 metres) plunge of the outer reef into the Pacific Ocean. The Great Barrier Reef is a tourist paradise today with many of the islands developed for this purpose. Some of the more accessible islands are Heron, Green and the Low Islands which are low coral cays; Magnetic Island off Townsville, Dunk Island and the Whitsunday Islands, especially Hayman and Lindeman, all reef fringed, higher-lying and rocky.

As we reached Rib Reef the boats were slung over the side to take advantage of the last two hours of daylight with one man in each boat using a deep line made up of sixty feet of piano wire which would sink well beneath the surface, and the other a light line of forty feet of fine cord backed by sixty feet of heavy nylon that trolled behind and above the other.

There were times when the fish bit consistently on the bottom line and ignored the other or vice versa. When the preference was for the former the men in the orthodox 35-foot fishing boats used two bottom lines without one fouling the other. A method not open to us in our narrow-beamed dories. For us it was trial with plenty of error. When fish refused to bite and lengthening and shortening of lines failed to produce results a cutback in speed might just bring them up. Still there were times when they refused to bite, no matter what we did.

All purpose-built fishing boats were steered by inboard tillers fitted with spring attachments operated by pressure applied by the knee but which, when withdrawn, set the boat in the turns necessary to reduce strain put on the line by a big fish and at the same time leave both hands free to pull in the line. This simple action also afforded a lone fisherman pulled over the side the opportunity to get back aboard his ever-circling vessel before being attacked by a shark. So far as we were concerned our outboard-ruddered and hand-steered boats precluded this safety measure.

By noon next day every fisherman on the coast was converging on Rib Reef. The theory was that when the fish continued biting in a small area they were rising from a heavy concentration feeding on the small fish attracted to the spot by one of the plankton-laden rips running out

223

from the reefs. By mid-afternoon at least two dozen boats were fishing over such a formation. It was a daunting sight for us with only limited experience of working alone with the whole wide ocean to ourselves to see the ease with which the fishermen steered their boats with only the occasional over-shoulder glance while they concentrated on their lines over the stern as they weaved through the others, crossing and re-crossing one another's paths in the circles that kept them over the fish.

Still fresh in my mind was Bill's warning that one lost fish streaming blood as it sounded (dived steeply) would take the whole school with it and end all fishing for the day. This prompted me to suggest to John that we operate on the outer fringes of the area until we had the hang of what was obviously an operation of immense skill. John's reaction was to seize the tiller and steer us right into the midst of the *mêlée* with the terse comment that we had as much right to fish there as those other bastards.

That we failed to ram half the other boats on our first run through was a tribute less to our seamanship than to the skilled evasive tactics of their cursing crews. Alas, worse was to follow. A double strike so concentrated our attention that we forgot to steer at all. An omission to which our attention was drawn by an irate fisherman holding aloft for all to see the 12-inch chewed-up remnant of what had been a 100-foot line in one outsized fist. In the other his heavy fish-stunning implement with which he promised to dong us two bastards should we ever cross his path again.

This gave rise to John's humorous aside: 'At least it made one of 'em speak to us.'

This gave me the hope that in the event of a recurrence John would be on the donging side of the boat, not me.

During the next few days we learned how to manoeuvre the boat without danger to others or breaking any more lines.

Rib Reef was the most beautiful of all the reefs. It could only be seen in its entirety from a small boat at high tide. Live coral growths in shades of blue, purple, black, red, yellow and green, all mixed to form a riot of colour over an immense area, were clearly visible through the crystal-clear water of the Great Barrier Reef. Gold and yellow, close to the surface, were avoided at all costs. The other colours in brilliant profusion in all the crevices and fissures inside and around the vast caves and canyons, which had taken shape within the huge growths attracted shoals of tiny multi-coloured fish swimming through the fairyland setting, vanishing under a projection one minute and indiscernible the next as they passed over a colour similar to their own. Trepang, beloved of the Chinese gourmet, and brightly coloured starfish dotted the golden sands that occurred between one coral growth and the next.

Each night after a hurried dinner, which bestowed scant praise on the excellent food cooked by Arthur, we baited light nylon lines to fish over the side for the sweetlip, dace, trevalli and parrot fish attracted by the jetisoned head and guts from fish caught during the day. By midnight we had gutted and iced down some forty-odd three- to five-pounders that sold on average at ten shillings each. But for scavenging sharks measuring from nine to twelve feet and their fast swimming nine-inch long sucker-shark attachments this could well have been more.

It was essential hooked fish should be drawn quickly to the surface or one of the dozen or more sharks, ceaselessly cruising beneath our boat would have it. The fast-swimming suckers were an even bigger nuisance.

They took the bait in the same way as an edible fish, and immediately the line began to draw them to the surface they made a dart for the side of the ship to which they attached themselves by the round flat sucker pad on their foreheads. Then they hung on with a tenacity nothing could break.

Experience taught us that letting a line go slack after a period of pulling would sometimes cause them to relax their hold sufficiently to be pulled in. Even then, given half a chance, a second hold could be secured and the whole performance repeated. The pad was normally used by the sucker to clamp itself to the underbelly of the much larger shark of which it was a tiny replica for free transportation and feed on the scraps dropping from the rapacious jaws of its host. We once observed two of them feasting on scraps pulled from between the teeth of a stationary larger shark, its mouth obligingly held wide open.

When trolling by day, sharks frequently positioned themselves over every school of fish being worked to bite mackerel off the line as it was being drawn in leaving only the head on the hook. Occasionally while doing this the sharks got hooked themselves.

The first indication that a shark was after a hooked fish came from the latter's unusual behaviour. It would sound sometimes deeply instead of its more usual swings from side to side. A leap from the water was a sure sign it was under attack from a shark. The only course then was to throw the whole line over the stern to give the hooked fish the play it needed and then haul in fast before the shark attacked again. Often in tribute to the great fight it had put up I felt an almost overwhelming urge to unhook such a fish and return it to the deep blue sea. Just what commercially-minded Bill would have thought and said of this would, at a guess, have been quite unprintable.

When a shark swallowed the hook with the fish it was pulled up to the stern with only minimum effort. If a few sharp jerks failed to free the hook then the line was cut close to the shark's nose. Alternatively, in the hope it would deter others, the line was tied to an empty debbie with marker attached and the shark left to tire or possibly release itself in its efforts to get free of the debbie. In the meantime we would use a spare line and recover the original later.

All too often when mackerel were plentiful the unsaleable red-fleshed bonito took our bait in a ratio of three to one. Hard fighters, their fierce jerkings bruised and stiffened our hands to such an extent that even with vigorous overnight massage it was still hard going when work recommenced at dawn next day.

Bought at five shillings a dozen our calico mittens gave us only slight protection. They did, however, to some extent, prevent sea-wet lines under pressure from big fish slipping and cutting into our fish-slimed, ever-wet hands. Under heavy pressure our nylon lines tended to jerk an infinitesimal bit at a time through tightly pinched fingers and thumbs. As the speed of withdrawal accelerated that part already drawn in and coiled at the feet whipped up loop by loop to flail the bare chest and face to cause excruciating pain. There was also the danger that any of the loops thrown around the neck or arms could separately strangle, strip skin from one or both hands or do all three at the same time.

The first time this happened to me, though flailed sightless at the time, I recalled Bill's advice that in this situation I should either throw the whole line over the stern or better still arrest its slip before one of the flying loops had me by the throat. I managed – I know not how – to apply the extra grip that stopped the slip.

Shark lines tied to both derricks were always left baited

with mackerel heads for the giant cod found only in these tropical waters. They averaged from two to four hundred pounds. When caught, the largest possible fillet was cut head to tail from each side. If the Fish Board could not take them they were sold to fried-fish shops. Although generally agreed by us Pommies aboard to be far superior to the dry-fleshed mackerel, cod was not popular in Queensland. So two cod fetched no more money that an average-sized mackerel. If a shark took the bait it was shot and dropped back in the hope that it would deter others. The belief that shark would not eat shark was called in question when one of the several sharks cruising under the boat took a huge bite out of another, just shot, as it sank to the bottom.

Once, standing at the rail with Bill, we saw a shark approaching from our seaward side. It came to rest within a foot of the vessel, opened wide its jaws and two baby sharks swam out.

Calling on the others on deck to 'Watch this' Bill gave a resounding open-handed smack on the ship's wooden side.

The shark's reaction was a swift half turn which brought it into line with its two offspring. In response, presumably to some signal known only to them, the baby sharks swam line-abreast like well-trained soldiers back into the opened parental mouth to be carried at speed in the direction from whence they had come.

Ask any Queensland fisherman why, at a time when sharks in large numbers were stripping our lines one after the other, they ignored the island fisherman skin-diving for trocus, the shell from which shirt buttons are made, only yards distant. You will invariably be told that these men are immune to attack by sharks. Certainly this belief was shared by the skin divers. They based their confidence of freedom from attack on the theory that since sharks were cowards at heart they only attacked anything that was defenceless. Judged by the non-chalance with which they trod water while emptying their pouches in between their average two-minute immersions they, like the fishermen, obviously believed this.

The theory of the immunity of the fishermen was called in question by an item in a Brisbane newspaper, supported by a photograph of an aging diver who had freed his head and shoulders from the jaws of a shark by reaching back and gouging its eyes until it released its hold. Large teeth-marks in the shape of a huge necklace extending halfway down the diver's chest were clearly discernible in the picture. When I showed the picture to divers for trocus working amongst us they merely grinned and carried on diving.

Bad weather was sometimes presaged by what fishermen called a Bite. This was when fish for a period of often up to three days appeared to go into a mad frenzy of biting on everything that moved – on the last day even bare hooks. This was accompanied by the rare sight of mackerel averaging in weight from twenty to sixty-odd pounds as they leapt out of the water in close pursuit of the butterfish on which they were feeding as to appear to be invisibly attached to their quarry. They rose, separated all the time by a gap of a few inches never widening nor shortening, to describe a perfect arc a hundred or more feet in the air. And then an unimaginable graceful descent ending in a splashless return to the ocean. The first time I saw this amazing spectacle I almost found myself looking for the invisible thread I imagined must be linking the tiny bottom fish to their three- to six-foot predators.

Three days' fishing filled the iceboxes on the smaller boats and our refrigerator each day with all it could freeze. As abruptly as it started the bite finished and, as expected, heavy weather drove the whole fleet into Townsville to discharge catches. Before leaving port next day we made a brief call at the pub for more of the treatment as before. This time, however, Annie the barmaid, gave us a smile as brief as it was discreet.

Before the season ended we had two more bites. The first was all to ourselves. This came about when Bill decided to run into port to discharge what fish we had instead of returning to the reefs with the rest after sheltering from a near cyclone that had stopped all fishing for two days. This decision had a welcome side effect as we discovered later. It came about when George, our engineer, rendered assistance to the crew of a disabled fishing boat we had sighted a few hours out from Townsville on our way to port.

Back on the reef the next day we found fishing so quiet that all the other boats were leaving for port. By dark we had the reef to ourselves. Two days later the biggest bite of the year started and by noon on each of the five days it lasted we had caught as many fish as our refrigerator could hold comfortably to be frozen down.

For a full eight days no other boats appeared on the scene. Assuming the bite to be general we thought the rest must be working fish nearer the coast. Finally, a lone 35-footer appeared to tell us of our great good fortune at having, with our superior speed, cleared the port before the others returned with such heavy loads that, added to those from the previous bite still unsold, had obliged the Fish Board to suspend its guarantee to buy all mackerel brought in by licensed fishermen until current stocks had been sold. Without this assurance not one boat dared to put out. In consequence the crews spent eight days and most of their previous earnings buying one another beers in the pub on the wharf.

When the local conversational gambit contained in the question, 'Do you coves like drinking with the flies?' was put to us in the pub by the would-be donger of John and me the next time in port, it effectively ended for us the ostracism we had known in the past. This, of course, had resulted from the aid George had given to the owners of the disabled boat several weeks before. From then on we were accepted by this tough, insular body of men as being acceptable members of their exclusive fraternity.

With the total inadequacy of our double-manned open boats ever in mind we gladly accepted an offer from retired naval architect Dave Stewart, the owner of a guest house on Magnetic Island, to build for us four decked-in dories during the coming off-season when I would be free to help. The scheme was to be financed by our senior partner, ex-China hand Bill Davies.

In the hope of raising spare working capital we decided to make one last trip out to the reefs despite the uncertain weather and the scarcity of fish.

Catches were poor and, as the white caps on the sea were whipped up by the increasing wind force, Bill surveyed the scene and decided to return to port. John, ever a trier, called for a last effort to find fish. As conditions worsened we ploughed, plunging and spray-swept, through ever rising seas, and with the mother ship straining at anchor, John finally agreed that home was best and we should make for Townsville.

With George, our engineer, temporarily helping out on a government ship, I was sent below to assist Tom with the engines while we manoeuvred clear of the reef. As I normally worked the winch that brought up the anchor I could visualise the sequence of movements on deck. At first the movements indicated the usual normality of operations but then there came an unusually long stop with the boat pitching heavily. Sensing that something above was amiss I risked a run up the hatch to find Cedric lying in the scuppers with blood on his head and John in the sea with blood flowing from a head wound.

From the bridge Bill yelled, 'Get that hook up.'

First we hauled John back on board. Arthur and I then each took a handle and winched in the slack in the chain as the bows were dipping but when the sharp rise as they lifted again tore the handle from my grasp I instinctively snatched my arm to the side. Arthur, however, unaccustomed to the winch pulled back too slowly to avoid a blow from the madly unwinding winch handle which broke his right arm. Only then did we realise that the violent pitching had broken the pawl on the winch and the anchor was snagged in coral on the bottom. The chain was secured to a stanchion and cut through with a hacksaw.

As we got clear of the reef the three fishing boats astern were let out one behind the other on long towing ropes, and we headed for port with John slightly delirious on his bunk and Ced and Arthur walking casualties. When we were halfway to port and right out in the open sea, the violence of the waves broke the tow line between the first and second boats.

As neither the skipper nor the engineer could leave the ship, the task of retrieving them fell to me. Getting off a heaving ship via the iron ladder over the stern into an even more madly pitching boat in bare feet to reduce the hazard of slipping, requires a sense of balance and agility I no longer possess.

For reasons best known to themselves, two boats standing close together in a rough sea never rise and fall in unison. The steep rise in one is always matched by an equally steep fall in the other, and the ideal moment to step from one to the other is during the fractional pause as each reaches the end of its separate movement. Otherwise it would be akin to stepping directly from one express lift into another while they were travelling in opposite directions.

Protected by some miraculous luck in seas that had me tossing high and then low like a shuttlecock as I lurched from one boat to the other to tether them together with our number one dory, I joined the frayed ends of the towing ropes in knots that had Bill wincing in sheer disbelief of their ability to hold anything together larger than a model boat on a pond. But they did.

Instead of the expected hero's acclaim as I stepped back on deck I was met with a barrage of Geordie good sense.

Arthur wanted to know, 'What in hell do you and that other silly bugger' (meaning Bill), 'think you are doing jeopardising the safety of the whole outfit, together with the neck of the only member qualified to help with the proposed boat building, simply to save two boats we no longer have use for.'

His sound Geordie reasoning so closely paralleled my own that I could only wish he had been on hand earlier to offer it before, rather than after the event.

We reached port safely and I joined Dave Stewart on Magnetic Island to work a sixteen-hour day, seven days a week in his large garden shaded by tall treets that atttracted a variety of multi-coloured parrots and parakeets amidst a profusion of tropical plants. Some of them, like the giant clams on the reefs that clamped a steel grip on any who trod on them, trapped the larger winged insects on which they fed.

An invitation to the other partners to spend Easter at the Stewart guesthouse coincided with an influx of farmers from the outback. One of them had fathered a small son so accustomed to the outback habit of alluding to anything in quantity such as men or steers as a 'mob' that he surprised even phlegmatic Dave when he called the sea he was seeing for the first time 'a big mob of water'.

No doubt inspired by our English presence, Mrs Stewart decided to serve all and sundry with our traditional egg-and-bacon breakfast. It was an expensive mistake. Even though egg-and-bacon breakfasts were unobtainable in the outback the novelty failed to catch on and, with a preference cultivated over a lifetime, they all asked for steak.

A week later we said our farewells to the Stewarts and took over our four new decked-in dories that for design and performance were a credit to Dave Stewart. Where else in the world outside Australia could we have found such a man, already fully occupied in the running of a large guesthouse, who could have volunteered to work such long hours day after day for the mere pittance we could afford to pay him? I cannot for the life of me think.

The next day we loaded the dories and sailed south to fish for mackerel and garfish in grounds off Gladstone, Bill's home town, a region familiar to him since childhood. It was still early in the season with fish only just appearing in thin runs. We scoured the seas out as far as the two unnamed cays (large sand masses rising all of sixty feet out of the sea and three times that length in diameter) some twenty hours out of port. We also reached the long Swain Reefs a few hours away in seas that from noon to dark got ever rougher.

I well remember so many years ago those many nights returning to the mother ship anchored in those lonely seas we seemed to have all to ourselves. We were guided by the masthead light as we carried in the dories mixed catches of mackerel, dolphin and baracuda, some weighing up to ninety pounds.

We arrived on the port side to discharge the heavy, slime-coated fish from the dories rolling wildly seemingly with the intent of dashing themselves to destruction against the bigger vessel which was also pitching so violently as to present just for an instant the deck at eye level and within seconds a view of the propellors ten feet above. Then, their decks scrubbed clean of slime, we dropped the dories back astern of the big ship before going aboard to eat the first meal since 5am. Arthur was the cook. Prior to his joining the consortium he had never cooked anything in his life. Our well-cleaned plates testified to the excellency of his meals and, safe in the knowledge that yet another hazardous day was over, and the next eight hours away, we retired to our bunks.

Clearly visible through the early-morning translucent water still undisturbed by the winds to come were giant mantas with spans large enough completely to envelop our wide-beamed 14-foot dories. We watched giant sea turtles making cautious ascents and soundless descents at our approach. Each one, probably a sole survivor of a batch of fifty or more not found by sea-borne islanders searching the sands for eggs, or luckier than the newly hatched hordes seized by swooping sea birds on those highly dangerous runs to the sea from the several holes in the sand in which their eggs were laid. Finally, those that made runs successfully found the gaping jaws of waiting fish. But the greatest predator of all was man – bigger, brainier, and the only hunter likely to end the lives of those who had miraculously lived from egg to the hugeness that made the giants immune to everything but their human predators.

Mindful of the lone fisherman whose boat had been tipped on its side by one of the large schools of whales seen at least ten times a day noisily tossing themselves out of the water, we gave the huge mammals right of way and as wide a berth as closeness to the next of their kind performing precisely the same snorting jumps permitted.

Ask a Queensland fisherman if there is such a thing as a killer whale and he'll laugh in your face and say, 'Just harmless bloody nuisances, that's all they are. If you get tipped over by one it's your own damn-fool fault for getting too close.'

In a bar with a sawdust-strewn floor in Bowen where we had called to offload fish and buy stores the response from the barmaid to a call from George for two whiskies was to place a bottle of whisky and one of water on the bar. When George, somewhat nonplussed, asked if this meant that we should help ourselves the barmaid merely gave an upward glance from her knitting as if to suggest why should we disturb the quiet of the otherwise empty bar with daft questions. So, assuming that this was normal practice, we helped ourselves.

This took my mind back to Shanghai where former US Navy sailor and fellow prisoner of mine, Joe Orapello, followed this practice in his three bars. Joe always maintained that the bar gained as those who took short measures far outnumbered those who were over-liberal in helping themselves.

From there we travelled in easy stages to Townsville via the Percy Islands, then owned by a local farmer but since sold to an English migrant couple, and points off the mainland coast where mackerel were caught by day and garfish at night. After sitting in the luminosity of several bays one night without a trace of garfish Bill handed me the oars to scull round a headland while he rolled a cigarette.

Skirting a crop of jagged rocks I was told to take a

narrow passage less than ten feet wide between those and what appeared in the half-light to be large smooth rocks. Even less impressed with my prowess as an oarsman than the rest I voiced the hope that I would not get the oars fouled in the rocks and bring us all to grief.

A quiet chuckle in the dark and then the question, 'Grief, did you say? Touch one of those and we'll all be shark shit by morning.'

A closer look made us aware of what Bill had known all along. Those great lumps that I thought were big smooth rocks were sleeping whales.

It was during a spell of bad weather at four in the morning when the discovery was made that due to the parting of the painter linking the first to the rest, we had lost three of our new dories. Since all four were there when checked by Arthur an hour earlier and recalling the time off Gladstone when one had travelled four miles with three of its watertight compartments damaged by a brush with a reef, we hoped that, despite the knocks they must have taken, the missing dories would remain afloat long enough to be found. The remaining dory was hastily loaded while Bill plotted the probable drift.

After searching in ever widening circles in rising seas for the rest of the day, we realised we could easily have passed the dories a dozen times without seeing their white-painted hulls in the white-capped waves, so we gave up the search while we still had fuel enough to get us home.

After a short talk we left for Gladstone where Bill said he was sure we could hire substitutes. Of the two we found available one was dangerously narrow in the beam but accepting the maxim that beggars could not be choosers, we hired both. Sailing up the coast in a slight sea Bill predicted bad weather and we anchored behind a hill on one of the islands on our route. Right through the night, despite our cover, the wind shrieked through the masts but died to a light breeze by morning.

As we put out towards the open sea next morning Bill again proved his uncanny weather-sense when he returned us to the same anchorage to sit out a near cyclone-force wind that raged all night before giving way to a calm that he correctly foretold would last out the week.

Already victualled and fuelled we went straight to Rib Reef and to Bill on this occasion went the coveted accolade for catching the record mackerel of the season. It's total weight was sixty-eight pounds without head and guts. It fetched £8 at the Fish Board, and to me went the totally unwanted distinction of landing the biggest – a sailfish, the most beautiful denizen of the sea with an estimated weight of around 300lb but of little commercial worth. It almost pulled me out of the boat and – to my eternal regret defeated my every attempt to free it from the hook – leaving me with no other option but to kill and haul it on to my boat.

With weeks to go before the end of the season and after several profitable bites, for reasons known only to themselves the fish stopped biting on garfish and concentrated their undivided attention on brightly coloured lures. Good results being essential, when they refused to take my lures I handed the narrow beamed boat over to John who proved the failure was mine in that he brought in fish as good as any.

Two days later the mackerel abruptly terminated the season a month early as they departed *en masse* – some thought for ever.

With more hope than good sense we returned south toe try for the large bottom-fish shoals reportedly abundant in that area in December. I was fortunate in being the only one to find one of these concentrations – if only for the experience.

Fishing a submerged crevice in one reef I pulled up three-pound sweetlip one after the other with a regularity bordering on the monotonous. As fast as I took one off the hook and cast back another took it. They were still biting when dangerously low at the stern I made back to the ship. The hope raised by this early success that we might return to port fully laden proved to be as illusory as ever. When the next haul produced less than a dozen we concentrated on the large barracuda that were plentiful there. After discharging these and returning the good dory, we bought the other for a nominal sum and returned to Townsville from where Bill and the other Australians returned to their homes. Reluctantly, ten debbies of the selfsame garfish for which we had paid £5 a tin the previous year were dumped over the side as being of no further use.

We gladly accepted a five-day job laying loose boards, dunnage, on the bottom holds of a large British freighter loading frozen meat, lead ingots and bulk sugar. Dunnage protects the cargo from shifting and from bilge water. While we laid our floorboards down below the regulars above lined higher holds with thick paper. We thought that temperatures in Townsville were high until we had experience of the intense heat five decks down in which we were to labour seemingly on a starvation diet. From the first day by the time we had made the wharf and found the canteen it was time to resume work. On the last day we did manage to get to the canteen in time to share out what potatoes and gravy our top deck mates were too full to eat. Even the extremely fit young fairground-booth boxer in our gang, who was staying with us for the duration of the job, had difficulty in treading a straight course as we trudged back to our ship after 14-hour days. Watching our somewhat erratic gait on the final night two policemen asked where they could get 'it', when in answer to their query as to what we'd been drinking Tom told them ginger ale.

Inspired no doubt by the fishing tales he'd heard while with us and alcoholically refreshed to near capacity, if appearances were anything to go by, our late boxer friend was seen inexpertly rowing a flattie into which fishing gear was loaded, happily beaming and bowing in polite acknowledgement of our shouted warnings – plainly mistaken for greetings – that ridges of sand we knew to be there would, unless he changed course, halt the erratic passage he was making in the general direction of the sea. Completely oblivious of the sandbanks and very shortly afterwards to the fact that he was aground on them he continued to go through the automatic motions of rowing.

Hilarious shouts of 'You're aground you Galah you're not moving,' directed at him by fishermen on the wharf were acknowledged with the same polite bows until, still sublimely unaware that he'd ever been aground at all, he recommenced his broken passage when by chance he was set back afloat by the bow wave of a passing launch and we lost sight in time of one of the nicest blokes it had been our good fortune to meet. We wished him good hunting and a safe return.

A tentative suggestion that we should carry chilled beef to the northern ports led to a tour of the meat plant. We started in the marshalling sheds where bullocks were contentedly cooling themselves under sprinklers. With no prompting at all a trained bull led them in single file down a narrow chute from which he made a quick left-hand exit and through a door hastily closed. The bullocks had to turn on the chute and this took them right into the abbatoir where each one was stunned, killed and moved before the appearance of the next in line.

After seeing a moving belt conveying a seemingly endless line of 12oz corned beef tins through the automatic processes of filling and sealing we followed the track upstairs to the final operation. There, six girls with percussion hammers were methodically tapping each tin as it filed past. One false note and a tin was instantly rejected. Imperfect seals, we were told, produced the decibel evidence they were so expert in hearing.

A later proposal sent to us from John in Sydney involved a firm in Santo in the New Hebrides which asked us to join them in the lucrative trocus trade there. We quickly accepted. There had been a revival in the demand for trocus consequent on the failure of a synthetic substitute for pearl buttons. This had boosted trocus price tenfold. We were to supply the ship and the New Hebrides firm the know-how. Arthur, Tom and I were to remain on the ship without pay to convert her to carry thirty-odd divers, re-caulk decks and do general maintenance.

A disclosure by Arthur that after the purchase of essential items the balance of funds would be sufficient only to buy four months' supply of bread, butter, tea and sugar for ourselves was eased in part when he produced thirty tins of cheap quince jam bought a few at a time and since forgotten. From then on it was jam three times daily with the exception of the time he bought a dinner of bacon and eggs with money filched from company funds to celebrate his birthday. A sole tin of strawberry jam unearthed in the galley and held in reserve provided a special treat for our Christmas dinner.

Our new skipper sent from Santo and also a bill arrived a few days before departure to buy fuel and stores which included for at least three jam-packed mortals a most mouth-watering sight of pre-cooked roasts, one each of beef, pork and mutton.

After finishing a job that had prevented me joining the celebratory meal in town, but still enabling me to have a last drink at the pub on the wharf after a hasty feed from the last of the jam, Arthur, Tom and I were given six weeks pay by old Bill, our senior partner. This would be useful to Tom and me as, unlike Arthur, we were to leave the ship at Santo.

Since our departure coincided with the arrival in town of the huge beef herds brought in annually from the far outback stations the pub was filled to capacity with the slim-hipped Aborigine cowboys, colourfully dressed, who had covered great distances driving the stock on to Townsville. Some of the journeys had lasted more than five months. The herds would end up ultimately, via the meat plant, on British tables and elsewhere in the form of corned beef.

Our fishermen friends joined the Aborigines in the pub. It was usual for them to take on temporary work in the meat plant during the off season. Their sincere good wishes for our future labours were in marked contrast to the hostility they showed us when we first arrived in Townsville. They warned us of impending bad weather and I was a little concerned when our new skipper confessed he had a tendency to suffer from sea sickness during the first twenty-four hours of any rough sailing. He reassured me, however, when he stressed that this had never been allowed to interfere with his duties. This recalled for me the time I had travelled on a ship captained by a sixty-five year old man who was always confined to his cabin for twenty-four hours at the commencement of every new voyage with sea sickness.

We completed loading, battening of hatches and checking the dories before turning in for two hours. To save time and fuel, instead of taking the usual route round the Great Barrier Reef just short of New Guinea, we were to take the little known Finders Passage through the reef that had been navigated some fifty years back by two small ships, the larger of which had touched bottom. In order to make passage through with the sun at its zenith we left port before dawn the next morning.

The smooth swell caused by the seasonal king tides that were much in evidence after Magnetic Island slowly subsided to a near flat calm as we approached the Great Barrier Reef. The sky was beautifully clear with only a light breeze blowing as we passed through Finders Passage into the Coral Sea.

From the golden sands beneath the sea there rose giant formations of coral that seemed to be within hand-touching reach in the transluscent waters. It carried my mind back to Lincoln Cathedral back in England as I first saw it at five o'clock on a summer's morning for all the coral structures in a uniform shade of brown appeared to be huge cathedrals lacking the symmetry imposed by man. In the seconds that passed between their first appearance over the bows and their silent disappearance beneath our keel it seemed to me that the topmost pinnacles were much too close for my liking. Perhaps I had misjudged the height owing to the magnification of the water. Yet I felt there was a dangerous nearness.

It was about that time the normally indefatigable Arthur, who had never been ill during his time with us, confessed to a feeling of giddiness reminiscent of an un-diagnosed illness he had had in India which had culminated in a state of coma with no visible sign of breathing. He requested that in the event of this being a recurrence we should make quite sure that he had passed the point of no return before slinging him over the side.

By midnight the ship was pitching steeply with the wind increasing in velocity so much that she was slipping down in the trough of one wave to be lifted high by the next. When this sequence was broken the bows, high in the air, crashed right under the succeeding wave so that we shipped solid walls of water that cascaded down the deck to strike the wheelhouse with such force as to convince me that, had it not been angled at both front and sides, nothing on earth could have prevented it being torn from its moorings and hurled over the stern. At the wheel I had the impression we were driving through solid green water and only the occasional glimpse of the madly dipping bows and the accompanying groans of the ship's timbers gave any indication we were still afloat as hour after hour we took this heavy pounding.

As the night wore on the vessel adopted a corkscrew motion as the rolling worsened. Even with legs braced wide apart I had to hold hard to the plotting table to avoid sliding first to one side and then to the other despite fixing my bare feet firmly to the steeply tilting deck. Dawn broke to a low overcast sky. Bill, who like Tom, was suffering from sea sickness, said he believed we were running through an extremely violent hurricane which, if the glass was to be believed, would not die out that day, nor for that matter, the next. Any doubts about that were dispelled on the third day when the wind veered right round the compass. By this time, tired and all too conscious of the long, steep rolls to port and, a lot later it seemed, those to starboard, as the wind changed frequently and there were heavy hammer blows to our sides, we realised that the centre of the hurricane lay not far ahead. Throughout this Arthur had lain inert in his bunk.

The nights seemed endlessly unreal, particularly as

darkness descended soon after 3pm and dawn never broke before 8am, a full three hours late. Even then there was only sufficient light to see the giant waves all about us instead of those engulfing the bridge. Later in the day with the wind veering every hour a hollow-eyed Arthur rose from his bunk to take the wheel. By then ravenously hungry I went to the refrigerator only to find that those choice cuts of meat had turned green as the burner, trimmed and set before leaving port, had snuffed out. This was yet another indication of the severe pounding we were taking since the refrigerator had never failed us before regardless of the weather. I broke open a tin of stew and opened the galley door to find that every pot and pan had broken clear of the storm-racks and the whole lot was crashing madly around the galley with a din not audible in the general clamour outside. Not once before even in the heaviest weather, had a single item been torn from these racks.

For the first time since leaving Townsville I went to sleep for an hour despite the noise of the seas crashing against the ship's sides. In the confined space below it sounded as if at least fifty big navvies were simultaneously striking the ship's sides with outsize sledge-hammers. Added to this there was now the disturbing rattle of the rudder chains racing full lock one way and then, after the briefest pause, going again full lock in the other. Back on the bridge I learned from Arthur that we had a following sea of such force that we had no steerway at all.

For the next six hours we managed to stay roughly on course by the following manoeuvre: as the head began to swing round to put us broadside to the wind, we discovered there was a momentary response just sufficient to check the head and start it to turn in the opposite direction. This movement in turn was checked again by the wheel, already spun through full lock and waiting to be spun back, to start the whole cycle again. Through this stratagem we avoided disaster.

The storm raged on and it did nothing to lighten the gloom to get Bill's professional opinion of what we already knew: that if the ship once got her side to the wind it would be curtains for all.

As the day wore on the raging seas appeared bent on breaking the ship's back as she made several side slips in quick succession keeled over at an impossibly steep angle by wind and waves into troughs between waves higher than the masthead.This often sucked us even lower into the voids left by their upward surge to the precipitous heights to which they were drawn by the ever veering wind before breaking to crash down over decks lifting from the last immersion. At the port scanner Bill could see the wave tops being trimmed of all spray.

By noon on the fourth day the wind appeared to be abating a little. We checked deck lashings and watched the masts swinging in an arc that looked as if it would never stop as they dipped even lower. We realised how much the ship had rolled during the preceding four days. The completely overcast sky since the first day had prevented Bill from getting a fix, and knowing that the ninety-mile long D'Entrecasteaux Reef lay somewhere ahead, we put out five more miles to counteract any drift or crabbing which might have set us on a collision course with this reef just submerged a few feet under water and from which we would set course direct for Santo.

Alas, shortly before 11pm with mountainous waves still engulfing the wheelhouse there was a discernible bump followed by loud rasping noises as the ship lifted and then slid to a stop. As Tom down below cut engines we realised we were aground on what could only be the D'Entrecasteaux Reef. At first with loud crunching

246

noises the ship started to slip back. This gave us hope she might re-enter the water stern first where the propellors – undamaged we hoped through Tom's quick action – might drag us clear of the reef. With her stern still fifty feet from the reef's edge we settled into a depression in the coral and stuck. When a break in the huge waves set her down on a coral head with such force as to hole her and list her on her side we saw the position was hopeless and two anchors were put out.

As the ship commenced to edge back a little at a time the unspoken question in all our minds was answered when after what seemed an eternity the slack in the chains took up and both anchors held fast. Relieved of the fear that the waves might sweep us stern first into the enormous vortex they had created as they surged back into the wind-driven sea, we sat out the rest of the night in the steeply tilted wheelhouse listening with one ear to the ship breaking up as it swung to and fro over the jagged coral within the narrow limits imposed by the anchors up front, with the other ear to the nerve-racking grind of the wheel ceaselessly spinning full lock both ways under pressure from the rudder, turning both ways with every swing of the stern.

Came the dawn we made the exasperating discovery that had we put out five miles plus twenty yards the previous day we would by now be close to Santo instead of where we were sitting high, but far from dry, on the extreme end of a reef ninety miles in length.

By mid morning we had the old narrow dory hanging from a crazily angled derrick but as it was lowered a sudden wave picked it up and dashed it to driftwood against the ship's side. Four hours later at low tide, with two of us standing neck deep on the reef pulling ropes to hold it clear of the ship, we got the good dory safely afloat and secured in our lee.

After a meal on the now half-flooded ship, and fearing that a freak wave might sweep her off the reef, we slept that night in the dory. As the only one who had had no sleep, I was allotted the position athwart the boat. Despite its all-night rolling that alternately immersed my feet and then half my head in the sea I slept, if only fitfully, most of the night. Ironically, the leaky decks caulked in Townsville, which had defied all previous efforts at sealing had not taken an ounce of water throughout the past several days.

By 3pm we had fitted a compass to the dory, loaded a tank of water, four small drums of diesel, what charts we needed and the Pacific Pilot with some tins of stew plus our personal papers and we set sail down Surprise Lagoon *en route*, we hoped, for French New Caledonia.

Arriving at Surprise Island about two hours later we found the narrow passage between the island and the reef impassable due to the heavy surf. So we turned about with the intention of sleeping the night again in the lee of the ship.

Heavy spray thrown back from the choppy seas and kept lively by the dying wind added to the difficulties we faced as we exerted all our efforts to avoid holing our craft during the long passage back up the lagoon bestrewn with dangerously high coral formations. Then the gathering darkness finally found us nowhere within sight of our mother ship. Yet, with the dogged perseverance of men too tired to think of anything else we continued to search back and forth in blinding spray, sometimes scouring almost entirely the section of the sea in which we thought she might lie. All four of us bleary-eyed, near to exhaustion, peered ahead sure that this time we would see the ship. Time and again we watched Bill, crouched in the bows, raise his arm once again for us to go about in yet another sweep. So we searched, ducking down out of the whipping spray until the sight of boiling surf in front gave warning that we must turn once again.

After what seemed to be an intolerable length of time I took the tiller from Arthur, whose eyes were so heavily shot with blood as to appear sightless. From then on I drifted into a dream world of my own, steering automatically and vaguely wondering how the church organ I could distinctly hear playing muted fugue-like music had found its way into this dark seething wilderness of stinging salt and wind-swept rock. So real it sounded as we sailed on – an illusion produced by the monotonous beat of the diesel engine, clear at times and fading at others to merge with wind and sea spraying back into our sore eyes and ears. Automatically we scanned the cream-capped waves for the half-submerged rocks in the waters all around.

Finally, Arthur's suggestion that we drop anchor in the lee of the reef and look for the ship the next day dragged us out of the torpor into which we had sunk. The engine was cut. A wax match held to Arthur's watch told us it was 9pm. Within minutes we were all asleep.

By morning the wind had died, and the ship, clearly discernible from where we had slept was boarded for the last time to re-fill our tank, and with a flat sea we had put Surprise and Huon islands behind us by late afternoon. By nightfall we had found another small island on which we slept.

Our objective was Pott Island which, according to the Pacific Pilot, had a mountain in its centre fringed by a French-owned copra plantation. This was the last island before French New Caledonia. We sailed on and with only one exception found small islands on which to sleep.

The exception was when we put through the Grand

Passage, a channel of small reefs discovered by Captain James Cook. Through this passage the current ran stronger than stated in the Pacific Pilot and the extra time taken set us in deep water at dark to ride out the night at sea anchor. While checking the engine next morning a vital locking nut forcefully ejected by a recoiling spring fortunately for us hit my bare chest and fell into the bilges. As the oars we had been obliged to fit to gain port clearance had been ditched the first day as useless encumbrances, Tom's slowly raised eyes were expressive of the thought running through mine: that drift as we may through these isolated reefs or for that matter in the open seas beyond, unless by some miraculous chance we were sighted by a Sydney to New Guinea Burns-Phillip ship making its bi-monthly northern run, our chances of survival were just about nil.

Ever present in our minds was the thought that just one small error could put us in a channel blocked by coral at its end. It was like probing one after the other a series of underwater alleys miles in length definable only with the sun above or behind until a way through was found. This in turn could branch off several ways before its end was reached. Luckily, with careful plotting and a bestowal of good fortune, we found our way through the sea-girt maze.

As we sailed through the stretch charted by Captain Cook our thoughts went back to those long dead, salt-pork-rationed seamen shanghaied to man the longboats from which these reefs were explored and charted. We wondered how often they had been forced to turn back to try again and again in their search for a passage through the labyrinthine maze, the extent of which had been unkown until they found it. At least we knew what they at first did not know and that was that, provided we could find it, we knew there was a way through. Little wonder, said Arthur, that those poor buggers of long ago were dreaming all the while o'Plymouth Hoe or, indeed, of anywhere else except these bloody reefs.

At a long-abandoned camp on one overnight stop we topped up our water with the scummy green liquid covering four feet of decomposed sea birds trapped over the years in a rusty old water-tank. We sieved the water through sand and then boiled it to kill off the small amount of remaining bacteria still visibly active. It was a wasted effort but it had one beneficial effect. Though its high and noxious stench had given way to a lesser but still unpleasant odour, we found just one measure of the coffee we had hastily picked up when leaving the old ship now made a darker brew than four did before.

I shall never forget the noontide landing on a tiny atoll and the lethargy into which we sank while sitting in the illusory shade of a crop of dry reeds on the beach. An hour must have passed before I noticed that the dory we had left at anchor was swinging with the tide in an arc that would ground its stern on jagged rocks near the beach. Though I was aware of the irreparable damage that would occur to propellor and shaft, I could not force myself to get to my feet to prevent it. Several times I tried counting to three and then to five but even that failed and this despite my knowing without a shadow of doubt that without the boat the next chance visitors to the atoll would find nothing more than a few bleached bones. In the absence of any of the stunted palms that annually drew islanders to such atolls it was anyone's guess when that would be.

Finally, with time running out I managed to rouse Tom from his torpor and to my everlasting shame he did what I should have done in the first place; he moved the boat. The light breeze that sprang up later restored us to something like normality. We even caught a mackerel which without salt we ate at our next island stop – let it be said without much relish. There we found clutches of dozens of turtle eggs each flanked by decoy nests. The eggs, probably unhatched the previous year were more like rubber than rubber itself.

Where the Pacific Pilot warned of impenetrable reefs ahead, we moved out into the open ocean to ride high and dry atop and in between glass-smooth waves flowing across our courses soundlessly to spend ourselves over reefs to our right that we could not see.

After a vote on whether we should play safe by continuing to Pott Island under the fine weather conditions prevailing it was decided one vote to three against that. Instead, we followed Bill's advice to save time and fuel by returning to the now navigable reefs. The principle followed was if you don't do as the captain suggests then why have one? So Bill had his way.

A flock of birds of the type that meet all ships Australia-bound days from the mainland appeared at noon on the fourth day. This was a sure indication we were nearing a large land mass that could only be our objective. The birds were insatiably curious. They flew two abreast from behind in a long line and, after matching their flight speed to ours, they mounted what seemed to be an eye-to-eye inspection of Bill or me, whoever was steering at the time. They hovered at a shoulder-level position until they were replaced by the next in line with repetitious regularity. All this was done in an eerie silence that became unnerving as the day wore on. They never rested. As fast as those at the front were replaced by those behind they retreated to the back of the queue to take another look. They avoided every effort to brush them away and we had to resign ourselves to the unblinking scrutiny as best we could. They left us just before dark but reappeared next day at full light. Shortly after I had taken over the tiller at 10am for the first of my four hours they slowly wheeled over the boat and flew out to sea.

It was about then I saw the contour of Pott Island so far distant it lacked even the clarity of a moorland peak on a misty day. Not wishing to raise false hopes in the others I checked the landfall in the Pacific Pilot and then willed myself to wait for a full hour before looking again to be sure that this time it was Pott mountain I could see. I roused the others and in the hope that the Pacific Pilot had it right and there was a French planter on the island, we had a double ration of our dwindling stew.

By late afternoon the island was clearly in view but it was three hours after dark, guided by a fire on the beach, before we penetrated the surrounding reefs to meet all six feet and four inches of the French planter who owned the island. From him we learned we had passed through one of the worst hurricanes in living memory. This became clearly evident the next day when he took us by Jeep to see 40-year-old copra palms scythed to the ground all round the island by ferocious winds of a velocity unknown before.

The planter, a most hospitable retired sea captain, ridiculed any idea we might have of going further by dory. He offered to accommodate us for a few days when his monthly visit to the mainland was due. Even with our dory in tow he said his launch would do the trip in a fraction of the time it would take us alone. Meanwhile, he fed us on game and fruit bat shot on the estate.

Strolling along the seashore one day with Bill we saw an island fisherman with a recently killed turtle in his boat. Asked how he had caught it, I gathered from questions put to him by Bill in the local patois, that he'd used our old friend the sucker shark hooked on a line and then lowered close to and just above the unwary turtle asleep on the seabed. The rest I knew. The sharp tug on the line and the speedy attachment of the sucker to the unfortunate turtle with such adhesive force as to bring both shark and turtle to the surface with no effort at all. Questioned about how the islanders caught the dugong, often seen swimming cradling a calf to its breast – whose near-human appearance had given birth to the legend of the mermaid – the lone islander fisherman's answers to my queries were just as evasive as those given by the shell divers on the Barrier Reef – from whose boats at night frequently emanated the succulent aroma of dugong steaks frying on deck. Penalties for killing both turtles and dugong in Australian waters could involve loss of boat plus heavy fines.

In reminiscent mood as the launch drew nearer to New Caledonia Bill recalled reading at school how a captain in the Royal Navy, who had first discovered the mineral-rich island, had been so unimpressed with its barren aspect that he sailed right round it twice before deciding to annex it for the British Crown only to find that a French unit had sighted it the day before and lost no time in claiming it for France.

We landed at Pume and were met by senior gendarme Brethes and his wife who gave us a meal that ran to eight courses and the whole of a piglet. We gladly accepted a lift on a truck owned by an old school friend of Bill's leaving that night for Noumea, the capital of the island. At the midday stop, regardless of our protests, we were given the last beers in place of the customary wine. The lady of the house was on the point of pouring wine when our driver told her we were Englishmen.

We arrived in Noumea in the middle of the night. The driver, ignoring all protest, woke the staff of a hotel and without any sign whatsoever of annoyance they signed us in and apologised that the rolls they served with the coffee for which we had not asked, were not oven-fresh.

254

They refused payment for the first beers in the bar next day and when this generosity was repeated in outside bars staffed by Melanesian girls we decided to keep to the hotel bar to avoid receiving the free drinks which in those pre-tourist times the locals could ill afford.

That Bill blamed himself for losing the ship was no reflection on his intelligence as he demonstrated clearly later in providing the answer to a problem put to us previously by our senior partner Bill Davies who first heard it when a passenger on the P&O ship *Canberra* sailing from Southampton to Sydney. Only two of the passengers got it right. I was the only one of our original crew of seven to join them in finding the correct answer.

The problem was this: On receipt of a plea for mercy put to him by the three surviving loyalist officers all lieutenants, the rebel general responded by showing them three stakes set in the form of a triangle and five uniformly sized discs, three white and two black. He told them they would be tied to the stakes facing inwards, their eyes would be covered while one of the five discs would be stuck on each of their foreheads. If after the blindfolds had been removed they could correctly give the colour of the disc on their own heads before sundown they would be reprieved. He warned that just one incorrect answer or attempt to communicate among themselves would result in immediate execution. Of the couple on the *Canberra* who came through the test one was a schoolgirl of fifteen and the other a retired army officer. Their times were twelve and ninety minutes respectively. My own time was ten minutes. In three minutes flat Bill had the correct answer. When their eyes were uncovered had one seen a black disc on the heads of each of the other two, he would have called for the general to tell him he had a white disc on his own head.

But when no one did, that effectively put one black disc out of play. After another period of reflection, each in turn came to the conclusion that not one of them was wearing a black disc, or the beholder would have called for the general. Again, when no one did, each one concluded that he could only have a white disc on his forehead. An intelligence conveyed to the general earned their instant release.

Through our insurers, Lloyds, we sold the dory to the highest bidder and before leaving New Caledonia we called on the French planter to thank him for his hospitality. He placed us further in his debt by giving us liberal pegs of Scotch whisky and food before we left to board the world's last operative Sandringham flying boat for the flight to Sydney.

We were met in Sydney by John who, with true Australian nonchalance drove us in our sea-stained overalls to the Wentworth, a top-flight hotel into which he had booked us. Over a crate of beer brought to our room by him and his friends we were advised to take jobs in one of the high-paying car plants.

We left the hotel next morning after an excellent breakfast marred for us somewhat by the awareness of the total unsuitability of our mode of dress which was probably, in the complete absence of any evidence of class consciousness in the attitude of those about us, more apparent to ourselves than to them. Tom and I took John's advice after buying new outfits from the downtown English store and renting rooms in Randwick with facilities for cooking.

Starting work on the assembly line the next morning and being tall I was assigned to the squad fitting rear windows. Tom worked on putting the cloth linings inside cars assembled from parts imported from Britain and Detroit in the USA.

A chance-in-a-million meeting with Cliff Webb with whom I had trained in the Shanghai Municipal Police depot and whom I had not seen for years, led to my early application for a job as a field officer with Desert Locust Control, an adjunct of the East African High Commission, which he had left after his recent marriage. In due course I received a reply telling me that should I ever be in Nairobi they would be ready to grant me an interview. So, with East Africa ever in mind, I worked long hours to earn the passage money. It was monotonous, repetitive work at the car plant. Most of the labour force was composed of Australians many of whom had been there all their lives. For economic reasons and the universal goal of keeping ahead of the Joneses some did two jobs such as delivering bread, emptying dustbins at running speed or tossing newspapers into front gardens while driving slowly down the centre of roads. The aim no doubt was to finish in good time to start work at the car plant or conversely make up time lost in leaving it.

Another encounter as improbable as that with Cliff Webb in Sydney occurred in a bar when I was asked by one of the most dinkum-looking Australian old timers I've ever seen whether the name Palethorpe meant anything to me. I said it did but it would mean nothing at all to him. Palethorpe was the name of a Yorkshire firm in England I told him, that produced tomato flavoured mincemeat and with that, the finest sausages in the world. This announcement brought a grin to the face of the questioner as wide as the harbour bridge, before saying that he had worked for Palethorpes from schooldays until 1920, the year he had migrated to Australia. He had guessed my origin from the accent I thought I no longer had when I'd been conversing at the bar. He told me he had never been able to convince an

Australian that there was such a thing as a tomato sausage. This reminded me of the many failures I had had with English southerners trying to convince them of the marriage between tomato and sausage meat inside the skin that was so popular up north.

Bill Brown, who drove me to work in his ancient two-seater on a cost-sharing basis, turned up one day at the wheel of a brand new Holden. The car, he told me, belonged to his brother, who owned a sheep station but who was seeking temporary work while staying with him in Sydney. The next morning I was introduced to a man in faded khaki slacks held up by a length of frayed rope. This was the brother now employed as a temporary sweeper at the car plant. The incongruity of it all struck me as bizarre. Here was a wealthy man who, within a week of his daughter having wrecked a brand new British MG car, had bought her another despite long waiting lists and high prices for imported cars. Yet here he was a menial – but a menial only to pass the time while staying in Sydney with his brother – a sweeper of floors and remover of garbage.

He reminded me of the old mining engineer returning from a holiday in England. A fellow passenger on the *Dymas* which brought me to Australia once said that there was no aristocracy as such in Australia but only the aristocracy of wealth. 'There it matters not who you are or what you are so much as what you've got in the bank.'

Stories of boomerangs returning to the hand of the thrower by city-bred Australians who had never set eyes on a boomerang had always been seen as far-fetched by me. That was until I saw it done by a small-town Aborigine. Clean shaven with hair parted down the centre and wearing sharply creased khaki shorts with bush jacket to match – a popular tourist attraction – he sent a boomerang flying round the small outback town square where he lived looking for all the world like a huge bat seeking somewhere to land. Unerringly the boomerang returned to the hand of the thrower seven times out of eight. The odd time out was when the boomerang seemed to lose last minute momentum and dropped at his feet, but still within reach.

The Australian tendency to spend an hour catching a horse to ride a distance that could be walked in five minutes was matched by another national habit: the urge to bet on anything that moved. I once experienced a prime example. Four men were seated in front of me on the Sydney cricket ground when there were differing opinions on what the likely score would be at close of play. Fivers were taken from each of the four and passed over the shoulder of the collector into my hands without a single glance to the rear. At the end of play the obvious winner of the bet reached back for the four fivers quite confident that no right-minded Australian – as he'd taken me to be – would ever sink so low as to walk off with stake monies placed in his care.

By December with funds boosted by overtime work I booked a passage to Aden on the Orient liner *Orontes,* on her last voyage before scrapping. A further forty pounds bought an air ticket from Aden to Nairobi. On receiving notice of my intention to leave, the plant foreman surprised me with attempts to dissuade me from going to New Guinea, where, not wishing him to think me quite mad I had stated I was bound for. Perhaps I was not quite so bad as I had imagined myself to be, but then perhaps I was. The dearth of labour in Sydney at the time was so acute that even an automaton who through sheer boredom, absent-mindedly fitted a standard glass in a special model at least twice a day was better than no automaton at all.

On the last day of the year, lighter in pocket by two thousand pounds than when I first set eyes on it, I watched the famous Last Pub in the World on the seaward end of the jetty in Freemantle slide past as we made out to sea. That was after the sight of three already homesick Sydneysiders complete with baggage, making a concerted last-minute – and dangerous – jump off the last gangway by then rising clear of the wharf.

Listening to the moans of Pommy migrants returning to UK whingeing about all things Australian, including the quality of the free accommodation most had occupied since arrival in the country, it struck me that, apart from John's casual allusion to me as not a bad sort of cove for a Pom when introducing me to his friends, I had never once been referred to as such. There had been times when jobs had been offered to me in preference to Australians better qualified than me. Perhaps the reason was simply this: I never committed the usual Pommy mistake of telling Aussies how much better things were done back home in England when so often the opposite was the case. For instance, in Australia the regulation that pedestrians should keep to the left of the pavement and strictly observed was infinitely superior to the free-for-all seen daily on ours.

Looking back on jobs offered there was the time at the start of the off season, I was asked by a fisherman, unaware of my commitment to build boats on Magnetic Island, to act as his offsider to fish around New Guinea. There was also an invitation to help in the delivery of a new powered yacht to Rabaul with air passage guaranteed back to Townsville. Also the invitation from an experienced gold prospector and, later, by three others who specialised in gold and sapphires, to join them on long tours to the outback. With generous government grants paid to licensed prospectors all I required in both instances was an initial outlay of £50 for my own tucker and tobacco. Both would supply everything else including transport and equipment.

The three sons of upstate farmers travelling to Britain to study new farming techniques, who threatened to punch the noses of any who referred to them as colonials, were living proof in the rural areas at least, that old impressions of Mother Country superiority died hard. The probability that their request for my future address, like most things aboard ship had been forgotten as soon as given could have been the reason why I never heard from them again. Or perhaps, who knows, they had done what they said they would do and in the doing had punched the wrong nose.

With only twenty-four hours to go to Aden there was an early morning tannoy announcement by the ship's captain to the effect that at 10am we would rendezvous with a sister ship of the P&O Orient Line – the passenger liner *Arcadia* outward bound to Sydney – to take off three stowaways who had illicitly boarded her in Aden. At 9.30am the majestic white painted-over-all *Arcadia* appeared over our bows. By 10am with passengers lining the rails of both ships, each ship lowered small powerboats to effect the exchange. Ten minutes later three crestfallen Arabs manacled together – their dreams of the good life in Australia now come to nought – appeared on deck to be transferred to the brig in the depths of the ship.

10

DESERT LOCUST CONTROL – EAST AFRICA AND ARABIA

When the Adenair flight via Hargeisa, the capital of the then British Somaliland, Djibuti and Mogadisho terminated in Nairobi all the hotels were full and I was glad that I had booked three nights at the New Stanley Hotel before leaving Aden. At Desert Locust HQ I learned that the senior officer was away from Nairobi for a week. In the meantime I took a room at the Queen's Hotel which I shared with a young German engineer towards whom I felt a detached sort of sympathy because of the magnitude of his task of promoting a car, the Volkswagen, in a territory completely dominated by British Austin cars. But that was back in 1955.

Following a successful interview at Locust HQ and a stiff medical I was posted to Saudi Arabia. Another Adenair flight took me to Jeddah where I was met by the senior officer and taken to Baraiman camp eighteen miles outside the city.

Desert Locust Control (DLC) had established an efficient system of control from the year of its founding. Accurate records of the movements of all the swarms, which had invaded Arabia and East Africa, had been compiled and from these a pattern of behaviour had emerged. The most important was that breeding occurred in roughly the same areas each succeeding year, though volume of rainfall or wind could cause variation in the pattern and often did.

The larger part of the vast areas controlled by DLC was sparsely populated. There were few roads and communications were nonexistent. Breeding on a large scale in these remote areas raised problems of some magnitude in moving men, vehicles and insecticides in sufficient quantity, and in time to combat breeding within the time limits imposed by nature. Breeding locusts bury their pods, each containing up to seventy eggs, in moist ground as they are laying. For this reason they follow the rains which not only assist in softening the otherwise sun-baked gound but provides the necessary warmth during the 12-14 days incubation period. At the same time this encourages the growth of the new vegetation on which the hoppers will feed. The hoppers, as they are known, remain confined to the ground as they develop through the five instar stages. Each stage terminating in turn as they shed their skins at seven-day intervals. At the third stage they change colour from black to green.

Throughout the five week period the hoppers, which are guided by the incidence of the vegetation most to their liking, will have spread to infest an area ten times the size of the original egg field. At the end of the fifth week the pink fledgling locust emerges from the skin cast for the last time. For about the next ten days they remain in the same area, making short erratic flights. Then, finally, small sections detatch themselves and begin the almost imperceptible drift which causes the rest to swarm about them before they fly away in search of new feeding grounds. This is an immature swarm which will, on changing colour to yellow, become capable of breeding. But when this will happen is anyone's guess.

To combat this breeding, field officers were equipped

with a personal Land Rover, a Dodge Power Wagon fitted with a winch, a five-ton Thornycroft diesel truck, a Redifon transmitter and positioned throughout the territories controlled by DLC a few weeks before incoming swarms were expected. This arrangement enabled us to familiarise ourselves with the area before the rains set in. We had maps, vehicle spares with workshop manuals and cash to cover wages and purchases of fuel and oil. We carried a well-equipped medical box complete with instruction on how to dispense its various contents. In Saudi Arabia where strict prohibition was in force, we had to forego alcohol.

In Baraiman I was handed a booklet on locusts to study and told that actual experience in the field, which would start immediately Jonah the transport officer had my vehicles ready, was the only effective way of learning the work. At the same time, tall, broad-shouldered, bearded and with an authoritative voice chief officer George Pemberton, a one-time British naval commander introduced me to Aisl, a foppishly dressed effeminate-looking young Arab government employee, who would act as my guide in the field but whose main function, George told me later, was to ensure that we in locust control, the only foreigners in Saudi allowed to roam the country at will, did not engage in any unauthorised prospecting for oil or gold. All other foreigners, be they American or British, were confined within a radius of five miles from their work place.

Next day as promised, rotund and overweight, loudly humorous ex-army sergeant major Jonah, the senior transport officer in Baraiman, presented me with my transport, the last remaining Land Rover and Dodge Power Wagon in camp. With the vehicles came the drivers. Slight of build, birdlike and volatile Sudani

(Sudanese) Bedouin goat herdsman turned driver, Mukta Maki, quick to anger and as quickly back to his old self, was to initiate me into the art of driving through seemingly bottomless fine sand without getting stuck. The far too raffish city-bred Eisa was to drive the Dodge. He, in common with the broad-shouldered young headman Ahmed, newly promoted to make up my team, had never left Jeddah before.

I was sent to assist Jeff Taylor in Bisha on the Arabian Highlands, the whole of which was heavily infested that year. Bisha lies due east of the Red Sea port of Jeddah.

By noon on the first day after leaving Baraiman we had crossed the wide coastal plain. We climbed the deeply eroded centuries-old road to Mecca which snaked its way up a 5,000 feet high escarpment to the highlands above and then forked two ways. The first, newly tarmac-adamed, went arrow-straight to Mecca. The second, a series of deep vehicular tracks into open desert was, according to Mukta, our road to Bisha. Or it would have been had not Aisl indicated that we continue along the dust-free tarmac road to Mecca for at least another hour before turning south for Bisha. Being our guide, he had his way. I grew more apprehensive as the miles sped past bringing Mecca, the holiest city in the Muslim world ever nearer by the minute. I knew that any Christian (infidel) who entered Mecca, whether by accident or design would suffer summary death by stoning. It was a great relief and considerable pleasure, therefore, when we were stopped by outer Mecca guards, who soundly berated guide Aisl for bringing an unbeliever (me) almost in sight of Mecca before herding us back the way we had come and heading us in the direction for Bisha.

There was actually a stoning during my sojourn in the

Highlands. An unfamiliarly light-skinned overseas Arab pilgrim, thought to be an infidel masquerading as a Muslim, suffered death by stoning. But, I was solemnly told by my informants, this man could be assured of a high place in Mohammed the Prophet's heavenly paradise – even before pronounced dead in Mecca.

Two hours later as we approached Bisha where Jeff Taylor's camp was sited I saw my first hoppers: a small band of first instars which appeared to me to be a group of wingless flies engaged in energetic jumping exercises on a patch of sand surrounded by flood waters. While Mukta, seated beside me in the Land Rover was identifying a palm-fringed town in the distance as Bisha I was anxiously studying the mile-wide expanse of flooded wadi we must ford to get there. Being the last arrival at Baraiman with the oldest transport in the DLC fleet our chances of crossing were slight. This question was resolved when we came across a convoy of our own Thornycrofts carrying urgently-needed bait who were confident they would make the crossing. With fan belt and sandals removed and following their experienced lead after being warned not to stall the engine, I took my first lesson in fording a flooded wadi – with Mukta seated beside me keeping a wary eye on the young driver following in my aging Dodge.

Driving through flowing brown water the illusion, in the absence of anything to mark the passage forward, is that it is not the water that is moving but that the vehicle is being drawn sideways upstream. This impression is broken only when the force of the water actually pushes the vehicle sideways in the opposite direction. As we came into the shallower water at the other side my Dodge stalled behind me and as I instinctively turned to go back loud shouts and urgent gestures from those on the bank signalled me to leave the water. During the few seconds of indecision I saw a Dodge which, from its colour I knew to be a government vehicle, drive down the bank at speed, take my stalled Dodge on its fender, and push it in the direction of the bank until its engine fired. Just as all three of us got onto dry land a high wall of flood water rushed down the wadi with sufficient force to have taken us with it. The truck had been sent by the Emir of Bisha in case it was needed. This was typical of the many kindnesses I was to experience while in Saudi.

In Bisha I was instructed by radio to proceed south towards the ill-defined Yemen border with two loads of bait and spent the next three weeks reconnoitring the southern extremes of those wildly beautiful Highlands, and from information coaxed from the equally wild Bedouin tribes we occasionally met, the area was cleared.

With the total absence of wells in this region water was our main problem. The drums brought from Bisha were conserved for tea making twice a day, cooking the one meal we had at night and topping up radiators. This was tacitly understood by everyone except Eisha the city-bred Dodge driver, who went all too often to the drum on his truck until everyone's attention was drawn to his selfishness by Mukta.

When he pointedly inquired of him whether he considered himself to be 'a man or boy', this had the desired effect of reducing his unwelcome swigs to four or less a day. This same driver compounded his offence by bringing ridicule on us all and wide grins of contempt-uous incredibility on the faces of a party of Bedouins by asking them for water. He was blissfully unaware that both they and their dogs lived entirely on milk from their camels and goats who were themselves sustained by dew absorbed during their early morning grazing and from water-bearing plants.

267

I was then moved to a point twenty miles off Jeff's camp where there was a heavy infestation. There was no shortage of water in Bisha nor diminution in the volume flowing down the wadi. One of the big Thornycrofts bringing up bait on the night of my arrival had stuck in the heavy silt in the middle of the wadi – and even after unloading defied all efforts to move it. We had been told at the time to carry on with the all-important control work and get it freed later. Work on a large American oil bowser similarly stuck had also been abandoned.

Returning to camp one day I learned that my Dodge driver had once more distinguished himself again over water. He had gone to the well to draw some and this time there were sheep herdsmen at the well head. Sheep were watered every second day and formed into compact squares whose symmetry they always maintained as though enclosed in invisible wires. At least that was how they were until my driver's blaring horn and loud demands that their owners should fill his drums stampeded them *en masse* across the open desert. He was speedily replaced by Mukta.

For reasons of economy the government guides, drivers and headman were brought from Jeddah but the bait spreaders were locally hired only as required. I was fortunate in hiring the only one available in the whole area on the first day and with careful use of our two vehicles managed to clear up a fair-sized area.

Hoppers do not normally feed between eleven and two o'clock in the afternoon. They prefer to spend this period clinging to any vegetation capable of suppporting them clear of the midday scorching hot sand.

While the rest were establishing camp on the first day I put four sacks of bait in the Land Rover and took the local coolie with me on a reconnaissance, baiting any bands of hoppers we saw until they stopped feeding. Then carried on to assess the full extent of the infestation in that general direction before returning to camp along a route different to the outward journey.

The following day the Dodge, guided by the coolie went over the same route and mopped up any bands we had been unable to bait the previous day. While this was being done I 'recced' another area with the headman and he acted as guide on the Dodge the next day. Working this system for three weeks from 5am to dark each day most of the bands were destroyed and due to their cannibalistic habits any remaining bands could reliably be left to do for themselves immediately they came across hoppers previously killed by the bait.

The bran bait we used was mixed with ICI Gamazine powder in Nairobi – and one speck of Gamazine from this bait which was spread thinly along the line of approach of a hopper band though quite harmless to man and beast, was sufficient to kill three hoppers – and frequently did. The first one actually eating the bait, the second which consumed the body of the first and that if eaten would in turn kill a third. The bait remained lethal for up to six weeks, a point not lost on the desert tribesmen and African bushmen in whose areas it was used. These men, though happy to see the marauding hopper bands killed off before their areas were denuded of vegetation, were apprehensive (or pretended to be) of the effect it might have on their grazing animals. A solemn declaration to the effect that while it was lethal to locusts it was quite harmless to man and all forms of animal life was a waste of time. Invariably the sceptics amongst them called for a demonstration by the field man to prove his good faith. The *modus operandi* was always the same. Half a mug of bait was taken from the open bag in use to prove the test genuine and then mixed with water. Though eaten in full view it did not convince them. They believed – despite our disclaimers – that we swallowed special pills from the medical box to counteract the poison before staging these demonstrations. One field man who dutifully gave five such demonstrations in the one day confessed to a slight feeling of intoxication but added, that there was not a cat-in-hell's chance of his ever becoming addicted to it.

A tiny crack in the bakelite casing of the petrol pump on my Land Rover, for which there had been no spare in Jeddah, finally fractured just as we were leaving for Wahdi Taballa. This left me no alternative to taking a chance on the Dodge which was necessarily left poised on the top of a hill every night due to a defective battery, the result of my old driver's lack of maintenance. In this we skirted the rough country dotted with thirty-foot-high sandy hillocks which lay directly in our path, by taking an old camel track which circled it. By late afternoon we had found and baited the hopper bands – the object of the recce.

All went well until we were at a point twenty-odd miles from the camp on our return when the engine stalled in soft sand in the bed of a narrow wadi. As our Dodges were fitted with front winches there was no starting handle. This left me with no alternative but to walk back to camp to get help from Jeff. The question I asked myself was – should I make that long safe detour by which we had come or take a chance by walking across those high hillocks without map or compass in the gathering darkness. I knew that if I missed the camp there was nothing but desert beyond. The time factor and the fact, due to its being Ramadan, that nobody had eaten since before dawn decided me. I was confident that Salam my ex-fisherman cook, would, as Mukta had done once before, place a hurricane lamp on an elevation as a guide for the last few miles into camp. And accordingly I set out with Ahmed the headman from Jeddah.

Walking across ground dotted with high hills there is a tendency to deviate as the higher hills are avoided. As darkness descended I remembered John Baldry's advice in the fishing days which was based on his wartime experience as a bomber pilot, to pick out as he did then, a star to steer by when the hypnotic effect of the twisting compass in the binnacle light, on returning at night from raids on Germany, induced a tendency to sleep. Although in my case there was no such tendency, I took an easily identifiable star as a guide to mark the course set from a mental picture summoned of the maps left in camp. I was careful to correct any deviation necessarily made round the higher hills by making a compensatory one in the opposite direction – as I knew to miss the camp would put us in country void of all habitation. Sublimely confident of my ability to walk straight to camp this possibility never once occurred to Ahmed whose fertile city-bred imagination, fearful of the desert and filled over the years with locust drivers' exaggerated stories of the wild men in this area was busily engaged in peopling every nook and gully with murderous assailants and the stealthy footsteps he imagined he could hear behind.

Some five hours later, with a lot of luck and a modicum of good judgment we could make out a faint light which appeared to be two miles ahead. But ten minutes later walked into camp to find it came from a moth-encrusted lamp standing on the camp table outside my tent. So much, I thought, for Red Sea fishermen.

At first light Mohamed the new guide, who after several strong hints to Jeddah had replaced Aisl, set off for Jeff's camp. Fortunately for all concerned he came across Jeff's Dodge on its way to my camp with a new petrol pump and battery which had arrived in Bisha late the previous night from Jeddah. The truck then went on

271

to Taballa and winched my Dodge clear of its bed of sand. With both he and the local coolie smothered in the previous night's mosquito bites, Mukta stormed across to berate me for the night's misfortunes, as though it had been me and not he who had stalled the Dodge. This continued until a swirling dust devil swept through camp hurtling everything moveable over a mile-wide area, for which, judging by his attitude, he also blamed me. I can see him now: bent slightly forward, hands on the tightly tied knees of the baggy white trousers which were habitually worn by all true believers like him. However, by dark with all our possessions recovered and the aroma of the night meals rising from the camp fires, he was again back to his old humorous self.

Driving across Wahdi Bisha to report to Jeff's camp that my area was clear I noted that only the top of the cab of the Thornycroft we had been obliged to abandon over a month ago was showing above the level of the now almost dry wadi bed. The same applied to the big American oil bowser bogged down at the same time. I was to do a reconnaissance of the whole Highlands to ensure that no hoppers remained, then free the truck from the wadi and take it into Jeddah on the twenty-ton Scammell which would be sent up for the purpose. Jeff, a one time electrical engineer and former amateur all-in wrestler in Yorkshire and the other field men were transferred to East Africa on temporary duty.

By the time I got back to the wadi only the air vent on the top of the cab was showing. As these vehicles had been specially built to give the high loading necessary to prevent the bottom layers of bags being immersed when fording flooded wadis, I realised we had a lot of digging to do. The promised Scammell and extra Dodges had brought coolies and Tanganyika jacks to assist in lifting the truck. This jack was a German invention used in the territory after which it was named. The jack itself was fitted upright on one end of a four-foot length of nine by three timber, and its long thread cranked up by a handle. The Americans had removed the bowser during my absence by lifting it out with a heavy crane mounted on a truck after coolies had dug it clear. Without such an aid I had only the jacks and without some form of solid foundation on which to stand them they would obviously sink into the mud when pressure was applied by cranking. When I sent a truck to get large flat stones for this purpose the suggestion put forward by Ibrahim the Scammell driver that we would not need these as the jacks would be more effective planted straight into the mud was dismissed as totally impracticable.

When sufficient sand had been removed from under the vehicle the jacks, each standing on a large flat stone, were wound up but instead of lifting the truck the expanding jacks merely pushed the stones deep into the mud. As even more and bigger stones were places on top of the first they in turn were wound down into the mud which was by then coating us all from head to foot and by dark, smothered with mosquito bites and nothing achieved, we called it a day.

Next morning as I was wondering what to do next Ibrahim's reiteration for the umpteenth time that we dispense with the stones decided me to let him try his idea if only to keep him quiet while I thought up something else. And accordingly the jacks were placed straight into the mud. As the cranked pressure was brought to bear the jacks sank as before but this time there was a fractional lift. The process continued for the rest of the morning and by noon we had the truck clear, despite having to winch the jacks out of the mud after each lift. Never once did this polite, self effacing Saudi driver so much as imply that he had 'told me so', for which I was profoundly grateful.

A hole in the wadi bed created by the flood waters was deepened to form a makeshift ramp and the Thornycroft was winched onto the Scammell by dark. The intention to start for Jeddah next day was cancelled due to the discovery that from the mosquito bites of the previous day the entire staff with the sole exception of Mukta were down with malaria. As usual the medical box and the pull of Jeddah had the desired effects and we arrived there next day.

A week in the locust control mess presided over by ex-Palestine Police Tich Harwood and I was able to dispense with the length of guy rope used for the past three months to hold my ever sagging shorts up – the result of living on thirty-day ration packs. Each pack contained six 12oz tins of corned beef, two of Irish stew, three mainly vegetable camp pies plus ten tins of standard-sized sardines, all rounded off with a tin each of Carr's digestive and tea biscuits and, not to forget, three bottles of Rose's lime juice.

Walking through the suq one night, which due to its being Ramadan opened only after dark, a tap on the shoulder drew my attention to a line of shining ryals which had fallen through a hole in the pocket of my slacks. The dense crowd through which I had been passing at the time had instinctively parted so that I could recover them with ease.

Later I was sent to the coastal area south of Jeddah to establish myself near Sabaya, twelve miles inland from the ancient port of Qizan and close to the Yemen border. With the exception of Mukta at the wheel of the Dodge I had been given an entirely new crew. Hussein: tall, slim, dignified and the most impressive guide in DLC. Aisl: older, more experienced and desert-bred had replaced Ahmed as headman. Vocal, English-speaking, liked by all, top driver in his class, Bartock joined us with his Thornycroft. With cheap meat and fish readily obtainable, both they and I were well content with this posting.

Driving down the coast the humid heat was intense. No demarcation line existed between land, sea and sky. All three were merged into an all-pervading haze. The track ran through a mixture of flour-like sand, Sabka salt flats, an eighty mile stretch of rocks ranging from very large to those the size of bungalows. The first threw up such clouds of fine dust that two-mile spacing between vehicles was necessary. Even then, eyes, ears and nostrils were filled with it. I had been warned in Jeddah and again by my drivers not to leave the iron-hard and deeply rutted track across the Sabka quicksands made tortuous by the original camel men who had made it in their search for ground sufficiently firm to bear their weight. And at all costs to avoid the illusory hard ground in between, which was nothing more than a sunbaked crust over bottomless mud. The eighty mile drive over the rocks was remarkable for the fact that no springs on my Land Rover, loaded with two-hundredweight of ryals each the size of a 10p piece, nor the Thornycroft, laden with twenty-six fifty-gallon drums of fuel, were broken as we lurched from one to the next.

When calling on Emirs to pay our respects we wore the red Bedouin headdress over the commonly used skull cap. Slacks replaced shorts, shirtsleeves were rolled down, and in conformity with the custom that hair be worn on the face, I sported a small moustache, plus a goatee beard. The Emir himself always presided over the meals which inevitably followed on these visits. Seated at his right side as guest of honour I was always the recipient of the tastier items as they were served. Especially the eyes for which I could never conjure up a liking and which,

275

after the first, under cover of a fold of my headdress I passed on to an appreciative Mukta. By pre-arrangement he always sat on my immediate right. Guests sat cross-legged in small semicircles on woven multi-coloured rugs. Care was taken not to present the soles of their feet towards the Emir and to eat only with the fingers of the right hand. The left – traditionally used to cleanse the anus with water or a handful of dry sand after a stool –was considered unclean. Large reed grass platters of mutton and rice constituted the main meal. There followed the ceremonial drinking of three small glasses of tea; the first sweet and black, the second flavoured with mint and the third filled with peanuts immersed in plain tea. The whole camp right down to the last coolie attended these functions and should any of them be within earshot of the Emir, he listened to their comments with the same unfailing courtesy he extended to the notables and without any sign of patronage.

When the servants appeared before one of these meals, each bearing the customary long spouted water jug for the hand washing ceremony, one guest was heard urging another to avoid the water jug being offered to the dirty Nazrani (Christian), being me. In dignified rebuke the Emir walked the whole length of the room, then pointedly washed his hands from the water jug under which I was washing mine. The remark passed by the notable was an allusion to our use of toilet paper in place of the customary water, or in its absence a smooth stone or clean sand.

On the several occasions I have stayed overnight at an aptly-named palace, every member of my staff slept on the thickly carpeted floor of the huge chamber allotted to us. Its three-feet-thick mud walls lined all round with brightly coloured Arab handmade rugs had kept the room cool even throughout the intense heat of the day.

Invariably, maize bread, freshly gathered dates and Carr's English tea biscuits were served for breakfast.

Sometimes, passing through a town only weeks after the last time I omitted to call on the Emir, almost invariably we were summoned to the palace not, I fancy, for the pleasure of seeing me so much as to hear what news Hussein the guide had gleaned at the several places we had visited in the interim.

For the first three months in Sabaya the Kharif, a hot seasonal wind, starting before dusk as no more than a slight air movement, slowly developing into a gale force wind by midnight before subsiding early next morning, left the atmosphere hazy with fine sand. Its moist humudity frayed the tempers of staff kept sleepless by cracking tent canvas and plagued by prickly heat to a point where minor differences flared into violent quarrels. Radio contact with Jeddah was made so difficult that messages were often relayed through other locust men camped in East Africa, unaffected by the Kharif.

It was while camped here in Sabaya that I experienced for the second time a quite severe earth tremor. On this occasion, through a vividly realistic dream I relived the last, right down to the violently rocking bed and the cries in the darkness. It was some time, though probably only seconds, before I realised that, as the shouts I could hear were hoarsely masculine and couched in Arabic and the creaks all about me consistent more with straining canvas than with groaning stonework, I was not, in this instance, elevated in a fifth floor room in the Hotel De Peking but in a tent on the Arabian Desert.

Fifty miles out on a week-long recce the staff's reaction when I told them I had forgotten to relock the large cash box in my tent after making a last minute payment was the Arabic equivalent of 'So what'. I was assured that no

277

one would even go near the camp in our absence let alone thieve from it. This proved to be the case months later when what remained in the box balanced my accounts to the last ryal.

Next day we crossed the near inaccessible country towards the Yemen border through sand so fine and deep, as to lead Mukta to exclaim, eyes and ears full of it, 'Atha mush rummel – Athi da-keek' (This is not sand –it's flour). Though the Land Rover took it in its stride, the final steep approach to the escarpment which was our objective defeated the first three attempts the Dodge made to breast it. But it made it on the fourth on to a vast trackless sandy plateau stretching a good five miles to the foot of the escarpment itself. Just discernible in the rays of the dying sun and nestling at the foot of the escarpment we could make out what appeared to be a small town, a mere dot on the map, without a name and the remotest in the country.

Even here, the official deputising for the absent Emir gave us a large palace room in which to sleep and a meal that night which was attended by all the local notables. A quiet word from Salam, my cook, next morning was to the effect that our host did not appear to have understood the advice he had given at their request as to how eggs should be fried. When two still-raw eggs floating in warm goat fat appeared I saw what he meant and judging by the expression on the face of the server it was pretty obvious that he thought the English had rather peculiar gastronomic tastes. But while extracting the eggs from the oil with freshly made maize bread I appreciated the effort that had gone into producing what they now considered to be a typical English breakfast towards the end of which, even in this remote town, came the inevitable Carr's biscuits.

Just as we were leaving, a lone figure, feet shackled

with a short iron chain to which was attached an iron cannon-ball sized weight, emerged from the town jail. When I asked what this was all about, I was told he was awaiting trial by the absent Emir and since no food was supplied in Saudi prisons he was being released for the day to beg for food in the town suq. Any question of escape with that huge weight chained to his legs, was virtually impossible.

More fortunate than he, South African-born, immensely strong and goatee-bearded Ron Talkon was sitting in his stationary Land Rover in the main street of Jeddah one day when a Saudi driven limousine backed into it. Both Ron and the Saudi driver of the other vehicle were immediately seized by police and confined in the city jail. Colleagues from Baraiman visited Ron twice each day with hot food, tea and cigarettes. The several Arabs with whom he shared his cell were likewise supplied by friends and relatives, their only sustenance.

That few in the more remote areas had ever seen a white man was evidenced by the number who came to the camp at each night stop invariably to ask Hussein the guide if they could take a closer look at me. Since the only other white I saw during that eight months on the coast was another locust man, passing through one day on his way to Jeddah from Aden, this was hardly surprising.

On one memorable occasion one of the crowd gathered around me after studying the front of the Land Rover was heard to remark to another, while pointing to the radiator grille: 'That's its nose,' then to the headlamps, 'Those are its eyes,' and to the front bumper, 'And that's its moustache.'

Once every year it was customary for King Saud, for a period of up to two weeks, to leave his palace in Ryhad and rule his kingdom from a round circus-sized marquee out in the desert. Everyone over a wide area was free to visit the King.

The year before my posting to Sabaya, Ron Talkon and a colleague were seated on the fifth tier of seats behind a tent pole and Ron complained to his colleagues he could not see the King. The sharp-eyed King, observing the whispered exchange, sent a minion to ask what had been said. On being told, he instructed that they be given seats with unimpeded views of the dais on which he sat and presented them with fifty ryals each.

At night when away from camp on recce we squatted round a fire made from twigs if available, reeds or donkey droppings if we came across them or, in the last resort, the reserve store kept under the truck seat and ate the meal cooked by Isle the headman by the light of the fire. The first meal since five that morning was either chopped mutton, goat or camel meat with sliced onions fried in goat fat mixed with rice and left to finish off in the raked embers. This we scooped out with the fingers of our right hands as we ate. Arab tea with plenty of sugar rounded off these meals which could not have been bettered in Soho.

As no rain had fallen for over eight months, driving over the sunbaked Sabka to Qizan, the last seaport this side of the Yemen border, was like driving over a never-ending series of inches deep furrows set in concrete. For this reason, when going there to buy fuel I sat with Bartock in the heavy Thornycroft, which gave a smoother ride than my short wheelbased Land Rover.

On a jetty by the fuel depot an enormously large Arab, whose wide shoulders levelled the top of my head and his slightly shorter but no less muscular brother, on learning that we wanted two dozen fifty-gallon drums of petrol and diesel agreed to load them for ten ryals. First they toppled them into the sea and then floated them to within twenty yards of the beach. There, the larger of the two took each in turn on his shoulders and carried it to the truck and placed it exactly where Bartock indicated on the high-loading body. This was a prodigious feat of strength matched only, as far as I know, by Taffy Woods, a husky six foot four inch tall one-time sparring partner of Tommy Farr who was briefly world heavyweight boxing champion in the 1930s. Taffy, a recruit with me in the Shanghai Municipal Police Training Depot, for a bet, once picked up unaided a similarly filled fifty-gallon drum and carried it a measured 100 yards before setting it down gently on the concrete-surfaced depot parade ground.

From there it was a short walk to the suq where Bartock conducted himself in a manner very unlike those many tourists seen in Aden in the past. They would hold aloft for all to see such bargains as wriggling snakes and crooked Charlie Chaplin walking sticks made of shells or wood, proudly boasting of having beaten the seller down to half his asking price and sublimely unaware that in anticipation of this the price had been doubled at their approach. Bartock in contrast bought meat for the whole camp without argument or comment. An Adani himself, he quietly passed from one stall to the next until the right price was quoted. For what, I was not at all sure until its presence beneath the writhing masses of flies on the stall was revealed by a magical wave of the hand of the vendor to be freshly killed mutton. The whole scene was enlivened by suq cafe waiters threshing the air above their heads with canes to prevent swooping crows clearing the trays they carried at shoulder level to waiting diners. Though I had seen it before in North Africa, I paused to watch a lone donkey lowering its head to receive friendly licks from the family dog balancing himself full stretch with one paw placed between the eyes of the donkey.

Every night while in camp in Sabaya, before retiring to my bed, came the nightly ritual of trying to pass water, a task made difficult by the intense heat. At 9am each day our whirling hygrometers, held three feet from the ground in the shade, gave a true reading of a few points above 100 degrees centigrade. All liquid swallowed during the day had immediately been expelled through pores in heavy sweats instead of, as was normal, passing wholly down into my bladder – and what little did, was soon almost pure acid. This could only be ejected with pain so great as to bring me to my toes, and often did to no avail. To put it off to the next night, with the accumulation of still more acid in the interim, would be a hesitant and fear ridden effort to pass what appeared to me to be more like tiny shards of broken glass than water.

To my dismay, almost eight months to the day after my arrival in Sabaya, the senior officer announced over the radio that since our tenure in Saudi had been terminated I should bid farewell on his behalf to all the coastal Emirs, then return to base. This was due, as I was to learn later, to the machinations of that arch Anglophobia who was frequently referred to by exiles from Egypt over which he ruled as Abdel Gamel Bloody Nasser. Grave, and I am positive, genuine expressions of real regret came from all sides when I made this news known. We were not permitted, on our way to Jeddah, to pass through a single town until we had joined the Emir in one last meal.

Back in Baraiman I felt rather like the Aden field man who for a period of two weeks after a long spell in the desert, refused to go near the base dining room until a signal from his boy indicated that everyone had eaten and left. Familiar with this tendency towards self effacement on the part of long absent desert men, base staff, particularly jocular senior transport officer, Jonah, drew me into every mealtime discussion to see how the return to normalcy had affected me.

I was to be transferred to Ethiopia. Those several would-be Lawrence of Arabia fanatics left of their own accord and the rest were discharged.

* * *

After a few days in Addis Ababa getting the necessary visas and passing the stiffest driving test I've ever known (which I learned later would have been waived on payment of a few Ethiopian dollars – then at eight to the pound) I flew to the Ethiopian DLC Headquarters in Dire-Dawa. This pleasant, sleepy town of wide avenues lined with tall, flamboyant trees, where no one ever seemed to hurry, is the biggest in Ethiopia. It is the head of the French controlled rail link with Djibouti, the port and capital of French Somaliland. The town had a number of Greek-owned shops and at least two Italian restaurants which catered in the main for the Italian and Greek businessmen who handled most of the commerce and the drivers of the huge trucks which carried their merchandise all over East Africa. Several pleasant hotels catered for the occasional visitors, chief of which was the Ras where most of the Europeans and Americans stayed, or called in for drinks at the quiet bar.

Ordinary bars known as tegbeits, for the less discerning seekers after quantity before quality, were patronised for this reason by DLC field staff. Drinks of all kinds, including a strong bottled beer from Addis and a good cheap local brandy, were available in these bars. This, with the distinctive type of music common to this part of Africa issuing from at least three different radios tuned into different stations in each of these bars with such force that it was best enjoyed at least two streets away, was in marked contrast to the quiet of the desert I had just left.

Possibly due to the failure of the rains in Arabia there was no locust activity anywhere in East Africa, but reports of heavy rain spreading through Ethiopia and the Ogedan preceded my posting to Mega in Southern Ethiopia.

After climbing the steep tarmac road which leads over the escarpment out of Dire-Dawa, we bought bags of potatoes and onions from the colourfully-dressed roadside vendors near Harar for distribution to the various locust camps we were to pass through in the next two weeks. By evening we were through the hills and had arrived at the large locust camp in Hargeisa, the capital of the then British Somaliland. Here I met a few more of that band of field men acknowledged throughout Arabia and East Africa by almost all and sundry as the absolute desert and bush experts, but dismissed by their principal employers, the Kenya farmers, as the unemployables of Africa, and by a Whitehall recruiting official as the roughs, toughs and adventurers of this world.

In its infancy, faced with an unprecedented infestation in Kenya, with a still bigger one threatening from surrounding territories, DLC sent its permanent men, already possessed of the essential visas, health documents and knowledge requiring no supervision, to stem the incoming tide. Meanwhile temporarily hired staff already in the country, but with no pressing commitments at the time, were hired to deal with the farmlands.

Regrettably, the farmers had not met Jonah the innovative head transport officer in Jeddah, Saudi Arabia. Nor had they met John Paget, one-time purser on the always unescorted Polish Government owned passenger ship *Batory,* who had, during the 1939-45 European war, survived crossing the Atlantic both ways no less than forty-nine times. Nor tall, well-built Hector McMichael who was now passing through Hargeisa on his return to Dira-Dawa after long treks in the rugged hills south of the Webi-Sibelli river's flood waters which had held him prisoner for months in complete isolation. Mac's complete lack of showmanship and self-effacing manner effectively masked that initiative and underlying strength of character which led him, a school leaver in his teens, to travel alone to Australia to become an outback sheep-station jackaroo, and subsequently work on construction sites in every state in the Commonwealth.

The first day's drive took our small party, comprising multilingual for that part of Africa, supervisor Abdel, slim-built Dodge driver Mahmoud and Mohamed my cook, out of Somaliland and through ever thickening bush to stop overnight at the now empty Wadare locust camp in the heart of the Ogedan. Dry and barren most of the year, but transformed almost overnight by the recent rains into an impressive wild beauty of dense leafy bush.

While my documents were being examined next day at a desolately lonely Ethiopian check camp, I sampled for the first time the hospitality of the garrison officers who were thirsty for news of the outside world – and freely generous with their cognac and the native-brewed teg, a mead-like drink made from honey produced in Ethiopia. As a consequence I arrived late at Kingsley-Heath's camp on the river Webi-Sibelli. There was a dream-like quality about the three meat courses, shot in anticipation of my arrival by this urbane, ex-Welsh Guards officer and now Kenya White Hunter, accompanied by cognac procured from the local gendarmerie, in the blaze of a leaping wood fire, which had guided me through tall dense trees to the riverside camp.

There followed several days driving along tracks through bush so dense that neglect in noting the sun's position before stepping off the road to spend a penny could, by reason of its very sameness once the direction of the track was in doubt, have serious consequences for the unwary.

Most of our driving was through very sparsely populated country and only a very occasional Somali bushman was sighted. These nomads, arms threaded along the spear resting on the back of their necks, a tiny water skin and meagre food supply swinging from spear or belt, long slim legs effortlessly bearing equally slim figures to their tribe's temporary grazing camps seven to ten days distant with an amazing economy of effort, were incontrovertibly the hardiest long distance bush walkers in Africa.

Three nights later we were in Dolo, an advance base camp which was presided over at the time by Taffy Saunders, one of the original field men in the organisation and Lulu, a full grown geranuk – the largest gazelle in Africa. Bought for a few shillings from a bushman who had found her when only a few days old, she was completely at ease with DLC staff. So much so that during the evening meal taken in the compound after dark she had stolen up to within neck-stretching distance behind my chair and half emptied my beer before Taffy had come to the end of his discourse on her somewhat catholic eating habits – which precluded nothing that was in any way edible. She liked tea, leaves and all and, as I had belatedly discovered, anything alcoholic.

At some stage during the reminiscing which invariably follows the first meeting with a character such as Taffy who, it transpired, had served in the Eritrean section of the BMA Police and had trained in Cyrenaica, an excited argument in the vicinity of my truck between his boy Suliman and mine presented Taffy, as host, with a problem of some delicacy. Suliman, it appeared, concerned at the rapid depletion of his master's stocks as more and more beer was consumed, had been caught by my cook Mohamed satisfying demand from a crate on the back of my truck. After solemnly considering the offences, Suliman was fined one dollar for his unauthorised unfastening of the tarpaulin on my truck to get at the beer, one more for stealing from a guest's truck, and given a two dollar rise in pay for showing such remarkable initiative in conserving his master's stocks. Lulu, meanwhile accustomed to these minor disturbances had daintily cleared all scraps from the dinner plates, emptied the dregs in the tea cups and licked the leaves from the bottom of the tea pot.

Realising that she was ill equipped to fend for herself if returned to the bush when the camp was closed pemanently a few months later, successful arrangements were made for her to be flown to Stockholm Zoo where, Taffy heard subsequently, she quickly adapted to her new surroundings.

Next day we passed through the two well ordered towns of Mandera and Moyale situated at each end of the boundary of the Northern Frontier Provinces of Kenya, neither of which permitted entry or egress during the hours of darkness. Wishing to make an early start the following day we passed through Moyale and crossed the border into Ethiopia.

While making camp for the night on a track so eroded by past rains that a convoy of double deck buses, passing through any of the resultant washouts, would have been invisible to a person approaching only ten yards away, a big diesel truck which had followed us out of Moyale in the late afternoon pulled up and requested permission to share our site. The dilemma this presented for two young Greek ladies was resolved by placing their bedrolls equidistant between my bed – they had waited to see where my boy would set it – and one of the large fires built to last all night and an equal number of yards from their fellow passengers sleeping round their own big fire.

The first month in Mega was spent in reconnaissance, but in common with the rest of East Africa no locusts were seen or reported in the whole vast area. We resigned ourselves temporarily to the routine life which pertained between locust campaigns, but in circumstances vastly superior to anything I had experienced before. With sheep costing less than three shillings with one recoverable on the skin, plenty of water, an absence of malarial mosquitoes and, due to the prevalence of big game, particularly leopard in the area, the staff were content to eat at night by the big fires made possible by the abundance of easily-gathered wood instead of making the usual nightly requests to go to the nearest village. Two leopards seen stalking past the camp early one morning made these night excursions even less attractive. To keep out the marauding wildlife a high six-foot deep barrier, made from a type of thorn bush liberally festooned with three-inch spike-like barbs, with a movable section for the vehicles to pass through, was always placed round a semi-permanent camp in areas such as this. These enclosures were known as 'saribas'.

Fresh from the desert there was a pleasurable sort of fascination in watching the blaze from our fires playing softly across the tall trees around us, and again on the several occasions in the night when more logs were added to deter the lions and leopards which abounded in this game-rich area. Since Dollo I had seen seven rare waterbuck, two kudu and a profusion of lesser game without leaving the car.

At the forty foot high bridge over the river Dua-Palma we were lucky in finding the very few crossbeams which had not fallen into the river far below were still positioned on our side of the bridge, just as the last vehicle to cross had left them. After driving both vehicles out onto the bridge as far as these beams permitted those at the rear were moved to the front to make an extension sufficiently long to permit of a further advance. This sounds easy, but try doing it without looking down into the fast flowing river far below while balancing yourself on a four inch wide girder! This manoeuvre, repeated twice, put us back on the track which three hours and sixty miles later brought us to our camp site at the foot of Mount Mega. A high sariba of bush with long sharp thorns, too deep for a lion to leap over, had been placed around our vehicles and tents by dark that night.

When sleeping out in the bush I pinned my faith on the theory that the breeze-induced movement of my mosquito net would be even more effective than the fire round which my staff slept. This was supported by the experience of a fellow locust man who wakened one morning to see innumerable paw marks left by a lion which must have circled his bed a dozen times in the night, but had not disturbed him.

Two miles distant, the town itself was a huddle of stone houses built round a Coptic church which on Sundays and Holy-days was filled with a mixed assembly of lounge-suited locals and horse-mounted worshippers in the more widely worn white jodhpurs and Norfolk type jackets.

The local Borana, whose main food was milk mixed with blood from the veins of their cattle which grazed on the waist-high grass in the area, were a friendly tribe. Their tribal wells which were unique in Africa were sunk in two sections the uppermost of which was a large thirty foot deep hole with trenches sloping down to hard mud drinking troughs at the bottom. The water was passed up hand over hand in giraffe skin buckets by a human chain of men and girls standing one above the other on steps cut in the wall of the well, accompanying their work with deep chested chanting so pleasing to the ear that whenever I saw the long plumed spears the men had thrust in the ground in the form of squares before descending the well, I paused to listen to the Paul Robeson-like chorus. The cattle arriving of their own accord went down to the well via one trench and after watering ascended by the other. We were made welcome twice a week to fill our drums from these troughs.

It was here that I first saw the tiny Bolo birds known, due to their concerted swooping motions when in flight, as Weavers. Like swarming bees they settled in such numbers as to first bend, and then break the branches of every tree in sight. Every effort made by the Kenya Government to control these pests which though light in weight, could devastate farmland just as quickly and completely as the locust, was frustrated by the unco-operative attitude of the Ethiopian Government foresters.

While watching the Weavers I picked up several dozen pinhead sized ticks from the long grass of the type which attach themselves to anything brushing against them, and then work their way under the skin to bloat themselves with blood to the size of a fingernail before dropping back to the ground. Recalling the advice given in Dire-Dawa, I applied a thick coat of engine grease and then waited to kill them as they emerged for air. When none of them did, I dismissed the advice as either a leg-pull or at best falacious and spent the rest of that day painfully squeezing them out through cuts made with a razor blade. After this the question previously put to me by a Borana girl who was covered from head to foot in animal fat as a protection against both cold and ticks, and wearing only a string belt from which hung a short strip of leather, as to whether I did not feel dirty clad in shirt and shorts did not sound quite so silly as it had at the time of asking.

The caves on the wooded slopes of Mount Mega just above our camp gave shelter to some of the hundreds of leopards in the area. Barely discernible under the thick coatings of dust which hid even their spots except at close quarters, five or six of them could always be seen sunning themselves on the ledges outside these caves. They were trapped by the Borana in holes cut out of the rocks under weighted slabs which covered the hole when they tugged at the bait inside, and later raised by the Borana at one end just sufficiently high to allow a spear to be thrust deep into the upturned snarling mouth obligingly presented to their captors. Reputed to be the best in the world, the skins were illicitly taken by camel to Mogadishio where, being unscarred either by bullet or spear, they commanded very high prices. One camel train stopped in deep bush by police was carrying no less than 117 such skins.

Less diligent than Ahmed in maintaining his sariba, the headman in a nearby village lost his second donkey in four months to a night marauding lion. Later, though probably considering it a lesser misfortune the headman in a village near Dib-Dibbi had his wife taken through a hole slashed in the family hut during his absence by the same ageing lion which had already killed seven others walking in the dry tug bed below.

All motorable tracks in Southern Ethiopia owed their existence to locust control and the one by which I went to Dib-Dibbi was no exception. In common with the rest it followed, through dense thorn and high bush, the route of the camel track it had originally been, until it was widened and straightened where possible by Ron Smith when coping with a major locust invasion the previous year. At least I didn't have, as he had, an average twenty punctures a day to mend with the prospect of many more to follow even after he had left the area, as the thorns embedded in his tyres and protective bands worked their way through to the tubes inside. Nor were my driver and supervisor scared out of their wits, as were his, when a herd of elephants attempting to stand their broken-down truck on its head, followed by four lions who repeatedly quartered the cab in search of the men they could smell inside, until the sound of Ron's Land Rover approaching in search of his overdue truck drove them away.

On my way back from Dib-Dibbi I called at Jed to look down at one of the deepest salt lakes in the world. Sited at the bottom of a crater so deep that it had taken the energetic Ron Talkon five hours to regain the summit after descending to view the workers at close quarters, who from the top had appeared to him as they did to me, like so many ants in a pond.

Several pleasant months later I was told by radio to meet Pete Hay in Moyale and return with him to base, from where I was to be transferred to Suiyun in the East Aden Protectorates. Faced with a fractured fuel pipe on the Dodge the day before leaving I was obliged to seek the help of Taffy Davis an ex-DLC mechanic presently constructing water pans for the Kenya Government some twenty miles south of the border. At five the next morning I drove through the same holes and washouts we had traversed on our way to Mega and by eleven Taffy had completed the repair. Hoping for an early start the next day I left immediately, and despite the time wasting transference of loose boards on the bridge over the Dua Palma, I arrived back in camp at 4pm anticipating hot tea and relaxation only to discover that in my absence the carburettor had suffered the same fate as the pipe. This left me with no alternative other than making another appeal to Taffy.

This time I took the driver with me to take turns at the wheel. He, however, claiming he had poor eyesight, forced me to take the wheel for the whole journey.

After skirting the now closed town of Moyale we arrived at Taffy's camp to be greeted with an incredulous expletive, but since we had been good friends in Saudi he did the job, and by midnight I was on my way back. Not all those green and amber eyes reflected that night in the beams of our headlights, alternately illuminating each side of the winding track, were those of lion or leopard, but the driver's nervous reaction to those that were tended to disprove his previous statement regarding his sight. But then, had I had nothing to do but look about me from a completely open car perhaps I would have done the same. That I was the only one to have made that risky Dua Palma bridge crossing by headlights not just once, but twice in one night was a distinction at the time at any rate, I could have well done without. We drove into camp as first light was breaking and within an hour were on our way back to Moyale.

Those who have lived in the bush are familiar with the coughing grunt of the male lion which scares his quarry into the path of his fanned out mates for them to kill, but few have heard one roar. My opportunity of joining those few was defeated by an overwhelming tiredness which

293

put me into a deep sleep immediately my head touched the pillow on the night I met Peter and despite my being a light sleeper, I failed to wake to the roars the rest told me next morning were emitted by a lion annoyed by our unwitting presence close to his hide.

The Adenair plane taking me to Aden to connect with their Dove flight to Suiyun touched down on Socotra just long enough for me to read from a board outside the British Agent's house the amusing answers to the questions most commonly put to him by passengers in transit, which went something like this – Yes, I am the only European on the island – Yes, you are the only other whites I ever see – No, I am not married – Yes, my supplies come from Aden by the weekly flight – Yes, I am quite happy here – No, I never feel lonely.

After the Dove had made its spectacular banking descent to the floor of the sheer thousand-foot drop Wahdi Hadramout I met Bob Hall, a one-time LRDG non-com and our most experienced desert man. Between long recces to check on any possible locust movements over the vast deserts of southern Arabia we lived in a house in Suiyun which in common with all others in that part of Arabia, was a monument to the ingenuity of the local artisan. Built from local sand and lime with fibrous palm trunks acting as beams, its original locks, still in perfect working order, were made of wood and operated by wooden keys which turned the intricate wooden wards of the locks themselves. A hole in the floor of an embrasure projecting from the water drum-fed shower room on the side of the house eliminated the necessity for the customary early morning walk into the bush, had there been any bush to walk into. So effective were the drying qualities of the desert sun on the sand beneath this embrasure that the only time I was made aware of it was when a visitor ignited the toilet paper scattered below with a carelessly dropped match. In the neighbouring town of Shiban similarly built houses rising to a height of twelve storeys were the rule rather than the exception.

Two sultans who held sway over life and death in their respective domains lived in palaces which in their oriental splendour might have strayed from the Arabian Nights. While I was there, our cook, Suliman, looked the wrong way at a girl in the harem of one of them and Bob was summoned to hear that Suliman had better be on the next Dove flight to Aden – or else. Not wishing to have a diplomatic row burst over our heads, Suliman duly left.

Until the 1950s the Rub-El-Khali had been impenetrable to motor transport until aided by one of its planes DLC found a way through the outer dunes and so enabled us to enter and explore an area hitherto penetrable only by camel. Even now only a few DLC men, the three British officers of the Hadrami Legion and some oil company geologists, flown in privately, have ever been in the 'Empty Quarter' as it is more commonly known. In order to penetrate the soft surrounding dunes I learned new driving techniques which entailed skirting the sloping shoulders of each dune in turn at high speed to lessen the tendency to side-slip into the hollows between, in which a vehicle could be irrevocably lost. Sometimes, due to wind pressures the blind side of a dune to which we were driving fell away into a sheer drop, and without warning the vehicle took off to land four square on the next dune in line. If a dune was soft, however, the vehicle would break the sand at the top and descend onto drift sand into which only a lightning change down could prevent sticking.

These same dunes presented a scene of total beauty when the slanting rays of the setting sun tinted and

softened those unshadowed by their westerly neighbours, with a golden sheen which was matched only by
the rays cast briefly from the east at dawn. The vast
pebble strewn plains inside, unbroken in this waterless
area by dry river beds and devoid of all forms of plant or
animal life suggested that it was once part of some
prehistoric sea. This impressive solitude with never so
much as a fly in evidence was broken on one occasion by
the track of a solitary migratory beetle whose faulty
navigation had put it off course, but apart from that no
other signs of life were ever seen.

Returning through Shibam we always called on Dr Eve
Hoeck, a German lady surgeon who managed the
hospital and was the only European in the town.

After leaving Aden, where we had taken delivery of five
new locust vehicles, we passed small parties of Indian
hajjis (pilgrims) on the waterless track trudging between
dunes which in the harsh sun-glare looked like mounds
of dried salt, unaware that they could be turned back by
the Saudis whose resources were annually taxed to the
limit by penniless pilgrims attempting the Haj. Many of
these who had started the Haj as young married couples
would on its conclusion arrive back home a family of
four.

In Makulla suq that night we had bowls of the fiery hot
curry introduced to the port centuries ago by Makulla-
based dhow masters who had traded as far east as
Sumatra and Australasia. The total absence of Europeans
in the port was reflected in suq prices which were even
lower than those in Crator. With our slightly enlarged
convoy we left the now empty government rest house by
the sea as the rays of the rising sun was clothing in
unimaginable beauty the centuries-old harbour and
surrounding hills in a sheen of burnished bronze which
gave only a hint of the heat to come.

At the half way mark we learned that the near middle aged newly arrived assistant agent met briefly on the way down had been shot dead within hours of our passage, and only weeks after his long sought after posting from Whitehall to Arabia had at last been granted.

There followed a day-long drive through high slate-blue rocky hills sparsely covered with a purple scrub, which gave them a wild beauty oddly reminiscent of the moorland hills at home except that these were void of all human and animal life.

After a freezing cold night part way up the escarpment we started the lengthy business of ascending to the top. To avoid the possibility of a multi accident we made the climb one at a time and when Bob in the lead reached the top I started up what seemed to be an endless series of roughly cut hairpins which got progressively steeper and tighter. I rounded the last one in my long wheel based Land Rover with three inches to spare between the sheer rock wall on my left and the 7,000 foot drop on my right. Ignoring this turn, the driver of the truck after me crawled straight ahead nose upwards into a shallow bay cut out of the rock face, and with the door wide open in case of any mistiming, applied both brakes. Meantime, the two Suiyun coolies riding in the back carried the two large stones they had ejected over the tailboard onto a short ledge cut out of the rock face in line with the track to the top, where they held them ready to place behind the rear wheels of the truck as it completed the reverse turning movement on to this ledge, which placed it nose pointing to the top and with its tail hanging in space.

When this hazardous exercise had been repeated with each of the three heavily loaded Thornycrofts all six vehicles settled down to traversing the plateau by a narrow track which deviated in a never-ending series of 'S' turns round the innumerable deep crevices and craters with which it was pitted. Many of these were so deep that the first and last vehicles, which on account of the blinding dust were spaced two miles apart, frequently passed each other in opposite directions separated only by the width of the crevice they were skirting at the time.

Once again, as we crossed these high tablelands I viewed without envy the tough loin-cloth-clad men walking their laden camels from The Hadramout to Behan and sometimes to Aden, and wondered anew how they managed to sleep during the four nights they would spend in these high altitudes shielded against the intense cold only by the warmth from their camels, and the single goat and camel hair blanket they strapped over one shoulder when travelling. Carrying, for the most part, the same loads and dressed like their forebears they could be seen squatting three times a week with their camels by the runways of the several Hadraumi airstrips to carry the air cargoes to their final destination.

Their eight days' detention and stripping, even to the fuel tanks and headlights but mercifully not the radiators when a quick thinking driver told them that trucks like camels could not work without water, of three loaded Thornycrofts returning alone from Aden on one occasion, was a mark of their disapproval for our encroachment on their centuries-old preserves, and in search of the money they imagined we had gained from it.

The rest of my service was in the Somalilands, Kenya, Ethiopia and the Ogedan where there was a heavy infestation at the time. I was sent to Mustahill on the banks of the river Webi-Sibelli to work the sparsely inhabited southern regions which were dominated by three tribes who traditionally evinced a marked antipathy towards each other, outsiders in general and

DLC in particular. With the heavy infestation of three years ago when they had been employed by the dozen as bait-spreaders still fresh in their minds, they grossly enlarged every hatching they came across. Reports of bands of record proportions requiring, according to them, forty men and thirty camels for twelve days would prove after a day long drive to be hardly worth baiting.

Conversely, reports supplied by the local police major, together with copious measures of his homemade teg, were always reliable, as were those from the Army Commander. He was said on the best authority available, which was DLC, to add homemade cognac to his already mind numbing version of teg just to give it some much needed extra strength.

When the nightly chantings, which sounded more like the ravings of a riotous mob than the religious recitals they were supposed to be, starting at midnight and ending with dog-like barkings at dawn, had prevented sleep for the umpteenth consecutive night I took the hint and moved up river to Callafo.

Returning from Emi, where according to the Somalis the British wrongly believe the remains of the Old Mad Mullar who was headline news in the 1920s as leader of the Somali rebellion lay buried, the Dodge windscreen was broken in a hail of stones simply because I had removed a barricade obstructing our path on the outward journey. The significance of a bugle call of all things in one of the remotest parts of Africa when we arrived to bait the just for once genuinely large hopper bands, became clear when thirty-odd members of the tribe which had reported them advanced from all directions to lay down the law according to them. I was to make no more unwelcome incursions into their area and in future pay on demand such sums as they required to do my job for me. My rejection of this together with a threat to throw them spears and all from the back of the Dodge they had boarded as of right ended amicably for once when he of the bugle gave us a run through all the calls he had learned when a bandsman in the one time Somali Scouts.

Within days of Jan's arrival in the wilds of Bar Magog the same upstarts who had once tried to oust me from the shade of a tree because they claimed that right as exclusively their own, took everything portable from his tent during his absence on recce. On returning to his camp next day after a police tracker led search had established that the culprits had crossed into Somalia before they could catch up with them, he found his transmitter smashed beyond repair and his tent slashed to ribbons.

Only a very few of the friendly Riverene tribe had ever left the river and the one I hired for a four day recce was not one of these. Stories of thirst crazed travellers in waterless bush thought up by my staff round the fire at night to relieve the monotony so heightened his inbred fears of it that when the river came in sight four days later, even though miles from his village, he leapt off the truck and left us without so much as a word.

The crocodile once as plentiful in Callafo as it still is in the river near Dolo and the nearby Dua Palma, where fourteen footers are an everyday sight, has been hunted here to near extinction. The only evidence of its limited presence now was a tendency on the part of the Riverene people to bathe in groups close to the banks, and for their dogs to drink on the run at widely spaced intervals, and then only a lick at a time. With their usual insouciance and disregard of reports of impending rain, Hargeisa told me to make once again, the obstacle strewn recce to Emi. As always, in order to avoid reprisals against my locally engaged supervisor I took it upon myself to remove the newly erected barrier blocking the only path through the forest of riverside trees into the open bush beyond. The threatened rain which had held off as we slowly winched our way across the permanent three miles wide swamp by the usual expedient of passing the winch wire through a spare wheel set in a shallow hole covered with earth, commenced to pour in torrents as we regained firm ground.

For its eighteen hours duration I sat under a tarpaulin undecided as to whether to return through the swamp if that were still possible, or continue in the hope that the rain had not yet flooded the two deep tugs which crossed the track some ninety miles ahead. Finally, influenced by the possible huge losses which could accrue to the Kenya farmers in the unlikely event of breeding having occurred since my last visit, by the plight of the staff who with their usual blind faith that Allah would provide had run out of food and forbidden by their religion to share mine and our reputation for always getting through, I pressed on when the rain eased off.

A tribute to the ingenuity of the wartime British Army, the manually propelled ferry used now only by DLC was just as we had left it on our last return from Emi. That is, except that now its bow or stern, whichever was which on a double ended ferry, was hard aground on top of the ramp, itself under several feet of fast flowing water. However, with our transport on deck after a lot of pushing and shoving and strenuous poling from the rear, and guided by its two overhead pulleys, we reached the Emi side without mishap.

When the seasonal camp where we set down the girl who had accompanied us from Callafo proved to be just short of the first of the tugs, and my main problem resolved by offerings of food for the crew I left them to it, and continued along the half flooded tree-overhung track to check the state of the first tug.

After several detours into the bush to avoid deep water on the track a lone bushman going the same way, who had invited me with a wave of his spear to follow him led me several times in and out of the trees until suddenly he stopped, and while holding the top branches of a dense thornbush clear of the car signalled with his spear that as the way was now clear I should go forward and then sweep back to the track. Since his idea of clear might not tally with my own I climbed onto the bonnet to see for myself and had I not, my mysterious disappearance literally from the face of the earth would have remained a mystery forever had I taken that carefully calculated nose-dive he had planned into the seemingly bottomless crevasse I saw yawning right under my feet. By the time I looked back his barely discernible outline was receding back into the bush from whence it came reflecting perhaps that he who tries and fails the first time, can always try again.

Joined by the Dodge at the tug, by then rapidly flooding, but through which I passed first try and delayed the truck only as long as it took to bury the wheel, rig the winch and reload. The next few miles would either allay or confirm the fear which had haunted me since Callafo that we might now be trapped without food or radio for the duration of the rains between this and the deeper vee-shaped tug which lay ten miles ahead. Its high water level, when we got to it, and rising by the minute was a clear indication that if we didn't cross then we never would. Recalling the nightmare occasion when his stalled Dodge had careered backwards from the top of the precipitous wall of this same tug with sufficient impetus to drive it half way up the even steeper side opposite, I told the driver to cut out any fancy driving and go straight through if he wanted to eat that night, or for that matter ever again. Then, pausing only long enough to check that he was in second gear and four wheel drive and kick off my sandals we made the crossing in the nick of time before the flood waters came boiling down from the hills in a huge wave twenty feet high. From there, lighter in heart than for days we drove by headlights through ever deepening floods into Emi where police Captain Ricardo kept me up half the night drinking his homemade teg.

Next day these same floods obliged us with the help of a police tracker to take to the hills to reach the track by which, before I learned that Mohd the driver was sickening with malaria, I had hoped to reach Wadere by nightfall. What with stops for aspirin and hot tea and our reduced rate of progress we were still only three parts there by nightfall. Time and again I steeled myself against the mute appeal of the doused headlights showing on and off in my wing mirror and waited in darkness round the next bend until the isolation of the bush at night, the pleas of the others and the overriding fear of the local tribes inclined Mohd to make still one more effort. Revived in part by an injection at the police post in Wadere when we arrived there late that night, he managed the last few miles to the locust camp where my report on Emi was listened to with such wrapped disinterest I wondered why I'd bothered to go.

Back by the Webbi two nights later the seldom heard hysterical laughter emanating from the trees across the river scared the life out of me and the staff too judging by their sudden silence until we realised that it came from our old friend the striped back laughing hyena.

About this time a liquid sprayer invented by John Sayer in Nairobi adapted for use on a Land Rover had proved so effective that it was soon to replace powdered

303

bait. My next move was to Berbera on the Somaliland coast where the tribes were more friendly, where due to the mile wide tugs emptying in hours instead of days we could always return to camp at night, and also dispense with the sundown to bedtime pacing up and down to avoid being eaten alive by the myriads of mosquitoes on the Webbi. Here I could sit outside my tent at night and watch the land crabs which were like miniature editions of the giant Saudi rock spiders which had clung to the walls of the tent at night regarding me with an unblinking fiery-eyed curiosity, tidying the beach, even to the extent of carrying away the still glowing cigarette ends flicked out of the tent.

Smaller and more densely populated than the other territories we worked, this posting was not popular with those like myself who preferred the remoter regions, but lying as it did in the path of the migratory swarms it was frequently the breeding ground for those legendary swarms so dense as literally to blot out the sun. After settling on every inch of ground in and around Berbera successive waves from one such swarm alighting on the busy port roads to devour those already reduced to pulp by passing trucks were themselves crushed and eaten by later arrivals who in turn were crushed.

Liquified in the sun, the grease from this accumulated pulp so impregnated the tarmac as to remain a hazard for days and a dark stain for months. These, seen later by others dispelled in part the disbelief with which reports such as this were usually received in Hargeisa. Also in doubt until I saw the damage myself was the local British doctor's statement that on his return to his flat for lunch he had seen locusts from this swarm, which had entered through open French windows, ravenously eating the sweat impregnated fabric on the arm and headrests of two old government issue armchairs. Before the heavy

layings resultant on these invasions one of the new
exhaust pressured liquid sprayers was fitted to all Land
Rovers. Fears that low gear driving through soft ground
with ground temperatures between 90 and 100 degrees
would overheat their engines proved groundless. So
heavy were the killings along the coast that the stench of
their decay, despite strong sea breezes, remained
powerful for weeks.

The largest, and I think the most beautiful, antelope in
Africa and this includes the kudu and waterbuck I have
ever seen near Mega, the oryx which still roams wild in
herds up to 300 on the plains of Southern Ethiopia like
the leopard, lion and elephant was now a dying species in
Somaliland. Said by Richard Burton, the first explorer, to
have been plentiful in the lush pastures which existed in
the 1800s the remaining three which appeared almost
tame on the two occasions I saw them owed their survival
to rigidly enforced protective laws. Their near extinction
had resulted from the extensive over-grazing which had
followed on the civilising influence of successive colonial
governments who had virtually stopped the inter-tribal
fighting which had formerly kept the population at a
level which the country could comfortably support.

The Kharif which creates an alien world of wind-
driven sand, straining bushes and rolling scrub was at its
peak when I was awakened, ears assailed by the whip
cracks of the fly striking the tent and the groans of
straining canvas by that instinct common to those who
live in the bush, that there was a lion in the tent. My
hastily switched on torch focused, not on the huge
snarling mouth I had expected to see, but on that of a
harmless civet cat scooping butter from an open tin left
on the table the previous night.

Drawn by the louder than usual screams and chatter
from dense trees near that same camp one afternoon I

came upon two gazelles furiously lashing out with their sharp hooves from within a circle of about twenty baboons who were making repeated attempts to snatch their newly born offspring. Their mode of attack before we broke it up was like that once described to me as common in the Sudan where it was not unknown for a large band to give way to a foot traveller until they were to each side and behind, then, after blinding him with dust kicked back in his face rend him apart with their teeth.

Credence to this may have been given by a personal encounter I once had in Ethiopia. After leaving the car to walk up a rocky defile, absently at first and then with growing unease I noticed that the scores of baboons flitting through the rocks on either side, were falling back, and some slightly behind me. Not anxious to test the validity or otherwise of this story I returned to the Land Rover with more haste than I'd left it.

With the run-down of the leopard who was their natural predator, long trails of iron-hard dome nuts it would need a hammer to break, discarded after one bite, marked their passage through the bush. By their habit of placing the first cob taken under one arm after only one bite and then letting it drop as they replaced it with a similarly bitten second which in turn was discarded as the arm opened again to take a third, whole crops were destroyed over night.

It was with some pleasure that I relieved four young bucks of their self imposed task of defending with their slashing hooves an old gazelle too feeble to keep up with the herd, by putting a shot through the head of a hyena out for a kill.

Another I shot was tearing the living flesh from the second loin of a sheep after reducing the first to a tangle of skin and torn sinew, as it leaned dejectedly against a sand bank within feet of its sleeping owner.

With all this in mind it is debatable whether the official in fastening himself in his Land Rover when he lost the ill-defined track and ran out of petrol on the wide waterless plain between Borama and Huddin had not exposed himself to a peril more real than that he had sought to avoid. This action, inspired by the dictum that it is easier for an air searcher to spot a vehicle in the bush than a thirst-crazed man on foot, was negated by the speedy return of his support driver, and his sighting the glow of stationary headlights soon after dark.

An old woman though probably still not forty, a girl of ten and her smaller brother setting out on this same vast plain towards the end of a long hot summer had been without water for nearly two days. Their tinder dry water skins testified to the truth of this, and their sheep were in a bad way. Although her own lips were dry and rimmed with dust the girl took the first hastily filled mug to her mother and the next to her brother, before drinking herself. Urged to make for the rain we had seen earlier moving in from the coast some ten miles distant the woman pointed out that they could only go as fast as their exhausted sheep could walk, and that would not be far. Beyond giving them water, tinned fruit and biscuits, the only items in my pack acceptable to a Moslem, there was nothing else we could do but leave them sitting there waiting for the rain to come to them.

The reason for the enigmatic smile never far from the face of the lean, straight-shouldered elder who lived in a sariba the size of a village and whose animals and possessions were fully commensurate with the fabulously wealthy estate he was reputed to own became clear when he anticipated a question still not fully translated by the interpreter, and made conscious of his slip by a direct question in English he admitted his familiarity

307

with the language. Amused at being caught out he went on to give a graphic account of the forty-odd years he had spent at sea, first as a galley boy and later as bosun on Cardiff-based freighters plying to the Far East and Australia. The high wages he had earned which as a Moslem he had not spent on drink were sent to his wife from the outset, and the land and animals she had purchased at intervals formed the basis for his present great wealth. Negligently balanced against his long spear, resplendent in brightly coloured lungi and short white jacket against the background of white sand and scrub, it seemed a far cry from the ports of the East and Australia we discussed and which he obviously knew better than I.

The area I took over in the dry season had such a foul water supply I wondered what I'd done to be sent there. Urine from the hundreds of sheep standing in squares at the only well for miles around, seeping down into the well's limited underground intake resulted in a mixture so foul that even when made into treble strength tea, one sip was enough. At least two beneficial side effects arose from this. There were no visitors from Hargeisa throughout the six weeks I was there which was a welcome change. The other was the solution to a problem which had dogged me for years.

Despite my having a cast-iron stomach which though it would take half rotten meat in its stride, would not take milk in any form. Explaining this for the umpteenth time since joining DLC when offered a share of the milk they were drinking in preference to the water, the staff said they had the answer to this. And they had at that. The camel milk they scrounged with their usual *sang-froid* from the first camel herd down the track had like all subsequent intakes, no adverse effects whatever.

The sudden stab of pain in my big toe and the thump

on my head was the more frightening as it was pitch-black at the time. The relief that came with the realisation that a snake bite had caused the one, and my heavy sandal's fall from the heights to which my reflex action had shot it for the other was as short lived as my first fear that the camp was under attack. The violent spasms which followed held me rigid for minutes on end and for the whole of that night, and most of the next day before reducing in frequency and strength during that night, and finally ceasing altogether without recourse to the serum I had lacked the guts to inject myself.

Opinions differ as to whether the frankincense and myrrh carried to Bethlehem by The Three Wise Men came from the straggly incense trees on the Saudi Tihama or their counterparts in Somaliland, which supplies most of the incense used in churches of the world. The bushes which grow from cracks in the porous rocks of the escarpment are self perpetuating and family owned. Still known as myrrh, the resin is camel-packed to Mait on the coast where it is stored in godowns age old, and redolent with its aromatic scent for shipment by dhow to Aden for world-wide distribution.

We arrived in Elyu, the last port this side of the old Italian Somaliland as a large sea-going dhow which had been careened on the beach was about to be returned to the water. A channel had been cut through the sand, everyone in the village was waiting to pull on a rope attached to the bow, and a man on a dais with two others holding reed pipes was standing over a drum. At a signal from the dhow master high on the bow, who I felt should have had a long whip in his hand to make the scene more authentically biblical in appearance, the rope was pulled tight and the band started to thump out, not the throbbing Eastern music I had expected, but the once popular and unmistakable tune which accompanied

'Lucy Locket lost her pocket, Kitty Fisher found it . . . .' As this schoolgirl jingle was repeated endlessly I found myself wondering whether they had got the tune from us or we from them, but knowing that it would start a dissertation as inconclusive as those relating to the Old Mad Mullar, or just who had the right to graze what in the Ogedan, I didn't ask.

Further down the coast Arab fishermen were making new nets complete with purse and wings in between hauling in sardines to add to those already drying on the beach. While some pulled grasses from nearby hammocks, others plaited them into ropes and netting mesh. Hands gnarled with age, the headman was attaching floats which he said came from Red Sea sponge beds, and rocks and pebbles with holes picked up while fishing, to act as sinkers. Their sole outlay according to him was the cost of a reel of twine to bind the hauling ropes to the net itself. A similar net we made in Sydney with free tuition from a Fisheries officer had cost in material alone all of £250.

Dawn temperatures were in the high 90s with humidity to match as we drove along the coastal plains, now evacuated by all but those too old to make the 9,000 foot climb up the Mait Pass to the plains above. Village huts stripped to their frames and with their contents lashed to their roofs looked more like platforms on stilts than anything else. At the foot of the pass I donned shirt and sweater. Uncomfortable at the time but necessary as I had discovered once before when passing through the cloud bank half way up, and the mists at the top wearing only shorts in a stripped down car. Since it made no kind of sense to hire a watchman for just one night we left the track at a point out of sight of anyone near it, and where the ground was sufficiently hard to leave no trace of our turn into the deepest bush we could find. A bushman turned cook, Mohd's smokeless fire was as impossible to see in that tangle of bush as a flea on a dog.

The failure of the wind to reverse direction after dark as it did last time gave me another cold awakening that night to find that instead of my bed being in the lea of the Land Rover as planned it was the other way round.

Cutting off corners by crossing the highland plains by compass when asked to make a fast run to a base near the Ethiopian border, I came upon the herd of wild asses seen only in Somaliland. Disturbed by my appearance they broke into a run in front of the car, a trait common to all wildlife in Africa. Every attempt to pass them was frustrated by a veer to whichever side of the herd the attempt was made. Finally, by making a wide turn to one side after a feint to the other I passed them, bigger and fatter than their domesticated brothers and still galloping, but by then not too sure where.

The series of moves which followed on three more years of shuttling between Somalia and Ethiopia took me by air to Nairobi, and from there to El Wak in the Northern Frontier Provinces of Kenya by road.

Marked with its Beau Geste-type police post near a tiny village in dense bush it was said to have a temperature of 130 degrees but was in fact cooler than the Somali plains I had just left. Only we and the police were permitted free movement up there but now, with the late rains expected, they were pulling out for its duration. Those who thought the camp in Somaliland had undrinkable water should have tried the selection offered in El Wak. A near dry well in limestone rock which took over an hour to fill a bucket of strong smelling sediment or what little water remained in a large pan which had been in constant use for three months by the locals as a public bath, launderette and immerse in and water their domestic animals by day, and as a slipper bath by the

311

local elephants by night.

I arrived in Moyale just too late to meet the seventy-year old temporary field man who had farmed in Kenya from the days when income seldom matched expenses. New machinery from home was bought from the proceeds of hunting trips on camel back into the then untracked bush. The two days' Land Rover drive from Nairobi to the Webbi was then a major event lasting weeks, and quinine the only relief for malaria. The two months he spent with us each year were motivated, it was strongly suspected, more by nostaligia than necessity. The seven lions drawn to his camp every night mentioned in his last radio report were still in evidence that night I camped on his old site and due no doubt to its proximity to a well used game trail leading to the river. While hunters pay Nairobi £250 for the first, and £500 for the second lion killed in Kenya proper, they were classed as vermin in the NFP and could be shot at will.

Reports of locusts laying near Moyale proved, after long searches, to be genuine just for once. Instead of laying in the ground as they usually did, these had laid in the foliage of the trees on which they had settled two days before giving thereby the myriads of birds this had attracted the feed of their lives. According to HQ this unusual behaviour on the part of the locusts was a certain indication that the swarm was a spent and dying force. Too late for a return to El Wak we placed the bedrolls which we always carried (in case of such a contingency) on the now vacant Moyale airstrip used once yearly by our airspray unit. The scene one night two years before was of a lone bull elephant shedding pots and pans to right and left as he trumpeted his way through their camp with the unit's log built cookhouse fast round his head after getting it stuck in the glassless window aperture while foraging inside. Though undisturbed by marauding elephants that night, the discovery next morning that two grown lions had left overnight pug marks close enough to us to have been of real concern, had we been awake to see them.

Driving along the steeply banked track to Nairobi two grey shapes which in the midday humid haze I took to be oryx climbed onto the road and stretched out shoulder to shoulder and head on to our approach. It was not until the gap between us had almost closed that I realised that those grey shapes seen in the distance had been fully grown lions. With neither room nor time for anything else (adopting the only course open to me) I kept the Land Rover, which was without canopy and had its windscreen bolted flat to the bonnet, creeping slowly forward until to my great relief the male, always the more tractable of the two, moved down the bank leaving me just sufficient room to pass between the steep fall on the left and his still recumbent mate on the right. Typically, apart from the slowly swivelling eyes about a foot from my own, not by so much as a flick of the tail did she betray any awareness of our passage. Nor did she, when I leaned slightly closer to cautiously steer the front and then the back wheels within an inch of first her extended forepaw and then her tawny flank without toppling the car down the left bank in the process.

A few days later, I went by air to Dire-Dawa to complete the last six months of my contract.

Back in London my belief that as the last field man, my days with DLC were numbered, proved correct when my letter of resignation to Nairobi was crossed in the post by one from them saying that for this same reason, my services were no longer required.

11

BED AND BREAKFAST HOTELS
IN LONDON AND ELSEWHERE

I had always had a yen to be self employed so on my return to the UK in December 1962 I made a tour round all the estate agents in the West End and Kings Cross in search of a bed and breakfast hotel. A business, I told myself, I could handle with ease. The first to be viewed was almost at the top of Sussex Gardens in the Paddington area. On a new twenty year lease at a reasonable rent the proprietor wanted £4,000 for it but was prepared to give a substantial reduction for a quick sale. It was too far from Paddington railway station for my liking so I carried on to the next, a freehold closer to the station for which £26,000 was asked. The estate agent who had taken me there told me that a potential buyer like myself with £10,000 cash available was a rarity and it would be easy to arrange a bank loan to cover the rest. He had on his books, he said, ten or more women with as little as £1,000 to their names anxious to buy and borrow the rest at 6%. At the start of the tourist boom three years later the first was sold for £9,000 and the second for £85,000 when a last minute bidder raised the anti by an additional £5,000.

Unfortunately as it turned out, I was put off buying a ten-bedroomed freehold in Kings Cross by the selling tactics employed by its proprietor. Only one room showed signs of occupancy at the time of viewing but on at least a dozen occasions within the space of the hour, while I was in conversation with the owner, his wife appeared to hand over fivers purportedly from newly arrived guests which he pointedly displayed before nonchalantly stuffing in his hip pocket, without either of them seeming to realise that the hotel should by then have been more than full. Three years later the place was sold for £62,000.

Finally, to my everlasting regret, I allowed a fast talking salesman to land me with a rundown eighteen-roomed hotel in the then no longer notorious Norfolk Square within sight of Paddington railway station on a twenty-one year lease with rent increases of £200 on the seventh and fourteenth years. I commenced business early in 1964 with a working capital a little in excess of £1,000 after borrowing £1,000 from my brother and double that amount from Lloyds Bank at 6% reducible. A popular sporting event having filled the hotel to capacity for the first weekend of my tenure, I moved in on the third day to learn that due to the failure of an immersion heater there was no hot water. A replacement from the Birmingham makers ordered by a plumber arrived broken next day. After a phone call to the firm I left Paddington next morning with the milk train and true to their promise they had me on the noon train with the broken part replaced and we had the heater installed by evening. To avoid a similar occurrence I had the heater changed every two years. Before handing over, the old owners had engaged a housekeeper who had learned the hotel business in her native Scotland.

Win taught me the quick hygienic methods of washing up without an accumulation of wet tea towels and how to make beds with minimum effort but in the first year, with the exception of holidaymakers sent by tourist firms in

315

the summer, Motor Show enthusiasts and the occasional football and school parties, she and Debby, the very efficient Irish lady who came in each day, managed without my amateur assistance apart from breakfast time – when I was permitted to make the toast.

Early in the second year before the Easter business then at fifteen shillings (75p) per night, I started to recoup some of the essential expenditure on new beds, decorating – which I learned to do myself – and replacement of threadbare carpets, most with big holes artfully hidden under beds. Regular loan repayments and additional advertising costs had reduced my bank balance to less than £200. According to accounts of business in preceding years given by neighbouring hoteliers they had often waited in vain for days on end for the ring on the doorbell which would give them their first guests for a week, but things were slowly looking up.

A lot of this door business came from American servicemen on weekend leave. After eliciting the information that there was a single room available they would want to see it.

This entailed a climb up five flights of stairs, hearing for the umpteenth time that the room was rather small, watching the reflective pokes at the bed which preceded removal of first the cover then the blankets followed by a request for a larger bed and, by inference, a bigger room on a lower floor. He would then follow the same procedure in a double room which for the convenience of couples with children was furnished with one or two single beds in addition to the double, but this time interest would be centred on the larger bed. Perhaps the view, the bed or carpet would not be to his liking, so another room would be made untidy before he thought it might be acceptable – but first he must see his friend waiting up the road after a further careful check had been made that the larger room would cost only four shillings above the rate quoted for the single. Having settled this point to his satisfaction he would then depart graciously promising to be back. His return with his friend after the two had completed a similar inspection of every neighbouring hotel and compared prices was just the preliminary to a further detailed inspection, this time for the benefit of the friend who would then condescend to take a second room.

The instruction regarding location of bathrooms and identity of the two keys for front and room door would be followed by an absorption which seldom extended to the announcement that breakfasts were not served after 8.45am, and that rooms should be vacated by 11am. Their aversion to early rising and non-compliance with repeated requests made through locked doors to vacate the rooms before noon was bad enough, but the staff's belated discovery, only minutes before they were due to finish work for the day, that not only had the double beds in the rooms of our selective friends been used but the singles too, made it more difficult than ever to get staff to continue Sunday working.

This tendency for thrift was not confined to single men. A hard driven bargain for a double bed in a room which contained a single often meant that both would be used and, if the stay was for several nights, the single would be carefully made up each day until the final departure timed to take place while we were busy with breakfasts. One couple put in a room with a double and two single beds on the strict understanding that the rates they had agreed to pay were for the use of the double bed used all three beds during the one night of their stay without, as far as we could see, having brought in any third party.

Whether it was an innocent misquote it was hard to

317

say, but if the opinion of the organiser of a party of out-of-town gents to the effect that his mates were the salt of the earth was genuine it was oddly at variance with the views of the staff when they drew my attention to the filthy condition of the rooms and toilets vacated next day. This determined me to eschew this type of business forthwith.

In sharp contrast the many school parties I accepted in those early days were always well conducted, well behaved, and for these reasons welcomed by the staff. Of these, the twenty ruddy-cheeked Eskimo schoolboys we had for ten days were perhaps the most notable. They were just as boisterous as any other boys away from home for the first time as was evidenced by the speed with which they acquired the knack of sliding at breakneck speed down the polished handrail from the fifth to the ground floor without any falling off and breaking their necks. This feat was the more commendable when we were told by their Swedish teachers that none had ever before been in a house with even one flight of stairs. With grandchildren of her own Win was delighted each morning when these boys lined up outside the basement kitchen to give a polite bow in unison as they thanked her for having given them breakfast before bounding upstairs to enter their coach for the day's outing. On their last day the self-styled canny Win showed her appreciation of this daily ritual by handing to each one a slab of Cadbury's milk chocolate bought with her own money.

Whether it was attributable to good luck or good judgment it is impossible to say, but despite the fact that payment in advance was demanded on only very rare occasions, over a span of ten years losses through non-payment of bills was minimal and amounted to less than £20. My initiation into the art of bilking was when an affable young man appeared at the door, requesting accommodation for four nights. On completing his business by noon on the fourth day, instead of walking out as he so easily could have done, he returned to the hotel and paid for the three nights I asked for and then made a further booking for ten nights starting the following week. A check on his room when he did not appear for breakfast on the last morning of his second booking revealed an unused bed, an unlocked portable gramophone case filled with old books and no affable young man.

A scruffily made out bearer cheque for fifteen shillings left by a man from the northern counties for a single one-night stay was such an obvious fake that I threw it away and forgot about it. Another one issued to the proprietress of another hotel for an advance booking put him in the hands of the police when the bank rejected it. Unfortunately for him while he was still in the hotel it transpired that the cheques were from a book he had found on a train.

Assuming that the well dressed couple brought by the proprietor of a nearby hotel to occupy a room we had vacant for two days were known to him, I accepted them without question. When deducting £6 from the credit side of the accounts following their departure two days later I could only hope that their declared intention, delivered in the dining room, that they would recommend the hotel to all their friends back home would slip their minds as completely as did the promise to settle their account immediately their bags were stowed safely in the gleaming new Rover saloon which had graced the front of the hotel for the past two nights.

About 2am one morning I was made aware of a less amusing admittance when I opened the door in response

319

to persistent rings on the night bell to find two police officers with a man who complained that a prostitute had lured him into one of our rooms and relieved him of his wallet. The room he indicated as the one concerned had been let during my temporary absence the previous evening by Win to what she described as a presentable young man but who was, in fact, a tout for a prostitute whose notoriety precluded any possibility of her being accepted in person. The following morning I was greatly relieved to find the keys issued to the young man of the night before in the letter box where he must have replaced them while we were busy with breakfast. That was the last time I ever permitted anyone, charming or otherwise, to be booked in my absence.

Almost permanently tired due to successive eighteen-hour days doing the decorating and improving so essential in those fiercely competitive pre-tourist boom days, I accepted Win's offer that she, refreshed from her regular afternoon sleep and a habitual late night reader, should on this one occasion admit the regular client who had phoned a warning that he would be later than usual. The relief with which I heard the bell ring at the anticipated time of arrival of the guest had barely registered when my semi-basement room light was switched on by a very frightened Win from whose incoherent speech and vague gesturings to the passage outside emerged the two intelligible words – the man. The barely discernible outline of a squat figure at the bottom of the stairs, observing my emergence from the room beat all records up the stairs – and was just a shadowy outline down the square by the time I reached the door. Handicapped by my bare feet I was obliged to give him best. This character, it transpired, whose ring had been answered in the belief that our elderly guest had arrived, refusing to accept that there were no vacant rooms and confronted by a woman he had thought to be alone, had used his superior weight to force open the door before following her down to what he obviously hoped would be an unoccupied basement.

The prominently displayed 'Hotel Full' sign did not deter one young man from repeatedly ringing the bell at 2am one morning because he believed that the sign was just a gimmick adopted by hoteliers for what reasons only he knew. So strong was his conviction, despite my disclaimer to the contrary, he told me he intended to continue ringing the bells of each of the remaining forty-odd hotels in the square despite their showing similar notices to mine. No hotelier dare ignore a ring on his night bell. The ringer could well be one of his own guests who had either lost, or forgotten to take his keys out with him.

It was probably because from the first day of her ten night visit the young American lady guest noticed that her habit of standing in front of the dining room fire holding the back of her skirt high, the better to warm her behind, was such a source of annoyance to Win that she continued to do it. On each of those days the appearance of the lady in question was heralded by a bristly Win expressing a desire to smack the brazen young madam. On the last morning that she announced the imminent departure of the lady with the rider that, perhaps, she was not after all such a bad young bairn was explained when I learned that a farewell kiss, wholly initiated by the bairn herself, plus no doubt an overgenerous tip, was the cause of this overnight transformation.

The newly installed self-closing fireproofed doors added to our work when guests forgot that they should either carry their yale key or set the snib on their lock when leaving their rooms, especially during the night.

Our advice to this effect was often recalled only when the click of the lock left them with no other course but to ring for me.

The absent-minded help I engaged while the Irish lady was on holiday was almost as bad. The master keys for the rooms given to her on her first day were not on the proper or any other hook on the board when she came to work the second day. Nor were they in her bag because she was sure she had not had it with her the previous day, or in any other likely or unlikely place she could have put them. So I assumed that as their most likely repository had since been emptied into the early morning refuse truck they were irretrievably lost. Within an hour of being handed the duplicate set she had locked them behind one of the four self-closing doors on the third floor but could not say which one. While standing on a rickety ladder above the fifty-foot drop to the basement below, making an attempt to get through the open window into the last of these rooms, I was told that the lady had found the original keys in the bag she had not after all left at home the day before.

Twice more in the month she was with us I was extremely lucky.

'Guess you'll be looking for these before long,' said one of our top floor guests as he tossed the chain of keys on his breakfast table. 'Wrapped themselves round my feet as I hopped into bed last night,' he said.

The next and thankfully the last time, they were clumped on the kitchen table with the comment from our laundry man, 'You'll be glad to get these back – found in the pocket of one of your staff's aprons in last week's laundry.'

The relief with which I viewed the loss of this rather pleasant lady was abruptly halted when ferry trouble prevented the Irish lady from resuming work the following Monday, the very day Win was due to take her first day off. She obligingly agreed to work until after the bulk of the breakfasts were served and then leave it to me. After verifying from the book that ten of our thirty-eight beds required complete changes I decided to do the rooms first. Despite the all too frequent descents to answer the phone in the hall I had the beds made, washbasins and glasses cleaned in all eighteen rooms and five bathrooms and toilets plus the morning's correspondence dealt with by 5pm. Two more hours washing up and resetting the tables ended just one more of those mythical short working days which had led me to engage in the hotel business.

Consequent on the series of visits to the hotel of what I suspected to be a representative of one of the multi-storied city hotels as breakfasts were being served, I was not altogether surprised when Win gave me notice of her intention to leave. She had, she said, accepted a job as head waitress at treble what I could afford to pay her. We wished her all the luck she deserved; and off she went.

Not much of a cook though an unusually efficient waitress, Win's departure put a welcome stop to requests from guests who had sampled her efforts in the past for reduced tariffs as they no longer required breakfasts. That, though she'd never have believed it, was when I took over the cooking and a Swiss *au pair* named Marian the more onerous duties of waitress.

It was said that when two locust men met conversation invariably centred on locusts, transport and females, in that order. The reversal in priorities in my new calling was apparent whenever two hoteliers got together. Each asked about the quality of the *au pairs* employed by the other, and this was followed more often than not by a heavy condemnation of those vociferous politicians who claimed that the girls were exploited by us. This popular concept was not shared by the girls themselves who came to us for the higher pay, shorter working hours free of child minding and freedom each day to attend language school. My early fears that foreign girls might be averse to working for single men made me stress my unmarried state when interviewing them but judging by the amusement this always invoked it obviously seemed to them to be verging on the ridiculous. Perhaps they considered that without a wife they could, and in retrospect I think they did, manage me rather more than I did them.

Long hours spent painting and decorating six days a week resulted in improved business in consequence of my membership of the British Travel Association, and heavy bookings from the Inland Revenue, in whose house magazine I advertised each month. Unlike their popular image, the tax officers proved to be amongst the most pleasant and agreeable of our guests. Unlike most hoteliers when the tourist boom bookings started in the mid-sixties, I considered that the costly advertising and correspondence this entailed was worth the effort. The type of person this attracted booked ahead, and their stated arrival times meant I knew when I could safely leave the hotel to do my outside business. They tended to be quiet and considerate of others especially as their home addresses were known. Cheques could be accepted without question, and above all it eliminated the constant haggling at the door at which I did not excel.

With the hotel only half full the two Swiss Ruths who replaced Marian who, fired by my stories about life in Australia, had emigrated there after ten months at the hotel, helped me to paint the staircase on Boxing Day because they liked painting. The remainder of their day off they spent at some place they called Fawltey Towers tending its old-age inmates. When sickness kept Debby at home for a month they cleaned her rooms under the impression, I heard later, that they were safeguarding her job.

Gerda, a teacher from Germany whose phoned application to replace the Ruths, who were returning home to train as air hostesses, was in such faultless English I rejected her on the grounds that I wanted a German girl capable of talking to our Continental guests and not the English girl I took her to be. A competent domestic worker, good at most things, Gerda's inability to serve the twenty-odd early risers who required breakfast at 7 am puzzled me until years later when I tried it myself. This dilemma was resolved from the second day when she enlisted the help of a German friend employed by a local family who gave her leave each day just long enough to serve these guests.

Still a rarity in London the scanty skirt hardly wider than a cummerbund worn by the blue-eyed blonde from Iceland (Father Christmasland she called it) who answered my request for a German-speaking girl made me so nervous of the reception I feared it would be accorded by our conservative-minded clientele – assuming that it was her normal attire – that I was averse to taking her despite serious staff shortages. In consequence I found myself stressing the dissuasive rather then the more persuasive aspects of the job I normally advanced in the hope of scaring her off. After a glance inside the semi-basement room proved that it was furnished and had a washbasin, my reference to its unsuitability was dismissed out of hand. When the prospect of rising early seven days a week to serve breakfasts followed by four hours domestic work with two hours telephone watch in the evening still failed to deter her – and I had ascertained from her work permit that unlike the majority of applicants she could be legally employed – I gave up and she moved in with a speed that could only have suggested that her bags had been left in the care of a friend waiting outside.

Again I was proved wrong. She spoke German and fluent French – which she had picked up while working six months in each country – both of which she and still another Swiss Ruth who came later, always spoke when together – and with understandable English she was amazingly popular. This was not entirely because of the shapely view presented when she bent to reach into the fridge but despite it – if the obvious pleasure of her humorous asides to the older guests whose comfort she always put first was any criterion.

Due to acute staff shortages when Hilda appeared on the scene I agreed to her demand that I should carry her hoover up the two flights of stairs to the rooms she was to clean on the doubtful premise that the effort was beyond her strength. Since neither of the other two girls were less feminine than she the cynical amusement with which they viewed the implementation of this promise each day undoubtedly contributed to its early discontinuance. The actual turning point came on the morning I found Hilda still sitting at the foot of the stairs after I had been delayed a good hour on the phone. My assumption that the sharp reproof which sent her leaping upstairs – hoover and all – with a speed which delighted the others had precipitated the notice I received a month later proved wide of the mark. My second assumption on the morning of departure that the huge pile of bacon and egg sandwiches she took to her room was nothing more than thrifty provision for her long journey back home was just as far off the target. Summoned later to say goodbye, I was somewhat bewildered to see six suitcase-laden girls emerging from Hilda's room, each of whom paused to shake hands and thank me, presumably for the sandwiches, before trooping out into the square in the wake of Hilda the resourceful.

Enlightenment came from Italian Rosa who with more animation than coherence told me that four days prior to this Hilda and six friends similarly employed in the square had accepted jobs at a West End hotel able to employ all of them and that I had been fortunate in being told the same day by Hilda of her intentions. What Rosa at the time did not know was the arrangement whereby the other six girls would secretly leave their own places of employment to gather in Hilda's room immediately they saw me leave the hotel on my usual walk to the newsagents and leave, I heard later, three puzzled hoteliers across the way without staff nor notice of their intentions.

Back after a brief absence one day I was relieved to hear from Marie that the pleasant young man in the lounge suit – who had undoubtedly watched me leave the hotel before calling to collect the gas bill – had not conned her into supplementing from her own pocket the few odd pounds in the cash box. On his insistence they had counted it before his quick check of the meter revealed, oddly enough, that it contained exactly the correct amount to settle the bill. Fearing success might inspire similar incursions on behalf of the other utilities from uncle Tom Cobbly and all, my short homily to the effect that these officials always wore uniforms and that bills were invariably paid by cheque was effectively exploded when she asked why, in that case, did I pay the bread and milk delivery men every Saturday in cash.

On two separate occasions while the staff of two inter-communicating hotels were busy in their base-ments serving seventy-odd breakfasts a similar character toured the rooms above requesting those who responded to his urgent knocks on their doors to hurry down if they wanted breakast. He asked them at the same time to leave their room doors open for the convenience of the room maids now making their rounds. Both times, with all the money and valuables left behind by those who complied with this request inside the most expensive suitcases he could lay hands on, he calmly left by the front door while his victims were still at breakfast.

While the proprietor of a similar hotel was cooking breakfasts in his basement kitchen four bogus workmen in blue overalls calmly untacked and removed his expensive hall and stair carpets. His headlong dash from the hotel – on being asked by the milkman why he was changing his new carpets so soon – was just too late and he reconciled himself to their loss after the newsvendor on the corner recalled seeing carpets similar to those he described being taken away in a plain van by blue-overalled men only minutes before.

Parisians both, Babette and Marie who worked at the hotel throughout the last two years of my tenure had a name for the French girl who, following a phoned request from Paris to join the staff, cried from the day of her arrival until her unlamented departure the next.

'Cretin,' they said, 'no one asked her to come.'

Contrariwise, there was the Amazon-sized mid-European girl hired from a local agency as a temporary stand-in for Marie while she was holidaying in France who refused to leave on Marie's return to London. Reminders that her agent had another job waiting for her went unheeded. Powerful arms akimbo, she blocked Marie's every attempt to enter the kitchen, implying thereby she could do all the serving without help. Finally, after a visit by the irate manager of her agency on the third day of her extended stay I was given a sudden dig in the back followed by a demand bordering on blackmail for money I could ill-afford but gladly paid to be shot of her despite her flat refusal to return her front door keys. The fear that she might reimpose her unwelcome presence on us later by using these keys, or that they might fall into the hands of some acquisitive early-morning room-door knocker or fast moving carpet removers, was lifted when they were dropped into my hand by a smiling Marie who had quietly removed them from the lady's unattended handbag while she had been in the kitchen dictating to me her terms for leaving.

I still hold in high regard the young American girl whom I found curled up on the floor outside the room she shared with two others, when checking the hotel early one morning. Not realising until she arrived back late at the hotel the night before that the keys provided for the room were in the possession of her room mates, from whom she had separated to join other friends on a day trip to Oxford, she had waited outside until admitted by guests returning from a late show. Then, rather than risk disturbing others by knocking on her own door or rousing staff, she had opted instead to sleep in the passage.

The evident enjoyment my *au pairs* got out of serving the late-sitting honeymooner with fresh supplies of butter, marmalade and what remained of the standard sized loaf he accounted for each morning after disposing of his own, and then most of his wife's share of toast, was ample compensation for the extra costs involved in those days of cheap food.

In the eighth year of my tenure, with a crop of varicose veins I could well do without, the result of working an average of eighteen hours every day of the year, I decided to sell and give Australia another go.

The place was soon swarming with those more intent on probing than buying; others who followed each of their four visits with all the family experts, with phoned requests for reductions in the price; and then those who brought their ten relations one at a time before deciding on the advice of one of them to buy a fried fish and chip shop instead.

Eventually I sold and booked a passage on the Shaw Savill passenger liner *Northern Star* to Sydney at the unbelievably low cost today of only £105 for a bunk in a two-berth cabin. The month-long voyage via Panama gave me a day in each of the ports of Las Palmas, Capetown, Durban and Curacao – the last stop before Sydney.

It soon became apparent that due to unprecedented inflation my capital was insufficient to purchase the type of hotel I'd had in mind. So, I booked a cheap passage on the Italian Sitmar Line ship *Fairsky*. An ageing wartime Liberty Ship which due to frequent breakdowns gave me the opportunity to explore Auckland, Wellington, Papeete, Balboa, Christobal and Panama before docking in London after a two days' stay in Lisbon.

It was remarkable that not once during the month I was in Sydney did anyone put to me the question asked by nearly everyone I met there back in the 1950s: 'What do the people in the "Old Country" think of Australia?' This time nobody asked, cared, or was even remotely interested.

The £8,000 gain I made on the sale of a London hotel I bought subsequently was almost totally lost when expenses for fireproofing and unsuspected dry rot treatment in a large house bought in Northants for conversion to hotel use, proving not to be a viable one, forced me to sell.

In my 67th year the re-sale of a third, with refunds of

capital gains tax, reduced the overall loss to virtually nought. It was then that I decided to retire and write these memoirs.

12

ACCOUNTS OF MY RECENT VISITS TO CHINA AND AROUND AUSTRALIA IN EXPO YEAR 1988

It is essential to have a passport valid for at least two months after the intended date of departure from China. A visa obtainable at the visa section – 31 Portman Place, London W1N 3AG – of the Embassy of the People's Republic of China. The current cost is £20. Travelling direct from the UK there are no health requirements but it is advisable to consult your doctor a month to six weeks before departure regarding what precautionary injections should be taken. In June 1987 I paid my first return visit to China flying Yugoslavair, Heathrow–Peking return. Traveller's cheques can be changed for FEC (Foreign Exchange Currency) at Peking Airport for which a receipt is given stating the amount changed and on what date. Great care should be taken that this is not lost; without it, any FEC still not spent on the day of departure from China will not be changed back into sterling or US dollars at the airport branch of the Bank of China.

My advice on leaving the airport building is to turn right and buy a FEC 2.50 ticket at the small kiosk and board one of the express coaches which will take you right into the city centre a journey of some ninety minutes. A taxi would cost anything up to 100 FEC.

When the coach makes its final stop, walk about sixty yards in the direction it is pointing where taxis for hire are queued. Ask to be taken to the Qioa Yuen Hotel on Dong Binile Road, Yu-An-Men-Wai, some six miles from central Peking. Alternatively, a taxi could be taken direct from the airport at much greater cost.

Like all the cheaper hotels in Peking there were no singles so, as rooms were charged on the number of beds they contained and the next was a twin, I was charged for two. A deposit of five FEC for the room key was required at the time of booking but returned when leaving.

The hotel was not palatial but adequate at the price charged. The rooms had plenty of hanging space. A writing table with overhead lamp, a chest of drawers big enough for two and a bench for luggage. Adjoining was a private hot and cold shower room with wc, a wash basin plus an adjustable four-armed drying rail for the convenience of those who did their own washing which could be relied upon to dry by next morning. The hotel had a private laundry which, provided there had been no rain that day, would return all items left with it twenty-four hours later. On the ground floor there was the kitchen and a fly-proofed dining room containing five tables each seating six with a squeeze, but four in comfort. Outside there were five long forms and tables to seat at least two dozen under a verandah. A large breakfast of ham, two fried eggs, four thick slices of toasted bread with butter and strawberry jam, or omelettes in all their forms with a large mug of tea or coffee, set me back only nine yuen. This was available from 6.30am till late afternoon when the waitresses started to take orders for dinner. This comprised all manner of meat, chicken, duck with fried or boiled rice or potatoes. The best value I found was the curried beef, but actually water buffalo to the uninitiated, with roast potatoes, onions and thick gravy and four slices of thick bread plus butter and jam, with a large tea, costing only nine yuen (one pound fifty pence sterling). Excellent Chinese-brewed bitter beer came at one yuen, fifty pence, the large bottle – best bring your own opener. Considering that the guests were in the main quite young they were extremely well behaved and ready at all times to converse with fellow guests and advise them how best to get to places they themselves had visited.

There were taxis aplenty in the forecourt from early morning. The charge for a run into the city was twelve yuen. For the energetic, bicycles could be hired in the hotel forecourt for a nominal sum. Care was taken to supply the right sized machine to fit each customer's leg and arm length. For sightseeing or going down to the city most guests used this inexpensive mode of transport. Every day, according to demand, for a charge of twenty yuen, twenty-seat minibuses took guests on visits to The Ming Tombs and Great Wall one day, and the the Summer Palace the next, and at night to see the renowned Peking Acrobatic Team perform their wonders for a flat rate of FEC 20. Though right on the outskirts of the city and parallel with a river it was quite safe to walk the adjacent country roads after dark. During my post-prandial strolls after dark I frequently saw young foreign girls from the hotel quite unconcernedly doing the same thing, as much as two miles from the hotel.

Room tariffs were on a sliding scale: £8pn for a twin, £5pn per bed in a family room containing three to five beds and £1pn for a sleeping space on the floor of a multi-occupied dormitory room in the semi-basement. It will be of interest to know that the cheapest double in a mid-Peking hotel in the off-season ranges upwards from £40pn. From July to October this price will be doubled.

In every direction as far as the eye could see a profusion of high rise buildings were springing up in Peking. It was with interest that I noted that all the huge gantries and cranes built to reach skyscraper heights were wholly produced in China. China had come a long way since our days. Workers were in great demand, with more job vacancies then there were men to fill them.

When I asked for a return air booking to Shanghai I was told that as returns were not allowed on internal flights, I should book the return flight when I reached Shanghai. As all economy class seats had been taken I paid £110 to travel first class to Shanghai. Shanghai itself had changed little except that the myriads of bright lights that had once made Nanking Road the most brilliantly illuminated thoroughfare in the world had been replaced by phosphorescent street lighting which only dimly dispelled the resultant gloom.

Every road leading to the Bund, particularly Nanking Road was crowded with well-dressed, obviously well fed shoppers, seemingly with unlimited money to spend, a high proportion of them sported imported Japanese cameras. Not a beggar was to be seen anywhere. All those with physical disabilities had some form of state supplied self-propelled wheelchair. For the Chinese – under the chairmanship of Deng Xiaoping – a complete metamorphosis.

Hundreds of camera-toting tourists, mainly German and American, on conducted tours, jostling their way up and down Nanking Road – stopping every few yards to take it in turn to photograph their parties – made progress along crowded pavements slower than it would otherwise have been. Further down Nanking Road, would-be diners at the world famous Sun-Ya restaurant were told that they must book at least four days in advance.

The artistically carved and delicately lacquered in bright blues, red and gold that had before been the fronts of the individual Chinese restaurants on both sides of Zhonglu (the last right turn off Nanking Road before the Bund), and which had collectively offered every provincial dish known to China, had been wantonly destroyed – their interiors gutted. On the grounds that they were Bourgeois Reactionaries their owners summarily evicted by Mao Tse-Tung's rampaging Red Guards during the 1965/68, so-called Cultural Revolution.

The 1920s and 1930s prestigious hotels, the green domed Cathay and the Palace Hotel facing each other on the bottom corners of Nanking Road with The Bund, formerly part of the far-flung Sassoon family Chinese empire, had emerged unscathed by the ravages of Mao Tse-Tung's Red Guards. A four lane traffic bridge – not there before – aligned with, and actually an extention of Nanking Road, now spanned the wide Wangpoo to give direct vehicular access from the Bund to Pootung on its opposite bank.

Asked where the thousands of rickshaws which formerly plied for hire in the streets of Shanghai had got to, the taxi driver taking me to the airport said they had been banned from the city's streets more than forty years ago. My economy class seat on the return flight to Peking had leg room just as spacious as that on the downward first class flight. Since both classes were given the same food, the only difference as far as I could see was that those travelling first class got theirs first. The return economy fare was £94. Tea and cakes were served after take off, and a four course hot meal before landing.

Resultant on the, in my opinion, ill-advised student uprising in Tianamen Square in central Peking the previous year all airlines offering budget-class fares, except China Air, had ceased to fly to China. Nobody wanted to go there now they all said. So, in June 1990 I flew economy, London to Peking return by China Air at a cost of £520.

Less than a third full the China Air DC10 flew to Peking in just under twenty-four hours, making one refuelling stop in the Arab Emirates where returning Peking-bound passengers bought their supplies of duty-free tobacco and drinks.

It was with some relief on passing through Tianamen Square *en route* to the Qiao Yuen Hotel in Feng-Tai to see it – save for a group of schoolchildren dancing in its vast centre, and two small squads of unarmed police drilling at each end – completely void of any student presence – or anyone else for that matter. A situation I'd hardly dared hope for. It being to the day the first anniversary of the student massacre of the previous year.

Reception staff at the Qiao Yuen Hotel welcomed me like a long lost rich uncle as well they might – despite two devaluations of the Chinese currency in the last twelve months the place was less than half full. Consequent on the 60% loss of China's tourist trade which followed on the students' revolt of the previous year the frenetic hotel and apartment building programme had come to an abrupt halt, adding thousands to those already out of work.

Getting a rail ticket to Shanghai entailed two twenty minute walks from the Beijing Hotel to Peking's impressive mainline railway station. First to fill in a form asking intended date of departure, whether by morning or late afternoon train and mode of travel by £54 soft sleeper, £28 soft seat, or by £17 hard seat – much favoured by foreign budget tourists for reasons of economy.

Returning three days later I handed over £54 for the soft sleeper I'd applied for and left Peking for Shanghai the next day, a twenty-three hour journey of some 900 miles. My four berth soft sleeper was shared with a middle-aged foreign lady and a Chinese businessman. A £1 feed of roast chicken, rice, cabbage and prawns and Chinese-brewed beer was brought to the compartment, or if preferred served in the dining car. There was a wc of the squatting variety at one end of the coach and a sit down type at the other. Next to this were four washbasins for the use of both sexes.

A female attendant standing at the door of the coach escorted each passenger to his allotted berth, took away his ticket and gave a plastic token in exchange. On alighting in Shanghai the same lady took back the token and then returned the ticket.

Then began the slow shuffle to the exit barrier manned, if that be the correct expression, by two uniformed females who, after a close scrutiny of tickets let passengers through the gate one at a time.

The China Internal Travel Service (CITS) 64 Nanking Road booked me a room in East Rainbow Mansions, a newly completed twenty-three-storey hotel on Yangshupu Lu, a twenty-five minute walk, or four trolley bus stops from the bottom of Nanking Road. Room tariffs per night ranged from £20 for a superior twin, for my well appointed 'Standard Twin' £17. Singles though seldom obtainable were £12. And 'Extra Bad' (as the hotel brochure reads) – a blanket and sleeping space on the floor in the basement – £3pn.

A substantial ham and eggs breakfast with all the trimmings cost only £1.50. A large bottle of Chinese-brewed bitter beer obtainable in the dining room bar, into which I was escorted by a uniformed waitress, cost yuen 1.70 – 40p our money. Since only Chinese-style food was served in the hotel I took my evening meal in a nearby restaurant.

Despite the high rate of unemployment, Chinese families with seemingly unlimited money to spend thronged the shops and stores on Nanking Road, but this year foreign tourists were not much in evidence. During my frequent forays into the city few were to be seen, some days the odd one or two – or at best six to a dozen. In stark contrast to my last visit when every student was keen to try out his English on me there was this time a tendency to avert eyes at my approach and give me as wide a berth as possible in the passing. Some, it was said, had been arrested by police for talking to foreigners.

Deda, on the corner of Sichuan Zong Lu and Nanking Road still, as of yore, served foreign style snacks and main meals at reasonable rates. The once world famous Sun Ya eating place on Nanking Road had closed its once well-patronised first floor restaurant and converted its much admired oak panelling foyer to a fast food takeaway. Inexpensive foreign food was still served at the old Keisling and Bader restaurant – now known as the Luzhou – at 473-7 Nanjing Road West. A newly-opened Kentucky Fried Chicken restaurant on the Bund in what once had been the Shanghai British Club – which in pre-war days boasted it had the longest bar in the world – now served a substantial fried chicken and mixed vegetable meal for only £1.50.

China 1991

With the help of the lady at the China Travel Service (CTS) 24 Cambridge Circus, London WC2 I arranged a three week tour of North China commencing 2 June, 1991. For £540 return a China Air DC10 flight of twenty-three hours saw me booking a two night stay at my usual Qiao Yuen hotel in Peking.

At 7am the third day as previously arranged with CTS in London I boarded a China Air British Trident 109 seat aircraft (now being built in China under licence) for the seven hour flight to Chongqing (Chunking – the war-time capital of China). Arrived there I was met by a CTS representative and taken to the prestigious Renmin Hotel for the night. At 6am next morning I was driven to the Yangtse River wharf and put aboard the passenger ferry Jiang Yu to sail through the spectacular 'Three Small Gorges', frequently mentioned by the old China hands of the early 1930s and the just as breathtakingly beautiful 'Lesser Gorges' before disembarking at Wuhan on the afternoon of the third day. Since there is no first class, only second class and steerage on these ferries, the fare Chongqing to Wuhan was FEC 563. As service was not included in this I was advised when boarding to tip the cabin stewardess not less than FEC 20 for each of the days I was likely to be on board or I'd get no service. Food was excellent and plentiful. Two large bottles of Chinese bitter beer were served with every meal including breakfast, and even two more without charge if requested. Beds in the two berth cabins were clean and comfortable. Fellow passengers were all American.

One night was spent at the Qingchuan Hotel in Wuhan before next day being put on the 90 minutes Trident flight to Shanghai.

At my request Mr Frank Chan the CTS agent for Shanghai who met me at the airport tried to get me a single room at the Pujiang Hotel 15 Huang Pu Lu. Formerly the wholly owned and British occupied Astor House Apartments, it was just a short walk along the Bund and then across Garden Bridge. No singles available that night they said, but with the promise of one for the following seven nights I took a £1pn bed in a five-bedded room – with space on the floor for five more which included a boiled egg breakfast next morning. When by noon next day the promised single had failed to materialise I went to the China International Travel Service (CITS) 64 Nanjing Road who reserved for me a single room at the Gao Yang Hotel, 879 Dong Da Nung Lu (formerly Yangtsepoo Road) some twenty minutes walk, or three trolleybus stops from the bottom of Nanjing Road. When I made a firm booking for seven nights their original quote of £16pn was reduced to £13pn. Breakfast of fried ham, two eggs plus all the usual trimmings cost less than £1. European type dinners being unavailable at the hotel, the evening meal was taken at a nearby cafe, where a large bottle of excellent Chinese-brewed beer cost only 1.50 yuen – 40p our money.

On my daily forays into town, as an old 'Shanghai-lander' whose six foot then made him a giant amongst men, I found that in general this was no longer the case. A point made even more apparent when being ushered into city hotels and department stores by doormen whose towering heights – six foot and more – put them head and shoulders above my own six foot. Just as surprising was the sight of upper-middle class Chinese couples standing shoulder to shoulder along Garden Bridge embracing and openly kissing, completely oblivious of everything and everyone but themselves. Another thing, Chinese women had *en masse* abandoned the long, split-sided gowns of yore in favour of exact replicas of the close fitting dresses and costumes as seen worn by visiting females from abroad – now manufact-ured in Shanghai and retailed at prices within reach of all.

The fast-receding, worldwide aversion to all things Chinese at the Tianamen Square student massacre of 1989 had brought tourists back in droves. A point made

341

manifest when I visited the famous 'Seven Crooked Bridge Temple' found by taking the first turn right after having passed the Kentucky Fried Chicken restaurant on the Bund then first left and on into the old city of Shanghai – where there were almost as many foreign sightseers as there were Chinese. These were mainly American and German, with a preponderance of the former.

Just why – since as all Chinese know devils cannot turn corners – the bridge to the Temple had seven crooks when only one would have sufficed, was as big a source of wonderment to foreign sightseers as it was to the younger, more enlightened Chinese.

Again, foreign tourists comprised the bulk of the audience the night I attended the Acrobatic Stadium 400 Nanjing Road West, to see the famous Shanghai Acrobatic Team performing gymnastic feats unequalled anywhere else in the world.

Curious as to how Christianity had fared in China under Communist rule I called in mid-week at the one-time Scottish Unitarian Church 53 Xizang Zong Lu, left turn off Nanjing Road East, to find it filled to capacity with devout Chinese worshippers. Fourteen Catholic churches are listed in the Shanghai telephone directory, the nearest of which for those staying in downtown hotels is 36 Sichual Nan Lu which is the continuation of Suchan Kong Lu a few minutes walk from the Peace Hotel. The third turn to the left off Nanjing Road East marked on its western corner by the Deda restaurant. At no. 36, the last of three Sunday Masses, preceded by a sermon in Chinese, is at 9am. The 9.30am Mass, the last of five starting at 4.30 at the Catholic Xujiahui Cathedral – built at the turn of the century by the St Franciscan priests and the most impressive church in Shanghai, was reached by boarding a no. 26 bus close to the bottom of the first road on the right of Nanjing Road when facing the river Wangpoo, alighting at its last stop at Xujiahui, then walking five minutes down the wide boulevard to the right. It is filled to capacity every Sunday with both young and old Chinese and resident and transitory foreigners. When I expressed surprise at this to one of the latter whom I took to be American, he said, 'Oh, this is nothing. At times like Christmas, Easter and Corpus Christi they flock here in their thousands to pack the cathedral until they overflow into all the adjoining roads.'

On the morning of my last day in Shanghai Mr Chan drove me to the station and presented me with the rail ticket for the next leg of my China trip which was Nanking. Only then did we learn that due to exceptionally heavy rain in the inter-land, the train's departure had been set back by four hours, to enable maintenance gangs to shore up miles of washed out track.

After a prolonged look round the extensive White Jade Bubba Temple in Anyuan Lu where I was amazed to see the otherwise modern-minded Mr Chan prostrate himself humbly before the good luck goddess, we repaired to a good class Chinese restaurant for lunch. Instead of as expected being given a disposable plastic knife and fork when I confessed to an ineptitude in the use of chopsticks, the proprietor, after a temporary absence, produced still in their original cardboard box an obviously just-purchased stainless steel 'made in Sheffield' carving knife and fork against which, when the bill for the meal was presented and despite the improbability of their ever being asked for again in that Chinese only district, no charge was made.

The train's arrival in Nanking coincided with that of another from Peking both with double decked coaches chock-a-block with foreign tourists. As they alighted from the trains in seemingly endless files they were herded by their respective flag-waving tour guides into the 'Foreigners Only' exit ramp, effectively blocking it to the exclusion of loners such as I. The result was that by the time I finally made it onto the station concourse the CTS representative, who should have met me with a soft sleeper ticket for that night's 8.10pm train to Peking and shown me the Chinese-built bridge across the River Yangtse plus Dr Sun Yat-Sen's memorial, had departed the station under the impression, the senior CITS officer on the station told me, that I'd missed the train in Shanghai. Thus, that night's 8.10pm train to Peking being fully booked, instead of a luxurious night's sleep in a soft sleeper bunk, I spent a most uncomfortable and seemingly endless night seated on a hard bench in the station's waiting room.

Next day, courtesy of the CITS officer on the station, at a cost of 100 yuen for a taxi I did the grand tour of Nanking. Back at the station, this same officer obtained for me a 'hard seat' ticket to travel on the 8.10 night train to Peking. Shortly before departure time the gates to the Peking-bound train were flung open to permit we hard-seaters and others who had paid less than a pound for the privilege of standing or, space permitting, squatting in the doorways and aisles of such hard-seat coaches as they could push and elbow their way into, to board.

The seats were not so hard as the name implied. In bench form without arm rests, and back to back, they were cushioned with a three inch thick covering of latex rubber to seat three on one side of the centre aisle and five on the other. After a glance at my ticket the female coach attendant conducted me to one of the latter to sit out the night between an English-speaking Chinese student in the seat next to the window and on the other, three similarly bilingual Chinese businessmen in charcoal grey lounge suits. Knee to knee and facing, flanked on his left side by three lieutenants, was a tall powerfully built army major.

On my arrival back in China three weeks before, it had soon become apparent that restrictions on conversing with foreigners, imposed by government decree the previous year, had been allowed to lapse into disuse.

Although on this and on previous trips to China I had met quite a number of mainly British young and middle-aged budget class tourists who had travelled the length and breadth of China hardseat, I was the one and only foreign 'hardseater' on this night's train. In consequence, even before we left Nanking station I was inundated with questions from not only the student and the three businessmen whose seat I shared but seemingly every other English-speaking passenger on the train all eager to know how present day China now stood in the eyes of the world. This went on until, to my great relief, it was broken up by the appearance of the coach stewardess with trays of £1 cartons of fried chicken and rice. Thereafter, at intervals during the night the student insisted that we change places to enable me, elbow resting on the sill of the window, to catnap at least some of the night away.

But that was not the end of it. At a word from the student as the train came to a halt in Peking station the major, despite my protests, hooked one huge finger through the handle of my case and, after slinging it along with his own two kit bags over his shoulder, made off up the long steeply rising exit ramp. By the time the student and I – he having matched his pace to mine – finally made the station exit the major was standing by the last taxi for hire on the busy concourse. Both paused just long enough to ensure that the driver knew the whereabouts of my hotel then hurried away, completely ignoring my grateful 'thank yous'.

The kindnesses extended to me by another student though briefer were just as memorable: as I passed through the archway beneath the huge portrait of Mao Tse-Tung in Tianamen Square, the sole entrance into the Forbidden City, heavy thunder and lightning made me retrace my steps and then turn left along the tree-lined Jianguo Wei Avenue and head for the Beijing Hotel at its western end. Less than half way there the rain commenced to bucket down with force sufficient to cascade through the dense foliage of the huge trees under which I had taken shelter and then on to me. Noting this, one of the three umbrella-toting students in a party of five standing under the next tree broke away from the rest to stand by me, his umbrella fully extended to give what shelter he could for both he and I.

As the rain got steadily worse he asked, 'You going to the Beijing Hotel?'

Then, pointing to the fast.rising flood water all about us said, 'We better go now while still possible.'

Fifteen minutes later, still with the lion's share of the brolly held over me with one hand and a tight grip on my left arm with the other, he guided me through ankle-deep flood water onto and up the steps of the East Wing of the Beijing Hotel. Then, pausing just long enough to roll up his, by then soaked, trouser legs, take off his shoes and sling them round his neck, he hurried back the way we had come to rejoin his friends – completely oblivious to all my words of thanks.

AUSTRALIA – Expo Year 1988

Before flying to Australia in Expo Year 1988 I inquired at NSW House, and the Queensland Tourist Office on the Strand about the cost of hotel accommodation in both these states. No one seemed to know, but after lengthy perusal of backroom files they both said £50 sterling or more per night, but not less.

So, to save on hotel expenses, and knowing that all economy, Cabin Class coach seats (my intended mode of travel) were fully reclining for sleeping at night with the help of Compas the UK agents for Australian State Railways then in London W1 (but since removed to PO Box 113, Peterborough PE1 1LE Tel: 0733 51780), I mapped out an itinerary which included all my intended stopovers for two separate journeys, to spend as many nights as possible on the two trains. This must be done at least a month before intended date of arrival in Australia, to enable Compas to discover from The Travel Centre, York St, Sydney, that there would be seats available on the requested dates and trains.

The answer was in the affirmative and on payment of the fares to Compas they issued the tickets which, me being a holder of a British passport and a permanent resident of the UK, cost me in London only one third of what I would have paid had I made the purchases after arrival in Australia.

On arriving in Sydney by Yugoslav Air, the cheapest airline flying to Sydney, I took an airport bus to Central Station in the city, a journey of ninety minutes. The fare 2.50 Australian dollars, to see if my London-made train reservations were in order and found that they were. Prominently displayed on the station's exit door was a list of 'Reasonably priced hotels'. Less than ten minutes walk from the station, I booked a single room in the 600-room Sydney Tourist Hotel, 400 Pitt Street, Sydney, whose locality and rates I had noted at the station exit. The charge – 20 Australian dollars pn, £40 sterling less than I'd been led to believe before leaving London. A ground floor self-selection restaurant served a large Australian breakfast and a several-course dinner at a cost of around two dollars for each.

That evening I crossed Pitt Street into Sydney's nearby Chinatown and, seeing an old 1870 established pub with a long bar, I went in and asked for a double Corio, the most popular whisky in the 1950s.

'Oh that,' said the head barman with the arms and shoulders of a blacksmith, 'went out of production years ago, it's all Scotch now, shipped out in bulk direct from Scotland.'

When I ordered a third double my money was pushed back across the bar counter.

'Have this on the house,' he said.

The only reason I could think of, was my Pommie accent. It was then I realised that I was drinking genuine Scotch at less than half the price prevailing in the UK.

Downtown Sydney had changed almost beyond recognition: multi-storied skyscrapers had replaced most of the old pubs I once knew. The once vehicle-clogged Martin Place was now a quiet pedestrian precinct. All day pub opening had put an end to the frenetic drinking of yore and with it the good-time girls in Kings Cross. The once-familiar clanging electric trams had given way to noiseless trolleybuses.

After four days spent rediscovering Sydney, which included a ninety minute long ferry trip as far as Bondi and then right round the harbour (reputedly the most beautiful in the world), I boarded the train for Townsville with stopovers both ways, at Brisbane, Bowan and Gladstone. As in Sydney, notices were posted on all three station exits listing local hotels who offered accommodation for the night with breakfast in the morning at twenty dollars or less per night. Both the fisherman's wharf and the old 'Pub on the wharf' in Townsville had gone for ever to make way for a major tourist attraction: an underwater simulation of The Great Barrier Reef, complete with shoals of multi-coloured fish. The whole of the old waterfront and another of my favourite pubs had vanished beneath a shopping plaza, the like of which I'd never expected to see in Townsville. It was much the same in other places. In Bowan I looked in vain for the pub with the sawdust-covered floor where customers were left to pour their own whiskies. Brisbane had spread to four times its former size and was now dotted with high rise buildings not there before.

Next came the 1,250 mile long journey on board the Sydney to Perth Indian Pacific to terminate for me at Kalgoorlie which, having seen Perth before, just a mass of identical skyscrapers and little else, would be of far greater interest to me. Kalgoorlie was the scene of one of the world's greatest gold rushes when gold was discovered there in 1893.

Right on the dot, the mile-long Indian Pacific pulled out of Sydney and slowly built up the express speed it would maintain throughout the steepest rail journey in the world to Katoomba, high up in the misty Blue Mountains of NSW, and from there to Broken Hill, one of the largest and richest silver, lead and zinc mines in the world. Three stops from there the train reached Ooldea to commence the longest stretch of straight railway line in the world, which extends for 478 km (300 miles) to Watson. The train then started its thirty-seven hour crossing of the waterless Nullarbor Plain. Passengers were mainly elderly. A more friendly crowd it would have been impossible to meet. A cafeteria Club Car for coach-class passengers served a selection of takeaway snacks, light meals and drinks with the request that they be consumed in the privacy of one's own car. However. a blind eye was turned on two of we loners who drank our beers in the comfort of the lounge bar itself.

It was nearing 8pm when we reached Kalgoorlie. It was

pouring with rain. A friendly taxi driver with two lady passengers already aboard undertook to find me a room for the night. The hotel where he dropped the ladies had no vacancies, nor had two others he tried. After a moment's thought and a fast ten minutes drive we turned into a wide shop-lined street, 'Main drag,' he said, at the top of which he turned right and stopped outside a large old fashioned pub, rushed inside in the ceaseless rain and seconds later from inside beckoned me into a foyer furnished on all sides with massive turn-of-the-century carved oak sideboards and nine feet high cupboards.

He said, 'Eighteen dollars with breakfast.'

When I offered a tip to repay all his trouble, he said, 'You've paid the fare on the clock, that's all I want.'

Next morning I was picked up at the hotel to join a sightseeing tour of the old gold mines in Kalgoorlie which ended at one of the last few still working. Eight at a time we were herded into the one cage then winched down the vertical shaft to see, far below, the miners at work. Nuggets suitably sized for conversion into ear or wedding rings were on sale in the mine's compound.

As arranged with Compas in London I re-boarded the Indian Pacific at Kalgoorlie on its return journey from Perth to Sydney, and left it at Adelaide. On the fifteen minutes walk from the station at Adelaide to the city itself I spotted what I'd been looking for: the Rapide Blue Coach Company's booking office and there was fortunate enough to secure the last seat on that night's coach to Sydney, which would take a different route to that of the train.

The coach stopped briefly at Wagga-Wagga – the mere mention of which by an Australian-born radio comedian of the 1930s threw his listeners into uncontrollable gales of laughter. But more importantly, Canberra, the capital city of Australia. There, to a running commentary from the relief coach driver, we saw more of this widely-sprawling city and environs in one hour than we would otherwise have seen on foot in a week.

It was the same again in Sydney. To a commentary by the other driver the coach threaded its way through the city dropping off individual passengers at their alighting points until it arrived at its terminal in Pitt Street, a mere minute's walk from the Sydney Tourist Hotel, where I pleasantly spent my last three days in the country.